SUPER HOROSCOPE
SAGITTARIUS

2012

NOVEMBER 23 – DECEMBER 20

BERKLEY BOOKS, NEW YORK

THE BERKLEY PUBLISHING GROUP
Published by the Penguin Group
Penguin Group (USA) Inc.
375 Hudson Street, New York, New York 10014, USA
Penguin Group (Canada), 90 Eglinton Avenue East, Suite 700, Toronto, Ontario M4P 2Y3, Canada
(a division of Pearson Penguin Canada Inc.)
Penguin Books Ltd., 80 Strand, London WC2R 0RL, England
Penguin Group Ireland, 25 St. Stephen's Green, Dublin 2, Ireland (a division of Penguin Books Ltd.)
Penguin Group (Australia), 250 Camberwell Road, Camberwell, Victoria 3124, Australia
(a division of Pearson Australia Group Pty. Ltd.)
Penguin Books India Pvt. Ltd., 11 Community Centre, Panchsheel Park, New Delhi—110 017, India
Penguin Group (NZ), 67 Apollo Drive, Rosedale, Auckland 0632, New Zealand
(a division of Pearson New Zealand Ltd.)
Penguin Books (South Africa) (Pty.) Ltd., 24 Sturdee Avenue, Rosebank, Johannesburg 2196,
South Africa

Penguin Books Ltd., Registered Offices: 80 Strand, London WC2R 0RL, England

The publishers regret that they cannot answer individual letters requesting personal horoscope information.

2012 SUPER HOROSCOPE SAGITTARIUS

PRINTING HISTORY
Berkley trade paperback edition / July 2011

Berkley trade paperback ISBN: 978-0-425-23943-8

Library of Congress Cataloging-in-Publication Data

ISSN: 1535-8992

PRINTED IN THE UNITED STATES OF AMERICA

10   9   8   7   6   5   4   3   2   1

Contents

THE CUSP-BORN
SAGITTARIUS

Are you *really* a Sagittarius? If your birthday falls around the fourth week in November, at the very beginning of Sagittarius, will you still retain the traits of Scorpio, the sign of the Zodiac before Sagittarius? And what if you were born near Christmas—are you more Capricorn than Sagittarius? Many people born at the edge, or cusp, of a sign have great difficulty determining exactly what sign they are. If you are one of these people, here's how you can figure it out once and for all.

Consult the cusp table on the facing page, then locate the year of your birth. The table will tell you the precise days on which the Sun entered and left your sign for the year of your birth. In that way you can determine if you are a true Sagittarius—or whether you are a Scorpio or Capricorn—according to the variations in cusp dates from year to year (see also page 17).

If you were born at the beginning or end of Sagittarius, yours is a lifetime reflecting a process of subtle transformation. Your life on Earth will symbolize a significant change in consciousness, for you are about to enter a whole new way of living or are leaving one behind.

If you were born at the beginning of Sagittarius, you may want to read the horoscope for Scorpio as well as Sagittarius, for Scorpio holds the key to many of your hidden weaknesses, sexual uncertainties, wishes, fantasies, and spiritual potentials. You are the symbol of the human mind awakening to its higher capabilities. You are preparing the way for the liberation of your soul into the realms of wisdom and truth. You leave behind greed, blind desire, and shallow lust, as you learn to create and understand yourself. You travel, see new places, see how people live, figure yourself out, acquire knowledge.

You may hide a stubborn and dangerous extremism and you may rely too much on luck, but at some crisis point in your life a change of consciousness will occur to shift your behavior patterns. New worlds open up, as you become aware of immortality and the infinite possibilities of your own mind.

If you were born at the end of Sagittarius, you may want to read the horoscope book for Capricorn as well as Sagittarius, for Capricorn is a deep part of your materialistic values. You were born with the need to bring your dreams into reality and put your talents and ambitions to practical use.

You need to conquer worry and depression and inhibition. You will learn to take life seriously, but without losing your sense of humor and hope. You must find a balance between believing nothing and believing too much. You need to find the firm middle ground between cynicism and idealism.

THE CUSPS OF SAGITTARIUS

DATES SUN ENTERS SAGITTARIUS (LEAVES SCORPIO)

November 22 every year from 1900 to 2015, except for:

November 21		November 23		
1976	1993	1902	1915	1931
80	1996	03	19	35
84	2000	07	23	39
88	2004	10	27	43
92	2008	11		
	2012			

DATES SUN LEAVES SAGITTARIUS (ENTERS CAPRICORN)

December 22 every year from 1900 to 2015, except for:

December 21						
1912	1944	1964	1977	1989	2000	2010
16	48	65	80	92	2001	2012
20	52	68	81	93	2002	2013
23	53	69	84	94	2004	2014
28	56	72	85	96	2005	
32	57	73	86	97	2008	
36	60	76	88	98	2009	
40	61					

THE ASCENDANT: SAGITTARIUS RISING

Could you be a "double" Sagittarius? That is, could you have Sagittarius as your Rising sign as well as your Sun sign? The tables on pages 8–9 will tell you Sagittarius what your Rising sign happens to be. Just find the hour of your birth, then find the day of your birth, and you will see which sign of the Zodiac is your Ascendant, as the Rising sign is called. The Ascendant is called that because it is the sign rising on the eastern horizon at the time of your birth. For a more detailed discussion of the Rising sign and the twelve houses of the Zodiac, see pages 17–20.

The Ascendant, or Rising sign, is placed on the 1st house in a horoscope, of which there are twelve houses. The 1st house represents your response to the environment—your unique response. Call it identity, personality, ego, self-image, facade, come-on, body-mind-spirit—whatever term best conveys to you the meaning of the you that acts and reacts in the world. It is a you that is always changing, discovering a new you. Your identity started with birth and early environment, over which you had little conscious control, and continues to experience, to adjust, to express itself. The 1st house also represents how others see you. Has anyone ever guessed your sign to be your Rising sign? People may respond to that personality, that facade, that body type governed by your Rising sign.

Your Ascendant, or Rising sign, modifies your basic Sun sign personality, and it affects the way you act out the daily predictions for your Sun sign. If your Rising sign indeed is Sagittarius, what follows is a description of its effects on your horoscope. If your Rising sign is not Sagittarius, but some other sign of the Zodiac, you may wish to read the horoscope book for that sign.

With Sagittarius on the Ascendant, the planet rising in the 1st house is Jupiter, ruler of Sagittarius. In this position Jupiter confers good health, a pleasing personality, a generous disposition, and an increased vitality. It also confers honors or wealth at some point in your lifetime. You may reap unexpected good fortune in times of hardship.

6

At some point, too, you may exile yourself from everyday life to serve a larger dedication. You will sacrifice for your ideals. Because you are zealous in your beliefs, you could make enemies behind your back. Again, the influence of Jupiter works to overcome the opposition.

You are the student, the idealist. Your need for wisdom is boundless. And you think big! You are not satisfied gathering concrete facts or analyzing practical information. You want to infer the grand patterns, to abstract, to generalize, and finally to generate new ideas. You are a visionary, a dreamer, a futurist. Philosophy, law, and religion attract you, for their truths go beyond the limits of everyday experience. Though you firmly hold your beliefs, you are not dogmatic. Rather, you romanticize them, and your method of persuasion is more seductive than shrill. You restless types are very adaptable, changing your ideas with each new discovery. Your mind is completely open.

With Sagittarius Rising you can be attracted to great causes. Your ideas are not generated merely to erect an impressive intellectual framework. Enlightened by your deep compassion, they become ideals in the service of humanity. There may be an inspirational quality to the causes you join or to the ideals you generate for a cause. Justice and mercy are concepts to be translated into action. You work hard to do that, but you are not rebellious or bossy or demanding. You are brave and forthright, without being reckless or combative. Cooperation and communication are important goals. You like working in groups; your friendly good humor is a model for all social relationships.

There is another you, a private you, that people do not necessarily know very well but may glimpse when you have gone out of their lives. That you is restless, opportunistic, seemingly rootless. You live so much in your mind that you don't want to be tied down by mundane obligations. In fact, you will escape from situations that limit your freedom of choice or action, even if you must dishonor a commitment to do so. You could shirk responsibility by flying off to some greener pasture, yet be no richer for the new experience. Carried to extremes, your quest for adventure could be self-indulgent, yet wasteful of yourself and selfish to the people around you.

Like the Archer, the zodiacal symbol of Sagittarius, you like to roam and hunt, though ideas and people may be your terrain and game. But some of you really prefer the outdoor life and sports. You certainly like to travel. Change recharges your happy-go-lucky nature. You like to get around but not get stuck in a rut, so just as swiftly as you appear on a scene, you disappear. Many jobs and places of residence are outcomes of your journeys.

The key words for Sagittarius Rising are buoyancy and expansiveness. Channel these forces into modes of industriousness so you do not waste your noble visions.

RISING SIGNS FOR SAGITTARIUS

Hour of Birth*	Date of Birth		
	November 21–25	November 26–30	December 1–5
Midnight	Virgo	Virgo	Virgo
1 AM	Virgo	Virgo	Virgo
2 AM	Libra	Libra	Libra
3 AM	Libra	Libra	Libra
4 AM	Libra	Libra; Scorpio 11/29	Libra
5 AM	Scorpio	Scorpio	Scorpio
6 AM	Scorpio	Scorpio	Scorpio
7 AM	Sagittarius	Sagittarius	Sagittarius
8 AM	Sagittarius	Sagittarius	Sagittarius
9 AM	Sagittarius	Capricorn	Capricorn
10 AM	Capricorn	Capricorn	Capricorn
11 AM	Capricorn; Aquarius 11/25	Aquarius	Aquarius
Noon	Aquarius	Aquarius; Pisces 12/3	Aquarius;
1 PM	Pisces	Pisces	Pisces
2 PM	Aries	Aries	Aries
3 PM	Aries	Taurus	Taurus
4 PM	Taurus	Taurus; Gemini 12/2	Taurus;
5 PM	Gemini	Gemini	Gemini
6 PM	Gemini	Gemini; Cancer 12/2	Gemini;
7 PM	Cancer	Cancer	Cancer
8 PM	Cancer	Cancer	Cancer
9 PM	Leo	Leo	Leo
10 PM	Leo	Leo	Leo
11 PM	Leo	Leo; Virgo 11/30	Virgo

*Hour of birth given here is for Standard Time in any time zone. If your hour of birth was recorded in Daylight Saving Time, subtract one hour from it and consult that hour in the table above. For example, if you were born at 6 AM D.S.T., see 5 AM above.

Hour of Birth*	Date of Birth		
	December 6–10	**December 11–16**	**December 17–22**
Midnight	Virgo	Virgo	Virgo; Libra 12/22
1 AM	Libra	Libra	Libra
2 AM	Libra	Libra	Libra
3 AM	Libra	Libra; Scorpio 12/14	Scorpio
4 AM	Scorpio	Scorpio	Scorpio
5 AM	Scorpio	Scorpio	Scorpio; Sagittarius 12/21
6 AM	Sagittarius	Sagittarius	Sagittarius
7 AM	Sagittarius	Sagittarius	Sagittarius
8 AM	Sagittarius	Capricorn	Capricorn
9 AM	Capricorn	Capricorn	Capricorn
10 AM	Capricorn; Aquarius 12/10	Aquarius	Aquarius
11 AM	Aquarius	Aquarius	Aquarius; Pisces 12/18
Noon	Pisces	Pisces	Pisces; Aries 12/22
1 PM	Aries	Aries	Aries
2 PM	Aries	Taurus	Taurus
3 PM	Taurus	Taurus	Taurus; Gemini 12/19
4 PM	Gemini	Gemini	Gemini
5 PM	Gemini	Gemini	Cancer
6 PM	Cancer	Cancer	Cancer
7 PM	Cancer	Cancer	Cancer; Leo 12/22
8 PM	Leo	Leo	Leo
9 PM	Leo	Leo	Leo
10 PM	Leo	Leo; Virgo 12/15	Virgo
11 PM	Virgo	Virgo	Virgo

* See note on facing page.

THE PLACE OF ASTROLOGY IN TODAY'S WORLD

Does astrology have a place in the fast-moving, ultra-scientific world we live in today? Can it be justified in a sophisticated society whose outriders are already preparing to step off the moon into the deep space of the planets themselves? Or is it just a hangover of ancient superstition, a psychological dummy for neurotics and dreamers of every historical age?

These are the kind of questions that any inquiring person can be expected to ask when they approach a subject like astrology which goes beyond, but never excludes, the materialistic side of life.

The simple, single answer is that astrology works. It works for many millions of people in the western world alone. In the United States there are 10 million followers and in Europe, an estimated 25 million. America has more than 4000 practicing astrologers, Europe nearly three times as many. Even down-under Australia has its hundreds of thousands of adherents. In the eastern countries, astrology has enormous followings, again, because it has been proved to work. In India, for example, brides and grooms for centuries have been chosen on the basis of their astrological compatibility.

Astrology today is more vital than ever before, more practicable because all over the world the media devotes much space and time to it, more valid because science itself is confirming the precepts of astrological knowledge with every new exciting step. The ordinary person who daily applies astrology intelligently does not have to wonder whether it is true nor believe in it blindly. He can see it working for himself. And, if he can use it—and this book is designed to help the reader to do just that—he can make living a far richer experience, and become a more developed personality and a better person.

Astrology and Relationships

Astrology is the science of relationships. It is not just a study of planetary influences on man and his environment. It is the study of man himself.

We are at the center of our personal universe, of all our relationships. And our happiness or sadness depends on how we act, how we relate to the people and things that surround us. The emotions that we generate have a distinct effect—for better or worse—on the world around us. Our friends and our enemies will confirm this. Just look in the mirror the next time you are angry. In other words, each of us is a kind of sun or planet or star radiating our feelings on the environment around us. Our influence on our personal universe, whether loving, helpful, or destructive, varies with our changing moods, expressed through our individual character.

Our personal "radiations" are potent in the way they affect our moods and our ability to control them. But we usually are able to throw off our emotion in some sort of action—we have a good cry, walk it off, or tell someone our troubles—before it can build up too far and make us physically ill. Astrology helps us to understand the universal forces working on us, and through this understanding, we can become more properly adjusted to our surroundings so that we find ourselves coping where others may flounder.

The Challenge of Love

The challenge of love lies in recognizing the difference between infatuation, emotion, sex, and, sometimes, the intentional deceit of the other person. Mankind, with its record of broken marriages, despair, and disillusionment, is obviously not very good at making these distinctions.

Can astrology help?

Yes. In the same way that advance knowledge can usually help in any human situation. And there is probably no situation as human, as poignant, as pathetic and universal, as the failure of man's love.

Love, of course, is not just between man and woman. It involves love of children, parents, home, and friends. But the big problems usually involve the choice of partner.

Astrology has established degrees of compatibility that exist between people born under the various signs of the Zodiac. Because people are individuals, there are numerous variations and modifications. So the astrologer, when approached on mate and marriage matters, makes allowances for them. But the fact remains that some groups of people are suited for each other and some are not, and astrology has expressed this in terms of characteristics we all can study and use as a personal guide.

No matter how much enjoyment and pleasure we find in the different aspects of each other's character, if it is not an overall compatibility, the chances of our finding fulfillment or enduring happiness in each other are pretty hopeless. And astrology can help us to find someone compatible.

Astrology and Science

Closely related to our emotions is the "other side" of our personal universe, our physical welfare. Our body, of course, is largely influenced by things around us over which we have very little control. The phone rings, we hear it. The train runs late. We snag our stocking or cut our face shaving. Our body is under a constant bombardment of events that influence our daily lives to varying degrees.

The question that arises from all this is, what makes each of us act so that we have to involve other people and keep the ball of activity and evolution rolling? This is the question that both science and astrology are involved with. The scientists have attacked it from different angles: anthropology, the study of human evolution as body, mind and response to environment; anatomy, the study of bodily structure; psychology, the science of the human mind; and so on. These studies have produced very impressive classifications and valuable information, but because the approach to the problem is fragmented, so is the result. They remain "branches" of science. Science generally studies effects. It keeps turning up wonderful answers but no lasting solutions. Astrology, on the other hand, approaches the question from the broader viewpoint. Astrology began its inquiry with the totality of human experience and saw it as an effect. It then looked to find the cause, or at least the prime movers, and during thousands of years of observation of man and his *universal* environment came up with the extraordinary principle of planetary influence—or astrology, which, from the Greek, means the science of the stars.

Modern science, as we shall see, has confirmed much of astrology's foundations—most of it unintentionally, some of it reluctantly, but still, indisputably.

It is not difficult to imagine that there must be a connection between outer space and Earth. Even today, scientists are not too sure how our Earth was created, but it is generally agreed that it is only a tiny part of the universe. And as a part of the universe, people on Earth see and feel the influence of heavenly bodies in almost every aspect of our existence. There is no doubt that the Sun has the greatest influence on life on this planet. Without it there would be no life, for without it there would be no warmth, no division into day and night, no cycles of time or season at all. This is clear and easy to see. The influence of the Moon, on the other hand, is more subtle, though no less definite.

There are many ways in which the influence of the Moon manifests itself here on Earth, both on human and animal life. It is a well-known fact, for instance, that the large movements of water on our planet—that is the ebb and flow of the tides—are caused by the Moon's gravitational pull. Since this is so, it follows that these water movements do not occur only in the oceans, but that all bodies of water are affected, even down to the tiniest puddle.

The human body, too, which consists of about 70 percent water, falls within the scope of this lunar influence. For example the menstrual cycle of most women corresponds to the 28-day lunar month; the period of pregnancy in humans is 273 days, or equal to nine lunar months. Similarly, many illnesses reach a crisis at the change of the Moon, and statistics in many countries have shown that the crime rate is highest at the time of the Full Moon. Even human sexual desire has been associated with the phases of the Moon. But it is in the movement of the tides that we get the clearest demonstration of planetary influence, which leads to the irresistible correspondence between the so-called metaphysical and the physical.

Tide tables are prepared years in advance by calculating the future positions of the Moon. Science has known for a long time that the Moon is the main cause of tidal action. But only in the last few years has it begun to realize the possible extent of this influence on mankind. To begin with, the ocean tides do not rise and fall as we might imagine from our personal observations of them. The Moon as it orbits around Earth sets up a circular wave of attraction which pulls the oceans of the world after it, broadly in an east to west direction. This influence is like a phantom wave crest, a loop of power stretching from pole to pole which passes over and around the Earth like an invisible shadow. It travels with equal effect across the land masses and, as scientists were recently amazed to observe, caused oysters placed in the dark in the middle of the United States where there is no sea to open their shells to receive the nonexistent tide. If the land-locked oysters react to this invisible signal, what effect does it have on us who not so long ago in evolutionary time came out of the sea and still have its salt in our blood and sweat?

Less well known is the fact that the Moon is also the primary force behind the circulation of blood in human beings and animals, and the movement of sap in trees and plants. Agriculturists have established that the Moon has a distinct influence on crops, which explains why for centuries people have planted according to Moon cycles. The habits of many animals, too, are directed by the movement of the Moon. Migratory birds, for instance, depart only at or near the time of the Full Moon. And certain sea creatures, eels in particular, move only in accordance with certain phases of the Moon.

Know Thyself—Why?

In today's fast-changing world, everyone still longs to know what the future holds. It is the one thing that everyone has in common: rich and poor, famous and infamous, all are deeply concerned about tomorrow.

But the key to the future, as every historian knows, lies in the past. This is as true of individual people as it is of nations. You cannot understand your future without first understanding your past, which is simply another way of saying that you must first of all know yourself.

The motto "know thyself" seems obvious enough nowadays, but it was originally put forward as the foundation of wisdom by the ancient Greek philosophers. It was then adopted by the "mystery religions" of the ancient Middle East, Greece, Rome, and is still used in all genuine schools of mind training or mystical discipline, both in those of the East, based on yoga, and those of the West. So it is universally accepted now, and has been through the ages.

But how do you go about discovering what sort of person you are? The first step is usually classification into some sort of system of types. Astrology did this long before the birth of Christ. Psychology has also done it. So has modern medicine, in its way.

One system classifies people according to the source of the impulses they respond to most readily: the muscles, leading to direct bodily action; the digestive organs, resulting in emotion; or the brain and nerves, giving rise to thinking. Another such system says that character is determined by the endocrine glands, and gives us such labels as "pituitary," "thyroid," and "hyperthyroid" types. These different systems are neither contradictory nor mutually exclusive. In fact, they are very often different ways of saying the same thing.

Very popular, useful classifications were devised by Carl Jung, the eminent disciple of Freud. Jung observed among the different faculties of the mind, four which have a predominant influence on character. These four faculties exist in all of us without exception, but not in perfect balance. So when we say, for instance, that someone is a "thinking type," it means that in any situation he or she tries to be rational. Emotion, which may be the opposite of thinking, will be his or her weakest function. This thinking type can be sensible and reasonable, or calculating and unsympathetic. The emotional type, on the other hand, can often be recognized by exaggerated language—everything is either marvelous or terrible—and in extreme cases they even invent dramas and quarrels out of nothing just to make life more interesting.

The other two faculties are intuition and physical sensation. The sensation type does not only care for food and drink, nice clothes and furniture; he or she is also interested in all forms of physical experience. Many scientists are sensation types as are athletes and nature-lovers. Like sensation, intuition is a form of perception and we all possess it. But it works through that part of the mind which is not under conscious control—consequently it sees meanings and connections which are not obvious to thought or emotion. Inventors and original thinkers are always intuitive, but so, too, are superstitious people who see meanings where none exist.

Thus, sensation tells us what is going on in the world, feeling (that is, emotion) tells us how important it is to ourselves, thinking enables us to interpret it and work out what we should do about it, and intuition tells us what it means to ourselves and others. All four faculties are essential, and all are present in every one of us. But some people are guided chiefly by one, others by another. In addition, Jung also observed a division of the human personality into the extrovert and the introvert, which cuts across these four types.

A disadvantage of all these systems of classification is that one cannot tell very easily where to place oneself. Some people are reluctant to admit that they act to please their emotions. So they deceive themselves for years by trying to belong to whichever type they think is the "best." Of course, there is no best; each has its faults and each has its good points.

The advantage of the signs of the Zodiac is that they simplify classification. Not only that, but your date of birth is personal—it is unarguably yours. What better way to know yourself than by going back as far as possible to the very moment of your birth? And this is precisely what your horoscope is all about, as we shall see in the next section.

WHAT IS A HOROSCOPE?

If you had been able to take a picture of the skies at the moment of your birth, that photograph would be your horoscope. Lacking such a snapshot, it is still possible to recreate the picture—and this is at the basis of the astrologer's art. In other words, your horoscope is a representation of the skies with the planets in the exact positions they occupied at the time you were born.

The year of birth tells an astrologer the positions of the distant, slow-moving planets Jupiter, Saturn, Uranus, Neptune, and Pluto. The month of birth indicates the Sun sign, or birth sign as it is commonly called, as well as indicating the positions of the rapidly moving planets Venus, Mercury, and Mars. The day and time of birth will locate the position of our Moon. And the moment—the exact hour and minute—of birth determines the houses through what is called the Ascendant, or Rising sign.

With this information the astrologer consults various tables to calculate the specific positions of the Sun, Moon, and other planets relative to your birthplace at the moment you were born. Then he or she locates them by means of the Zodiac.

The Zodiac

The Zodiac is a band of stars (constellations) in the skies, centered on the Sun's apparent path around the Earth, and is divided into twelve equal segments, or signs. What we are actually dividing up is the Earth's path around the Sun. But from our point of view here on Earth, it seems as if the Sun is making a great circle around our planet in the sky, so we say it is the Sun's apparent path. This twelvefold division, the Zodiac, is a reference system for the astrologer. At any given moment the planets—and in astrology both the Sun and Moon are considered to be planets—can all be located at a specific point along this path.

Now where in all this are you, the subject of the horoscope? Your character is largely determined by the sign the Sun is in. So that is where the astrologer looks first in your horoscope, at your Sun sign.

The Sun Sign and the Cusp

There are twelve signs in the Zodiac, and the Sun spends approximately one month in each sign. But because of the motion of the Earth around the Sun—the Sun's apparent motion—the dates when the Sun enters and leaves each sign may change from year to year. Some people born near the cusp, or edge, of a sign have difficulty determining which is their Sun sign. But in this book a Table of Cusps is provided for the years 1900 to 2015 (page 5) so you can find out what your true Sun sign is.

Here are the twelve signs of the Zodiac, their ancient zodiacal symbol, and the dates when the Sun enters and leaves each sign for the year 2012. Remember, these dates may change from year to year.

ARIES	Ram	March 20–April 19
TAURUS	Bull	April 19–May 20
GEMINI	Twins	May 20–June 20
CANCER	Crab	June 20–July 22
LEO	Lion	July 22–August 22
VIRGO	Virgin	August 22–September 22
LIBRA	Scales	September 22–October 22
SCORPIO	Scorpion	October 22–November 21
SAGITTARIUS	Archer	November 21–December 21
CAPRICORN	Sea Goat	December 21–January 20
AQUARIUS	Water Bearer	January 20–February 19
PISCES	Fish	February 19–March 20

It is possible to draw significant conclusions and make meaningful predictions based simply on the Sun sign of a person. There are many people who have been amazed at the accuracy of the description of their own character based only on the Sun sign. But an astrologer needs more information than just your Sun sign to interpret the photograph that is your horoscope.

The Rising Sign and the Zodiacal Houses

An astrologer needs the exact time and place of your birth in order to construct and interpret your horoscope. The illustration on the next page shows the flat chart, or natural wheel, an astrologer uses. Note the inner circle of the wheel labeled 1 through 12. These 12 divisions are known as the houses of the Zodiac.

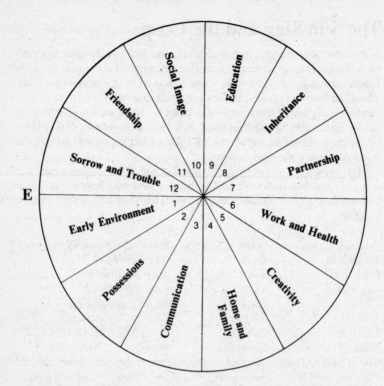

The 1st house always starts from the position marked E, which corresponds to the eastern horizon. The rest of the houses 2 through 12 follow around in a "counterclockwise" direction. The point where each house starts is known as a cusp, or edge.

The cusp, or edge, of the 1st house (point E) is where an astrologer would place your Rising sign, the Ascendant. And, as already noted, the exact time of your birth determines your Rising sign. Let's see how this works.

As the Earth rotates on its axis once every 24 hours, each one of the twelve signs of the Zodiac appears to be "rising" on the horizon, with a new one appearing about every 2 hours. Actually it is the turning of the Earth that exposes each sign to view, but in our astrological work we are discussing apparent motion. This Rising sign marks the Ascendant, and it colors the whole orientation of a horoscope. It indicates the sign governing the 1st house of the chart, and will thus determine which signs will govern all the other houses.

To visualize this idea, imagine two color wheels with twelve divisions superimposed upon each other. For just as the Zodiac is divided into twelve constellations that we identify as the signs, another twelvefold division is used to denote the houses. Now imagine one wheel (the signs) moving slowly while the other wheel (the houses) remains still. This analogy may help you see how the signs keep shifting the "color" of the houses as the Rising sign continues to change every two hours. To simplify things, a Table of Rising Signs has been provided (pages 8–9) for your specific Sun sign.

Once your Rising sign has been placed on the cusp of the 1st house, the signs that govern the rest of the 11 houses can be placed on the chart. In any individual's horoscope the signs do not necessarily correspond with the houses. For example, it could be that a sign covers part of two adjacent houses. It is the interpretation of such variations in an individual's horoscope that marks the professional astrologer.

But to gain a workable understanding of astrology, it is not necessary to go into great detail. In fact, we just need a description of the houses and their meanings, as is shown in the illustration above and in the table below.

THE 12 HOUSES OF THE ZODIAC

1st	Individuality, body appearance, general outlook on life	Personality house
2nd	Finance, possessions, ethical principles, gain or loss	Money house
3rd	Relatives, communication, short journeys, writing, education	Relatives house
4th	Family and home, parental ties, land and property, security	Home house
5th	Pleasure, children, creativity, entertainment, risk	Pleasure house
6th	Health, harvest, hygiene, work and service, employees	Health house
7th	Marriage and divorce, the law, partnerships and alliances	Marriage house
8th	Inheritance, secret deals, sex, death, regeneration	Inheritance house
9th	Travel, sports, study, philosophy, religion	Travel house
10th	Career, social standing, success and honor	Business house
11th	Friendship, social life, hopes and wishes	Friends house
12th	Troubles, illness, secret enemies, hidden agendas	Trouble house

The Planets in the Houses

An astrologer, knowing the exact time and place of your birth, will use tables of planetary motion in order to locate the planets in your horoscope chart. He or she will determine which planet or planets are in which sign and in which house. It is not uncommon, in an individual's horoscope, for there to be two or more planets in the same sign and in the same house.

The characteristics of the planets modify the influence of the Sun according to their natures and strengths.

Sun: Source of life. Basic temperament according to the Sun sign. The conscious will. Human potential.

Moon: Emotions. Moods. Customs. Habits. Changeable. Adaptive. Nurturing.

Mercury: Communication. Intellect. Reasoning power. Curiosity. Short travels.

Venus: Love. Delight. Charm. Harmony. Balance. Art. Beautiful possessions.

Mars: Energy. Initiative. War. Anger. Adventure. Courage. Daring. Impulse.

Jupiter: Luck. Optimism. Generous. Expansive. Opportunities. Protection.

Saturn: Pessimism. Privation. Obstacles. Delay. Hard work. Research. Lasting rewards after long struggle.

Uranus: Fashion. Electricity. Revolution. Independence. Freedom. Sudden changes. Modern science.

Neptune: Sensationalism. Theater. Dreams. Inspiration. Illusion. Deception.

Pluto: Creation and destruction. Total transformation. Lust for power. Strong obsessions.

Superimpose the characteristics of the planets on the functions of the house in which they appear. Express the result through the character of the Sun sign, and you will get the basic idea.

Of course, many other considerations have been taken into account in producing the carefully worked out predictions in this book: the aspects of the planets to each other; their strength according to position and sign; whether they are in a house of exaltation or decline; whether they are natural enemies or not; whether a planet occupies its own sign; the position of a planet in relation to its own house or sign; whether the sign is male or female; whether the sign is a fire, earth, water, or air sign. These are only a few of the colors on the astrologer's pallet which he or she must mix with the inspiration of the artist and the accuracy of the mathematician.

How To Use These Predictions

A person reading the predictions in this book should understand that they are produced from the daily position of the planets for a group of people and are not, of course, individually specialized. To get the full benefit of them our readers should relate the predictions to their own character and circumstances, coordinate them, and draw their own conclusions from them.

If you are a serious observer of your own life, you should find a definite pattern emerging that will be a helpful and reliable guide.

The point is that we always retain our free will. The stars indicate certain directional tendencies but we are not compelled to follow. We can do or not do, and wisdom must make the choice.

We all have our good and bad days. Sometimes they extend into cycles of weeks. It is therefore advisable to study daily predictions in a span ranging from the day before to several days ahead.

Daily predictions should be taken very generally. The word "difficult" does not necessarily indicate a whole day of obstruction or inconvenience. It is a warning to you to be cautious. Your caution will often see you around the difficulty before you are involved. This is the correct use of astrology.

In another section (pages 78–84), detailed information is given about the influence of the Moon as it passes through each of the twelve signs of the Zodiac. There are instructions on how to use the Moon Tables (pages 85–92), which provide Moon Sign Dates throughout the year as well as the Moon's role in health and daily affairs. This information should be used in conjunction with the daily forecasts to give a fuller picture of the astrological trends.

HISTORY OF ASTROLOGY

The origins of astrology have been lost far back in history, but we do know that reference is made to it as far back as the first written records of the human race. It is not hard to see why. Even in primitive times, people must have looked for an explanation for the various happenings in their lives. They must have wanted to know why people were different from one another. And in their search they turned to the regular movements of the Sun, Moon, and stars to see if they could provide an answer.

It is interesting to note that as soon as man learned to use his tools in any type of design, or his mind in any kind of calculation, he turned his attention to the heavens. Ancient cave dwellings reveal dim crescents and circles representative of the Sun and Moon, rulers of day and night. Mesopotamia and the civilization of Chaldea, in itself the foundation of those of Babylonia and Assyria, show a complete picture of astronomical observation and well-developed astrological interpretation.

Humanity has a natural instinct for order. The study of anthropology reveals that primitive people—even as far back as prehistoric times—were striving to achieve a certain order in their lives. They tried to organize the apparent chaos of the universe. They had the desire to attach meaning to things. This demand for order has persisted throughout the history of man. So that observing the regularity of the heavenly bodies made it logical that primitive peoples should turn heavenward in their search for an understanding of the world in which they found themselves so random and alone.

And they did find a significance in the movements of the stars. Shepherds tending their flocks, for instance, observed that when the cluster of stars now known as the constellation Aries was in sight, it was the time of fertility and they associated it with the Ram. And they noticed that the growth of plants and plant life corresponded with different phases of the Moon, so that certain times were favorable for the planting of crops, and other times were not. In this way, there grew up a tradition of seasons and causes connected with the passage of the Sun through the twelve signs of the Zodiac.

Astrology was valued so highly that the king was kept informed of the daily and monthly changes in the heavenly bodies, and the results of astrological studies regarding events of the future. Head astrologers were clearly men of great rank and position, and the office was said to be a hereditary one.

Omens were taken, not only from eclipses and conjunctions of the Moon or Sun with one of the planets, but also from storms and earthquakes. In the eastern civilizations, particularly, the reverence inspired by astrology appears to have remained unbroken since the very earliest days. In ancient China, astrology, astronomy, and religion went hand in hand. The astrologer, who was also an astronomer, was part of the official government service and had his own corner in the Imperial Palace. The duties of the Imperial astrologer, whose office was one of the most important in the land, were clearly defined, as this extract from early records shows:

> This exalted gentleman must concern himself with the stars in the heavens, keeping a record of the changes and movements of the Planets, the Sun and the Moon, in order to examine the movements of the terrestrial world with the object of prognosticating good and bad fortune. He divides the territories of the nine regions of the empire in accordance with their dependence on particular celestial bodies. All the fiefs and principalities are connected with the stars and from this their prosperity or misfortune should be ascertained. He makes prognostications according to the twelve years of the Jupiter cycle of good and evil of the terrestrial world. From the colors of the five kinds of clouds, he determines the coming of floods or droughts, abundance or famine. From the twelve winds, he draws conclusions about the state of harmony of heaven and earth, and takes note of good and bad signs that result from their accord or disaccord. In general, he concerns himself with five kinds of phenomena so as to warn the Emperor to come to the aid of the government and to allow for variations in the ceremonies according to their circumstances.

The Chinese were also keen observers of the fixed stars, giving them such unusual names as Ghost Vehicle, Sun of Imperial Concubine, Imperial Prince, Pivot of Heaven, Twinkling Brilliance, Weaving Girl. But, great astrologers though they may have been, the Chinese lacked one aspect of mathematics that the Greeks applied to astrology—deductive geometry. Deductive geometry was the basis of much classical astrology in and after the time of the Greeks, and this explains the different methods of prognostication used in the East and West.

Down through the ages the astrologer's art has depended, not so much on the uncovering of new facts, though this is important, as on the interpretation of the facts already known. This is the essence of the astrologer's skill.

But why should the signs of the Zodiac have any effect at all on the formation of human character? It is easy to see why people thought they did, and even now we constantly use astrological expressions in our everyday speech. The thoughts of "lucky star," "ill-fated," "star-crossed," "mooning around," are interwoven into the very structure of our language.

Wherever the concept of the Zodiac is understood and used, it could well appear to have an influence on the human character. Does this mean, then, that the human race, in whose civilization the idea of the twelve signs of the Zodiac has long been embedded, is divided into only twelve types? Can we honestly believe that it is really as simple as that? If so, there must be pretty wide ranges of variation within each type. And if, to explain the variation, we call in heredity and environment, experiences in early childhood, the thyroid and other glands, and also the four functions of the mind together with extroversion and introversion, then one begins to wonder if the original classification was worth making at all. No sensible person believes that his favorite system explains everything. But even so, he will not find the system much use at all if it does not even save him the trouble of bothering with the others.

In the same way, if we were to put every person under only one sign of the Zodiac, the system becomes too rigid and unlike life. Besides, it was never intended to be used like that. It may be convenient to have only twelve types, but we know that in practice there is every possible gradation between aggressiveness and timidity, or between conscientiousness and laziness. How, then, do we account for this?

A person born under any given Sun sign can be mainly influenced by one or two of the other signs that appear in their individual horoscope. For instance, famous persons born under the sign of Gemini include Henry VIII, whom nothing and no one could have induced to abdicate, and Edward VIII, who did just that. Obviously, then, the sign Gemini does not fully explain the complete character of either of them.

Again, under the opposite sign, Sagittarius, were both Stalin, who was totally consumed with the notion of power, and Charles V, who freely gave up an empire because he preferred to go into a monastery. And we find under Scorpio many uncompromising characters such as Luther, de Gaulle, Indira Gandhi, and Montgomery, but also Petain, a successful commander whose name later became synonymous with collaboration.

A single sign is therefore obviously inadequate to explain the differences between people; it can only explain resemblances, such as the combativeness of the Scorpio group, or the far-reaching devotion of Charles V and Stalin to their respective ideals—the Christian heaven and the Communist utopia.

But very few people have only one sign in their horoscope chart. In addition to the month of birth, the day and, even more, the hour to the nearest minute if possible, ought to be considered. Without this, it is impossible to have an actual horoscope, for the word horoscope literally means "a consideration of the hour."

The month of birth tells you only which sign of the Zodiac was occupied by the Sun. The day and hour tell you what sign was occupied by the Moon. And the minute tells you which sign was rising on the eastern horizon. This is called the Ascendant, and, as some astrologers believe, it is supposed to be the most important thing in the whole horoscope.

The Sun is said to signify one's heart, that is to say, one's deepest desires and inmost nature. This is quite different from the Moon, which signifies one's superficial way of behaving. When the ancient Romans referred to the Emperor Augustus as a Capricorn, they meant that he had the Moon in Capricorn. Or, to take another example, a modern astrologer would call Disraeli a Scorpion because he had Scorpio Rising, but most people would call him Sagittarius because he had the Sun there. The Romans would have called him Leo because his Moon was in Leo.

So if one does not seem to fit one's birth month, it is always worthwhile reading the other signs, for one may have been born at a time when any of them were rising or occupied by the Moon. It also seems to be the case that the influence of the Sun develops as life goes on, so that the month of birth is easier to guess in people over the age of forty. The young are supposed to be influenced mainly by their Ascendant, the Rising sign, which characterizes the body and physical personality as a whole.

It is nonsense to assume that all people born at a certain time will exhibit the same characteristics, or that they will even behave in the same manner. It is quite obvious that, from the very moment of its birth, a child is subject to the effects of its environment, and that this in turn will influence its character and heritage to a decisive extent. Also to be taken into account are education and economic conditions, which play a very important part in the formation of one's character as well.

People have, in general, certain character traits and qualities which, according to their environment, develop in either a positive or a negative manner. Therefore, selfishness (inherent selfishness, that is) might emerge as unselfishness; kindness and consideration as cruelty and lack of consideration toward others. In the same way, a naturally constructive person may, through frustration, become destructive, and so on. The latent characteristics with which people are born can, therefore, through environment and good or bad training, become something that would appear to be its opposite, and so give the lie to the astrologer's description of their character. But this is not the case. The true character is still there, but it is buried deep beneath these external superficialities.

Careful study of the character traits of various signs of the Zodiac are of immeasurable help, and can render beneficial service to the intelligent person. Undoubtedly, the reader will already have discovered that, while he is able to get on very well with some people, he just "cannot stand" others. The causes sometimes seem inexplicable. At times there is intense dislike, at other times immediate sympathy. And there is, too, the phenomenon of love at first sight, which is also apparently inexplicable. People appear to be either sympathetic or unsympathetic toward each other for no apparent reason.

Now if we look at this in the light of the Zodiac, we find that people born under different signs are either compatible or incompatible with each other. In other words, there are good and bad interrelating factors among the various signs. This does not, of course, mean that humanity can be divided into groups of hostile camps. It would be quite wrong to be hostile or indifferent toward people who happen to be born under an incompatible sign. There is no reason why everybody should not, or cannot, learn to control and adjust their feelings and actions, especially after they are aware of the positive qualities of other people by studying their character analyses, among other things.

Every person born under a certain sign has both positive and negative qualities, which are developed more or less according to our free will. Nobody is entirely good or entirely bad, and it is up to each of us to learn to control ourselves on the one hand and at the same time to endeavor to learn about ourselves and others.

It cannot be emphasized often enough that it is free will that determines whether we will make really good use of our talents and abilities. Using our free will, we can either overcome our failings or allow them to rule us. Our free will enables us to exert sufficient willpower to control our failings so that they do not harm ourselves or others.

Astrology can reveal our inclinations and tendencies. Astrology can tell us about ourselves so that we are able to use our free will to overcome our shortcomings. In this way astrology helps us do our best to become needed and valuable members of society as well as helpmates to our family and our friends. Astrology also can save us a great deal of unhappiness and remorse.

Yet it may seem absurd that an ancient philosophy could be a prop to modern men and women. But below the materialistic surface of modern life, there are hidden streams of feeling and thought. Symbology is reappearing as a study worthy of the scholar; the psychosomatic factor in illness has passed from the writings of the crank to those of the specialist; spiritual healing in all its forms is no longer a pious hope but an accepted phenomenon. And it is into this context that we consider astrology, in the sense that it is an analysis of human types.

Astrology and medicine had a long journey together, and only parted company a couple of centuries ago. There still remain in medical language such astrological terms as "saturnine," "choleric," and "mercurial," used in the diagnosis of physical tendencies. The herbalist, for long the handyman of the medical profession, has been dominated by astrology since the days of the Greeks. Certain herbs traditionally respond to certain planetary influences, and diseases must therefore be treated to ensure harmony between the medicine and the disease.

But the stars are expected to foretell and not only to diagnose.

Astrological forecasting has been remarkably accurate, but often it is wide of the mark. The brave person who cares to predict world events takes dangerous chances. Individual forecasting is less clear cut; it can be a help or a disillusionment. Then we come to the nagging question: if it is possible to foreknow, is it right to foretell? This is a point of ethics on which it is hard to pronounce judgment. The doctor faces the same dilemma if he finds that symptoms of a mortal disease are present in his patient and that he can only prognosticate a steady decline. How much to tell an individual in a crisis is a problem that has perplexed many distinguished scholars. Honest and conscientious astrologers in this modern world, where so many people are seeking guidance, face the same problem.

Five hundred years ago it was customary to call in a learned man who was an astrologer who was probably also a doctor and a philosopher. By his knowledge of astrology, his study of planetary influences, he felt himself qualified to guide those in distress. The world has moved forward at a fantastic rate since then, and yet people are still uncertain of themselves. At first sight it seems fantastic in the light of modern thinking that they turn to the most ancient of all studies, and get someone to calculate a horoscope for them. But is it really so fantastic if you take a second look? For astrology is concerned with tomorrow, with survival. And in a world such as ours, tomorrow and survival are the keywords for the twenty-first century.

SPECIAL OVERVIEW 2011–2020

The second decade of the twenty-first century opens on major planetary shifts that set the stage for challenge, opportunity, and change. The personal planets—notably Jupiter and Saturn—and the generational planets—Uranus, Neptune, and Pluto—have all moved forward into new signs of the zodiac. These fresh planetary influences act to shape unfolding events and illuminate pathways to the future.

Jupiter, the big planet that attracts luck, spends about one year in each zodiacal sign. It takes approximately twelve years for Jupiter to travel through all twelve signs of the zodiac in order to complete a cycle. In 2011 a new Jupiter cycle is initiated with Jupiter transiting Aries, the first sign of the zodiac. As each year progresses over the course of the decade, Jupiter moves forward into the next sign, following the natural progression of the zodiac. Jupiter visits Taurus in 2012, Gemini in 2013, Cancer in 2014, Leo in 2015, Virgo in 2016, Libra in 2017, Scorpio in 2018, Sagittarius in 2019, Capricorn in 2020. Then in late December 2020 Jupiter enters Aquarius just two weeks before the decade closes. Jupiter's vibrations are helpful and fruitful, a source of good luck and a protection against bad luck. Opportunity swells under Jupiter's powerful rays. Learning takes leaps of faith.

Saturn, the beautiful planet of reason and responsibility, spends about two and a half years in each zodiacal sign. A complete Saturn cycle through all twelve signs of the zodiac takes about twenty-nine to thirty years. Saturn is known as the lawgiver: setting boundaries and codes of conduct, urging self-discipline and structure within a creative framework. The rule of law, the role of government, the responsibility of the individual are all sourced from Saturn. Saturn gives as it takes. Once a lesson is learned, Saturn's reward is just and full.

Saturn transits Libra throughout 2011 until early autumn of 2012. Here Saturn seeks to harmonize, to balance, to bring order out of chaos. Saturn in Libra ennobles the artist, the judge, the high-minded, the honest. Saturn next visits Scorpio from autumn 2012 until late December 2014. With Saturn in Scorpio, tactic and strategy combine to get workable solutions and desired results. Saturn's problem-solving tools here can harness dynamic energy for the common good. Saturn in Sagittarius, an idealistic and humanistic transit that stretches from December 2014 into the last day of autumn 2017, promotes activism over mere dogma and debate. Saturn in Sagittarius can be a driving force for good. Saturn tours Capricorn, the sign that Saturn rules, from the first day of winter 2017 into early spring 2020. Saturn in Capricorn is a consolidating transit, bringing things forth and into fruition. Here a plan can be made right, made whole, then launched for success. Saturn starts to visit Aquarius, a sign that Saturn corules and a very good sign for Saturn to visit, in the very last year of the decade. Saturn in Aquarius fosters team spirit, the unity of effort amid diversity. The transit of Saturn in Aquarius until early 2023 represents a period of enlightened activism and unprecedented growth.

Uranus, Neptune, and Pluto spend more than several years in each sign. They produce the differences in attitude, belief, behavior, and taste that distinguish one generation from another—and so are called the generational planets.

Uranus, planet of innovation and surprise, is known as the awakener. Uranus spends seven to eight years in each sign. Uranus started a new cycle when it entered Aries, the first sign of the zodiac, in May 2010. Uranus tours Aries until May 2018. Uranus in Aries accents originality, freedom, independence, unpredictability. There can be a start-stop quality to undertakings given this transit. Despite contradiction and confrontation, significant invention and productivity mark this transit. Uranus next visits Taurus through the end of the decade into 2026. Strategic thinking and timely action characterize the transit of Uranus in Taurus. Here intuition is backed up by common sense, leading to fresh discoveries upon which new industries can be built.

Neptune spends about fourteen years in each sign. Neptune, the visionary planet, enters Pisces, the sign Neptune rules and the final sign of the zodiac, in early April 2011. Neptune journeys through Pisces until 2026 to complete the Neptune cycle of visiting all twelve zodiacal signs. Neptune's tour of Pisces ushers in a long period of great potentiality: universal understanding, universal good, universal love, universal generosity, universal forgiveness—the universal spirit affects all. Neptune in Pisces can oversee the fruition of such noble aims as human rights for all and liberation from all forms of tyranny. Neptune in Pisces is a pervasive influence that changes concepts, consciences, attitudes, actions. The impact of Neptune in Pisces is to illuminate and to inspire.

Pluto, dwarf planet of beginnings and endings, entered the earthy sign of Capricorn in 2008 and journeys there for sixteen years into late 2024. Pluto in Capricorn over the course of this extensive visit has the capacity to change the landscape as well as the humanscape. The transforming energy of Pluto combines with the persevering power of Capricorn to give depth and character to potential change. Pluto in Capricorn brings focus and cohesion to disparate, diverse creativities. As new forms arise and take root, Pluto in Capricorn organizes the rebuilding process. Freedom versus limitation, freedom versus authority is in the framework during this transit. Reasonableness struggles with recklessness to solve divisive issues. Pluto in Capricorn teaches important lessons about adversity, and the lessons will be learned.

THE SIGNS OF THE ZODIAC

Dominant Characteristics

Aries: March 21–April 20

The Positive Side of Aries

The Aries has many positive points to his character. People born under this first sign of the Zodiac are often quite strong and enthusiastic. On the whole, they are forward-looking people who are not easily discouraged by temporary setbacks. They know what they want out of life and they go out after it. Their personalities are strong. Others are usually quite impressed by the Ram's way of doing things. Quite often they are sources of inspiration for others traveling the same route. Aries men and women have a special zest for life that can be contagious; for others, they are a fine example of how life should be lived.

The Aries person usually has a quick and active mind. He is imaginative and inventive. He enjoys keeping busy and active. He generally gets along well with all kinds of people. He is interested in mankind, as a whole. He likes to be challenged. Some would say he thrives on opposition, for it is when he is set against that he often does his best. Getting over or around obstacles is a challenge he generally enjoys. All in all, Aries is quite positive and young-thinking. He likes to keep abreast of new things that are happening in the world. Aries are often fond of speed. They like things to be done quickly, and this sometimes aggravates their slower colleagues and associates.

The Aries man or woman always seems to remain young. Their whole approach to life is youthful and optimistic. They never say

die, no matter what the odds. They may have an occasional setback, but it is not long before they are back on their feet again.

The Negative Side of Aries

Everybody has his less positive qualities—and Aries is no exception. Sometimes the Aries man or woman is not very tactful in communicating with others; in his hurry to get things done he is apt to be a little callous or inconsiderate. Sensitive people are likely to find him somewhat sharp-tongued in some situations. Often in his eagerness to get the show on the road, he misses the mark altogether and cannot achieve his aims.

At times Aries can be too impulsive. He can occasionally be stubborn and refuse to listen to reason. If things do not move quickly enough to suit the Aries man or woman, he or she is apt to become rather nervous or irritable. The uncultivated Aries is not unfamiliar with moments of doubt and fear. He is capable of being destructive if he does not get his way. He can overcome some of his emotional problems by steadily trying to express himself as he really is, but this requires effort.

Taurus: April 21–May 20

The Positive Side of Taurus

The Taurus person is known for his ability to concentrate and for his tenacity. These are perhaps his strongest qualities. The Taurus man or woman generally has very little trouble in getting along with others; it's his nature to be helpful toward people in need. He can always be depended on by his friends, especially those in trouble.

Taurus generally achieves what he wants through his ability to persevere. He never leaves anything unfinished but works on something until it has been completed. People can usually take him at his word; he is honest and forthright in most of his dealings. The Taurus person has a good chance to make a success of his life because of his many positive qualities. The Taurus who aims high seldom falls short of his mark. He learns well by experience. He is thorough and does not believe in shortcuts of any kind. The Bull's thoroughness pays off in the end, for through his deliberateness he learns how to rely on himself and what he has learned. The Taurus person tries to get along with others, as a rule.

He is not overly critical and likes people to be themselves. He is a tolerant person and enjoys peace and harmony—especially in his home life.

Taurus is usually cautious in all that he does. He is not a person who believes in taking unnecessary risks. Before adopting any one line of action, he will weigh all of the pros and cons. The Taurus person is steadfast. Once his mind is made up it seldom changes. The person born under this sign usually is a good family person—reliable and loving.

The Negative Side of Taurus

Sometimes the Taurus man or woman is a bit too stubborn. He won't listen to other points of view if his mind is set on something. To others, this can be quite annoying. Taurus also does not like to be told what to do. He becomes rather angry if others think him not too bright. He does not like to be told he is wrong, even when he is. He dislikes being contradicted.

Some people who are born under this sign are very suspicious of others—even of those persons close to them. They find it difficult to trust people fully. They are often afraid of being deceived or taken advantage of. The Bull often finds it difficult to forget or forgive. His love of material things sometimes makes him rather avaricious and petty.

Gemini: May 21–June 20

The Positive Side of Gemini

The person born under this sign of the Heavenly Twins is usually quite bright and quick-witted. Some of them are capable of doing many different things. The Gemini person very often has many different interests. He keeps an open mind and is always anxious to learn new things.

Gemini is often an analytical person. He is a person who enjoys making use of his intellect. He is governed more by his mind than by his emotions. He is a person who is not confined to one view; he can often understand both sides to a problem or question. He knows how to reason, how to make rapid decisions if need be.

He is an adaptable person and can make himself at home almost anywhere. There are all kinds of situations he can adapt to. He is a person who seldom doubts himself; he is sure of his talents and his ability to think and reason. Gemini is generally most satisfied when he is in a situation where he can make use of his intellect. Never short of imagination, he often has strong talents for invention. He is rather a modern person when it comes to life; Gemini almost always moves along with the times—perhaps that is why he remains so youthful throughout most of his life.

Literature and art appeal to the person born under this sign. Creativity in almost any form will interest and intrigue the Gemini man or woman.

The Gemini is often quite charming. A good talker, he often is the center of attraction at any gathering. People find it easy to like a person born under this sign because he can appear easygoing and usually has a good sense of humor.

The Negative Side of Gemini

Sometimes the Gemini person tries to do too many things at one time—and as a result, winds up finishing nothing. Some Twins are easily distracted and find it rather difficult to concentrate on one thing for too long a time. Sometimes they give in to trifling fancies and find it rather boring to become too serious about any one thing. Some of them are never dependable, no matter what they promise.

Although the Gemini man or woman often appears to be well-versed on many subjects, this is sometimes just a veneer. His knowledge may be only superficial, but because he speaks so well he gives people the impression of erudition. Some Geminis are sharp-tongued and inconsiderate; they think only of themselves and their own pleasure.

Cancer: June 21–July 20

The Positive Side of Cancer

The Moon Child's most positive point is his understanding nature. On the whole, he is a loving and sympathetic person. He would never go out of his way to hurt anyone. The Cancer man or woman is often very kind and tender; they give what they can to others. They hate to see others suffering and will do what they can to help someone in less fortunate circumstances than themselves. They are often very concerned about the world. Their interest in people generally goes beyond that of just their own families and close friends; they have a deep sense of community and respect humanitarian values. The Moon Child means what he says, as a rule; he is honest about his feelings.

The Cancer man or woman is a person who knows the art of patience. When something seems difficult, he is willing to wait until the situation becomes manageable again. He is a person who knows how to bide his time. Cancer knows how to concentrate on one thing at a time. When he has made his mind up he generally sticks with what he does, seeing it through to the end.

Cancer is a person who loves his home. He enjoys being surrounded by familiar things and the people he loves. Of all the signs, Cancer is the most maternal. Even the men born under this sign often have a motherly or protective quality about them. They like to take care of people in their family—to see that they are well loved and well provided for. They are usually loyal and faithful. Family ties mean a lot to the Cancer man or woman. Parents and in-laws are respected and loved. Young Cancer responds very well to adults who show faith in him. The Moon Child has a strong sense of tradition. He is very sensitive to the moods of others.

The Negative Side of Cancer

Sometimes Cancer finds it rather hard to face life. It becomes too much for him. He can be a little timid and retiring, when things don't go too well. When unfortunate things happen, he is apt to just shrug and say, "Whatever will be will be." He can be fatalistic to a fault. The uncultivated Cancer is a bit lazy. He doesn't have very much ambition. Anything that seems a bit difficult he'll gladly leave to others. He may be lacking in initiative. Too sensitive, when he feels he's been injured, he'll crawl back into his shell and nurse his imaginary wounds. The immature Moon Child often is given to crying when the smallest thing goes wrong.

Some Cancers find it difficult to enjoy themselves in environments outside their homes. They make heavy demands on others, and need to be constantly reassured that they are loved. Lacking such reassurance, they may resort to sulking in silence.

Leo: July 21–August 21

The Positive Side of Leo

Often Leos make good leaders. They seem to be good organizers and administrators. Usually they are quite popular with others. Whatever group it is that they belong to, the Leo man or woman is almost sure to be or become the leader. Loyalty, one of the Lion's noblest traits, enables him or her to maintain this leadership position.

Leo is generous most of the time. It is his best characteristic. He or she likes to give gifts and presents. In making others happy, the Leo person becomes happy himself. He likes to splurge when spending money on others. In some instances it may seem that the Lion's generosity knows no boundaries. A hospitable person, the Leo man or woman is very fond of welcoming people to his house and entertaining them. He is never short of company.

Leo has plenty of energy and drive. He enjoys working toward some specific goal. When he applies himself correctly, he gets what he wants most often. The Leo person is almost never unsure of himself. He has plenty of confidence and aplomb. He is a person who is direct in almost everything he does. He has a quick mind and can make a decision in a very short time.

He usually sets a good example for others because of his ambitious manner and positive ways. He knows how to stick to something once he's started. Although Leo may be good at making a joke, he is not superficial or glib. He is a loving person, kind and thoughtful.

There is generally nothing small or petty about the Leo man or woman. He does what he can for those who are deserving. He is a person others can rely upon at all times. He means what he says. An honest person, generally speaking, he is a friend who is valued and sought out.

The Negative Side of Leo

Leo, however, does have his faults. At times, he can be just a bit too arrogant. He thinks that no one deserves a leadership position except him. Only he is capable of doing things well. His opinion of himself is often much too high. Because of his conceit, he is sometimes rather unpopular with a good many people. Some Leos are too materialistic; they can only think in terms of money and profit.

Some Leos enjoy lording it over others—at home or at their place of business. What is more, they feel they have the right to. Egocentric to an impossible degree, this sort of Leo cares little about how others think or feel. He can be rude and cutting.

Virgo: August 22–September 22

The Positive Side of Virgo

The person born under the sign of Virgo is generally a busy person. He knows how to arrange and organize things. He is a good planner. Above all, he is practical and is not afraid of hard work.

Often called the sign of the Harvester, Virgo knows how to attain what he desires. He sticks with something until it is finished. He never shirks his duties, and can always be depended upon. The Virgo person can be thoroughly trusted at all times.

The man or woman born under this sign tries to do everything to perfection. He doesn't believe in doing anything halfway. He always aims for the top. He is the sort of a person who is always learning and constantly striving to better himself—not because he wants more money or glory, but because it gives him a feeling of accomplishment.

The Virgo man or woman is a very observant person. He is sensitive to how others feel, and can see things below the surface of a situation. He usually puts this talent to constructive use.

It is not difficult for the Virgo to be open and earnest. He believes in putting his cards on the table. He is never secretive or underhanded. He's as good as his word. The Virgo person is generally plainspoken and down to earth. He has no trouble in expressing himself.

The Virgo person likes to keep up to date on new developments in his particular field. Well-informed, generally, he sometimes has a keen interest in the arts or literature. What he knows, he knows well. His ability to use his critical faculties is well-developed and sometimes startles others because of its accuracy.

Virgos adhere to a moderate way of life; they avoid excesses. Virgo is a responsible person and enjoys being of service.

The Negative Side of Virgo

Sometimes a Virgo person is too critical. He thinks that only he can do something the way it should be done. Whatever anyone else does is inferior. He can be rather annoying in the way he quibbles over insignificant details. In telling others how things should be done, he can be rather tactless and mean.

Some Virgos seem rather emotionless and cool. They feel emotional involvement is beneath them. They are sometimes too tidy, too neat. With money they can be rather miserly. Some Virgos try to force their opinions and ideas on others.

Libra: September 23–October 22

The Positive Side of Libra

Libras love harmony. It is one of their most outstanding character traits. They are interested in achieving balance; they admire beauty and grace in things as well as in people. Generally speaking, they are kind and considerate people. Libras are usually very sympathetic. They go out of their way not to hurt another person's feelings. They are outgoing and do what they can to help those in need.

People born under the sign of Libra almost always make good friends. They are loyal and amiable. They enjoy the company of others. Many of them are rather moderate in their views; they believe in keeping an open mind, however, and weighing both sides of an issue fairly before making a decision.

Alert and intelligent, Libra, often known as the Lawgiver, is always fair-minded and tries to put himself in the position of the other person. They are against injustice; quite often they take up for the underdog. In most of their social dealings, they try to be tactful and kind. They dislike discord and bickering, and most Libras strive for peace and harmony in all their relationships.

The Libra man or woman has a keen sense of beauty. They appreciate handsome furnishings and clothes. Many of them are artistically inclined. Their taste is usually impeccable. They know how to use color. Their homes are almost always attractively arranged and inviting. They enjoy entertaining people and see to it that their guests always feel at home and welcome.

Libra gets along with almost everyone. He is well-liked and socially much in demand.

The Negative Side of Libra

Some people born under this sign tend to be rather insincere. So eager are they to achieve harmony in all relationships that they will even go so far as to lie. Many of them are escapists. They find facing the truth an ordeal and prefer living in a world of make-believe.

In a serious argument, some Libras give in rather easily even when they know they are right. Arguing, even about something they believe in, is too unsettling for some of them.

Libras sometimes care too much for material things. They enjoy possessions and luxuries. Some are vain and tend to be jealous.

Scorpio: October 23–November 22

The Positive Side of Scorpio

The Scorpio man or woman generally knows what he or she wants out of life. He is a determined person. He sees something through to the end. Scorpio is quite sincere, and seldom says anything he doesn't mean. When he sets a goal for himself he tries to go about achieving it in a very direct way.

The Scorpion is brave and courageous. They are not afraid of hard work. Obstacles do not frighten them. They forge ahead until they achieve what they set out for. The Scorpio man or woman has a strong will.

Although Scorpio may seem rather fixed and determined, inside he is often quite tender and loving. He can care very much for others. He believes in sincerity in all relationships. His feelings about someone tend to last; they are profound and not superficial.

The Scorpio person is someone who adheres to his principles no matter what happens. He will not be deterred from a path he believes to be right.

Because of his many positive strengths, the Scorpion can often achieve happiness for himself and for those that he loves.

He is a constructive person by nature. He often has a deep understanding of people and of life, in general. He is perceptive and unafraid. Obstacles often seem to spur him on. He is a positive person who enjoys winning. He has many strengths and resources; challenge of any sort often brings out the best in him.

The Negative Side of Scorpio

The Scorpio person is sometimes hypersensitive. Often he imagines injury when there is none. He feels that others do not bother to recognize him for his true worth. Sometimes he is given to excessive boasting in order to compensate for what he feels is neglect.

Scorpio can be proud, arrogant, and competitive. They can be sly when they put their minds to it and they enjoy outwitting persons or institutions noted for their cleverness.

Their tactics for getting what they want are sometimes devious and ruthless. They don't care too much about what others may think. If they feel others have done them an injustice, they will do their best to seek revenge. The Scorpion often has a sudden, violent temper; and this person's interest in sex is sometimes quite unbalanced or excessive.

Sagittarius: November 23–December 20

The Positive Side of Sagittarius

People born under this sign are honest and forthright. Their approach to life is earnest and open. Sagittarius is often quite adult in his way of seeing things. They are broad-minded and tolerant people. When dealing with others the person born under the sign of the Archer is almost always open and forthright. He doesn't believe in deceit or pretension. His standards are high. People who associate with Sagittarius generally admire and respect his tolerant viewpoint.

The Archer trusts others easily and expects them to trust him. He is never suspicious or envious and almost always thinks well of others. People always enjoy his company because he is so friendly and easygoing. The Sagittarius man or woman is often good-humored. He can always be depended upon by his friends, family, and coworkers.

The person born under this sign of the Zodiac likes a good joke every now and then. Sagittarius is eager for fun and laughs, which makes him very popular with others.

A lively person, he enjoys sports and outdoor life. The Archer is fond of animals. Intelligent and interesting, he can begin an ani-

mated conversation with ease. He likes exchanging ideas and discussing various views.

He is not selfish or proud. If someone proposes an idea or plan that is better than his, he will immediately adopt it. Imaginative yet practical, he knows how to put ideas into practice.

The Archer enjoys sport and games, and it doesn't matter if he wins or loses. He is a forgiving person, and never sulks over something that has not worked out in his favor.

He is seldom critical, and is almost always generous.

The Negative Side of Sagittarius

Some Sagittarius are restless. They take foolish risks and seldom learn from the mistakes they make. They don't have heads for money and are often mismanaging their finances. Some of them devote much of their time to gambling.

Some are too outspoken and tactless, always putting their feet in their mouths. They hurt others carelessly by being honest at the wrong time. Sometimes they make promises which they don't keep. They don't stick close enough to their plans and go from one failure to another. They are undisciplined and waste a lot of energy.

Capricorn: December 21–January 19

The Positive Side of Capricorn

The person born under the sign of Capricorn, known variously as the Mountain Goat or Sea Goat, is usually very stable and patient. He sticks to whatever tasks he has and sees them through. He can always be relied upon and he is not averse to work.

An honest person, Capricorn is generally serious about whatever he does. He does not take his duties lightly. He is a practical person and believes in keeping his feet on the ground.

Quite often the person born under this sign is ambitious and knows how to get what he wants out of life. The Goat forges ahead and never gives up his goal. When he is determined about something, he almost always wins. He is a good worker—a hard worker. Although things may not come easy to him, he will not complain, but continue working until his chores are finished.

He is usually good at business matters and knows the value of money. He is not a spendthrift and knows how to put something away for a rainy day; he dislikes waste and unnecessary loss.

Capricorn knows how to make use of his self-control. He can apply himself to almost anything once he puts his mind to it. His ability to concentrate sometimes astounds others. He is diligent and does well when involved in detail work.

The Capricorn man or woman is charitable, generally speaking, and will do what is possible to help others less fortunate. As a friend, he is loyal and trustworthy. He never shirks his duties or responsibilities. He is self-reliant and never expects too much of the other fellow. He does what he can on his own. If someone does him a good turn, then he will do his best to return the favor.

The Negative Side of Capricorn

Like everyone, Capricorn, too, has faults. At times, the Goat can be overcritical of others. He expects others to live up to his own high standards. He thinks highly of himself and tends to look down on others.

His interest in material things may be exaggerated. The Capricorn man or woman thinks too much about getting on in the world and having something to show for it. He may even be a little greedy.

He sometimes thinks he knows what's best for everyone. He is too bossy. He is always trying to organize and correct others. He may be a little narrow in his thinking.

Aquarius: January 20–February 18

The Positive Side of Aquarius

The Aquarius man or woman is usually very honest and forthright. These are his two greatest qualities. His standards for himself are generally very high. He can always be relied upon by others. His word is his bond.

Aquarius is perhaps the most tolerant of all the Zodiac personalities. He respects other people's beliefs and feels that everyone is entitled to his own approach to life.

He would never do anything to injure another's feelings. He is never unkind or cruel. Always considerate of others, the Water

Bearer is always willing to help a person in need. He feels a very strong tie between himself and all the other members of mankind.

The person born under this sign, called the Water Bearer, is almost always an individualist. He does not believe in teaming up with the masses, but prefers going his own way. His ideas about life and mankind are often quite advanced. There is a saying to the effect that the average Aquarius is fifty years ahead of his time.

Aquarius is community-minded. The problems of the world concern him greatly. He is interested in helping others no matter what part of the globe they live in. He is truly a humanitarian sort. He likes to be of service to others.

Giving, considerate, and without prejudice, Aquarius have no trouble getting along with others.

The Negative Side of Aquarius

Aquarius may be too much of a dreamer. He makes plans but seldom carries them out. He is rather unrealistic. His imagination has a tendency to run away with him. Because many of his plans are impractical, he is always in some sort of a dither.

Others may not approve of him at all times because of his unconventional behavior. He may be a bit eccentric. Sometimes he is so busy with his own thoughts that he loses touch with the realities of existence.

Some Aquarius feel they are more clever and intelligent than others. They seldom admit to their own faults, even when they are quite apparent. Some become rather fanatic in their views. Their criticism of others is sometimes destructive and negative.

Pisces: February 19–March 20

The Positive Side of Pisces

Known as the sign of the Fishes, Pisces has a sympathetic nature. Kindly, he is often dedicated in the way he goes about helping others. The sick and the troubled often turn to him for advice and assistance. Possessing keen intuition, Pisces can easily understand people's deepest problems.

He is very broad-minded and does not criticize others for their faults. He knows how to accept people for what they are. On the whole, he is a trustworthy and earnest person. He is loyal to his friends and will do what he can to help them in time of need. Generous and good-natured, he is a lover of peace; he is often willing to help others solve their differences. People who have taken a wrong turn in life often interest him and he will do what he can to persuade them to rehabilitate themselves.

He has a strong intuitive sense and most of the time he knows how to make it work for him. Pisces is unusually perceptive and often knows what is bothering someone before that person, himself, is aware of it. The Pisces man or woman is an idealistic person, basically, and is interested in making the world a better place in which to live. Pisces believes that everyone should help each other. He is willing to do more than his share in order to achieve cooperation with others.

The person born under this sign often is talented in music or art. He is a receptive person; he is able to take the ups and downs of life with philosophic calm.

The Negative Side of Pisces

Some Pisces are often depressed; their outlook on life is rather glum. They may feel that they have been given a bad deal in life and that others are always taking unfair advantage of them. Pisces sometimes feel that the world is a cold and cruel place. The Fishes can be easily discouraged. The Pisces man or woman may even withdraw from the harshness of reality into a secret shell of his own where he dreams and idles away a good deal of his time.

Pisces can be lazy. He lets things happen without giving the least bit of resistance. He drifts along, whether on the high road or on the low. He can be lacking in willpower.

Some Pisces people seek escape through drugs or alcohol. When temptation comes along they find it hard to resist. In matters of sex, they can be rather permissive.

Sun Sign Personalities

ARIES: Hans Christian Andersen, Pearl Bailey, Marlon Brando, Wernher Von Braun, Charlie Chaplin, Joan Crawford, Da Vinci, Bette Davis, Doris Day, W.C. Fields, Alec Guinness, Adolf Hitler, William Holden, Thomas Jefferson, Nikita Khrushchev, Elton John, Arturo Toscanini, J.P. Morgan, Paul Robeson, Gloria Steinem, Sarah Vaughn, Vincent van Gogh, Tennessee Williams

TAURUS: Fred Astaire, Charlotte Brontë, Carol Burnett, Irving Berlin, Bing Crosby, Salvador Dali, Tchaikovsky, Queen Elizabeth II, Duke Ellington, Ella Fitzgerald, Henry Fonda, Sigmund Freud, Orson Welles, Joe Louis, Lenin, Karl Marx, Golda Meir, Eva Peron, Bertrand Russell, Shakespeare, Kate Smith, Benjamin Spock, Barbra Streisand, Shirley Temple, Harry Truman

GEMINI: Ruth Benedict, Josephine Baker, Rachel Carson, Carlos Chavez, Walt Whitman, Bob Dylan, Ralph Waldo Emerson, Judy Garland, Paul Gauguin, Allen Ginsberg, Benny Goodman, Bob Hope, Burl Ives, John F. Kennedy, Peggy Lee, Marilyn Monroe, Joe Namath, Cole Porter, Laurence Olivier, Harriet Beecher Stowe, Queen Victoria, John Wayne, Frank Lloyd Wright

CANCER: "Dear Abby," Lizzie Borden, David Brinkley, Yul Brynner, Pearl Buck, Marc Chagall, Princess Diana, Babe Didrikson, Mary Baker Eddy, Henry VIII, John Glenn, Ernest Hemingway, Lena Horne, Oscar Hammerstein, Helen Keller, Ann Landers, George Orwell, Nancy Reagan, Rembrandt, Richard Rodgers, Ginger Rogers, Rubens, Jean-Paul Sartre, O.J. Simpson

LEO: Neil Armstrong, James Baldwin, Lucille Ball, Emily Brontë, Wilt Chamberlain, Julia Child, William J. Clinton, Cecil B. De Mille, Ogden Nash, Amelia Earhart, Edna Ferber, Arthur Goldberg, Alfred Hitchcock, Mick Jagger, George Meany, Annie Oakley, George Bernard Shaw, Napoleon, Jacqueline Onassis, Henry Ford, Francis Scott Key, Andy Warhol, Mae West, Orville Wright

VIRGO: Ingrid Bergman, Warren Burger, Maurice Chevalier, Agatha Christie, Sean Connery, Lafayette, Peter Falk, Greta Garbo, Althea Gibson, Arthur Godfrey, Goethe, Buddy Hackett, Michael Jackson, Lyndon Johnson, D.H. Lawrence, Sophia Loren, Grandma Moses, Arnold Palmer, Queen Elizabeth I, Walter Reuther, Peter Sellers, Lily Tomlin, George Wallace

LIBRA: Brigitte Bardot, Art Buchwald, Truman Capote, Dwight D. Eisenhower, William Faulkner, F. Scott Fitzgerald, Gandhi, George Gershwin, Micky Mantle, Helen Hayes, Vladimir Horowitz, Doris Lessing, Martina Navratalova, Eugene O'Neill, Luciano Pavarotti, Emily Post, Eleanor Roosevelt, Bruce Springsteen, Margaret Thatcher, Gore Vidal, Barbara Walters, Oscar Wilde

SCORPIO: Vivien Leigh, Richard Burton, Art Carney, Johnny Carson, Billy Graham, Grace Kelly, Walter Cronkite, Marie Curie, Charles de Gaulle, Linda Evans, Indira Gandhi, Theodore Roosevelt, Rock Hudson, Katherine Hepburn, Robert F. Kennedy, Billie Jean King, Martin Luther, Georgia O'Keeffe, Pablo Picasso, Jonas Salk, Alan Shepard, Robert Louis Stevenson

SAGITTARIUS: Jane Austen, Louisa May Alcott, Woody Allen, Beethoven, Willy Brandt, Mary Martin, William F. Buckley, Maria Callas, Winston Churchill, Noel Coward, Emily Dickinson, Walt Disney, Benjamin Disraeli, James Doolittle, Kirk Douglas, Chet Huntley, Jane Fonda, Chris Evert Lloyd, Margaret Mead, Charles Schulz, John Milton, Frank Sinatra, Steven Spielberg

CAPRICORN: Muhammad Ali, Isaac Asimov, Pablo Casals, Dizzy Dean, Marlene Dietrich, James Farmer, Ava Gardner, Barry Goldwater, Cary Grant, J. Edgar Hoover, Howard Hughes, Joan of Arc, Gypsy Rose Lee, Martin Luther King, Jr., Rudyard Kipling, Mao Tse-tung, Richard Nixon, Gamal Nasser, Louis Pasteur, Albert Schweitzer, Stalin, Benjamin Franklin, Elvis Presley

AQUARIUS: Marian Anderson, Susan B. Anthony, Jack Benny, John Barrymore, Mikhail Baryshnikov, Charles Darwin, Charles Dickens, Thomas Edison, Clark Gable, Jascha Heifetz, Abraham Lincoln, Yehudi Menuhin, Mozart, Jack Nicklaus, Ronald Reagan, Jackie Robinson, Norman Rockwell, Franklin D. Roosevelt, Gertrude Stein, Charles Lindbergh, Margaret Truman

PISCES: Edward Albee, Harry Belafonte, Alexander Graham Bell, Chopin, Adelle Davis, Albert Einstein, Golda Meir, Jackie Gleason, Winslow Homer, Edward M. Kennedy, Victor Hugo, Mike Mansfield, Michelangelo, Edna St. Vincent Millay, Liza Minelli, John Steinbeck, Linus Pauling, Ravel, Renoir, Diana Ross, William Shirer, Elizabeth Taylor, George Washington

The Signs and Their Key Words

		POSITIVE	NEGATIVE
ARIES	self	courage, initiative, pioneer instinct	brash rudeness, selfish impetuosity
TAURUS	money	endurance, loyalty, wealth	obstinacy, gluttony
GEMINI	mind	versatility	capriciousness, unreliability
CANCER	family	sympathy, homing instinct	clannishness, childishness
LEO	children	love, authority, integrity	egotism, force
VIRGO	work	purity, industry, analysis	faultfinding, cynicism
LIBRA	marriage	harmony, justice	vacillation, superficiality
SCORPIO	sex	survival, regeneration	vengeance, discord
SAGITTARIUS	travel	optimism, higher learning	lawlessness
CAPRICORN	career	depth	narrowness, gloom
AQUARIUS	friends	human fellowship, genius	perverse unpredictability
PISCES	confinement	spiritual love, universality	diffusion, escapism

The Elements and Qualities of The Signs

Every sign has both an *element* and a *quality* associated with it. The element indicates the basic makeup of the sign, and the quality describes the kind of activity associated with each.

Element	Sign	Quality	Sign
FIRE	ARIES LEO SAGITTARIUS	CARDINAL	ARIES LIBRA CANCER CAPRICORN
EARTH	TAURUS VIRGO CAPRICORN	FIXED	TAURUS LEO SCORPIO AQUARIUS
AIR	GEMINI LIBRA AQUARIUS		
WATER	CANCER SCORPIO PISCES	MUTABLE	GEMINI VIRGO SAGITTARIUS PISCES

Signs can be grouped together according to their element and quality. Signs of the same element share many basic traits in common. They tend to form stable configurations and ultimately harmonious relationships. Signs of the same quality are often less harmonious, but they share many dynamic potentials for growth as well as profound fulfillment.

Further discussion of each of these sign groupings is provided on the following pages.

The Fire Signs

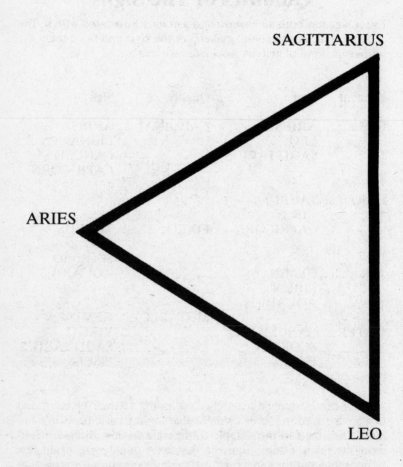

This is the fire group. On the whole these are emotional, volatile types, quick to anger, quick to forgive. They are adventurous, powerful people and act as a source of inspiration for everyone. They spark into action with immediate exuberant impulses. They are intelligent, self-involved, creative, and idealistic. They all share a certain vibrancy and glow that outwardly reflects an inner flame and passion for living.

The Earth Signs

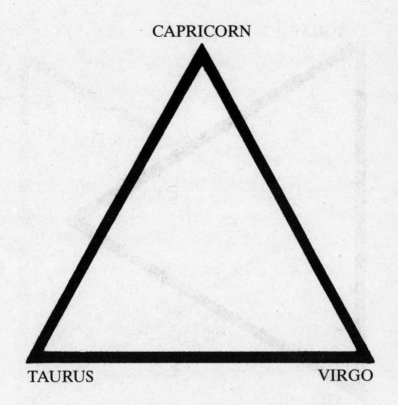

CAPRICORN

TAURUS

VIRGO

This is the earth group. They are in constant touch with the material world and tend to be conservative. Although they are all capable of spartan self-discipline, they are earthy, sensual people who are stimulated by the tangible, elegant, and luxurious. The thread of their lives is always practical, but they do fantasize and are often attracted to dark, mysterious, emotional people. They are like great cliffs overhanging the sea, forever married to the ocean but always resisting erosion from the dark, emotional forces that thunder at their feet.

The Air Signs

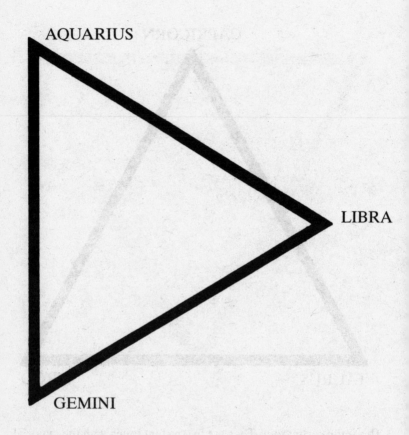

AQUARIUS

LIBRA

GEMINI

This is the air group. They are light, mental creatures desirous of contact, communication, and relationship. They are involved with people and the forming of ties on many levels. Original thinkers, they are the bearers of human news. Their language is their sense of word, color, style, and beauty. They provide an atmosphere suitable and pleasant for living. They add change and versatility to the scene, and it is through them that we can explore new territory of human intelligence and experience.

The Water Signs

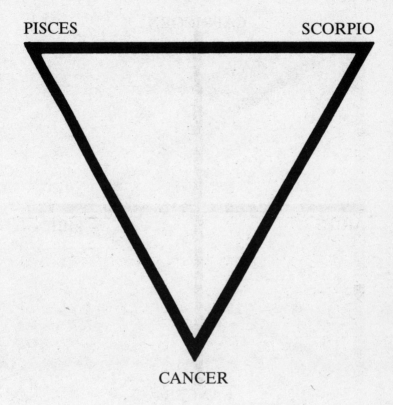

PISCES   SCORPIO

CANCER

This is the water group. Through the water people, we are all joined together on emotional, nonverbal levels. They are silent, mysterious types whose magic hypnotizes even the most determined realist. They have uncanny perceptions about people and are as rich as the oceans when it comes to feeling, emotion, or imagination. They are sensitive, mystical creatures with memories that go back beyond time. Through water, life is sustained. These people have the potential for the depths of darkness or the heights of mysticism and art.

The Cardinal Signs

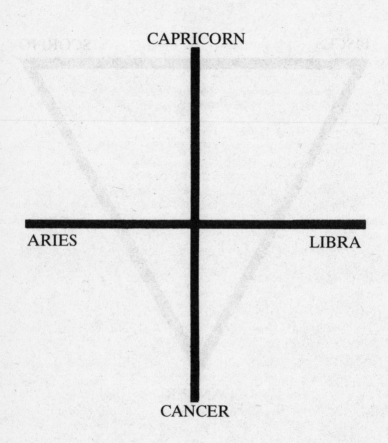

CAPRICORN

ARIES

LIBRA

CANCER

Put together, this is a clear-cut picture of dynamism, activity, tremendous stress, and remarkable achievement. These people know the meaning of great change since their lives are often characterized by significant crises and major successes. This combination is like a simultaneous storm of summer, fall, winter, and spring. The danger is chaotic diffusion of energy; the potential is irrepressible growth and victory.

The Fixed Signs

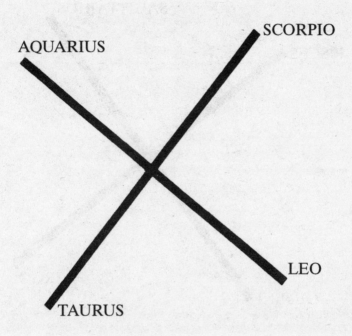

Fixed signs are always establishing themselves in a given place or area of experience. Like explorers who arrive and plant a flag, these people claim a position from which they do not enjoy being deposed. They are staunch, stalwart, upright, trusty, honorable people, although their obstinacy is well-known. Their contribution is fixity, and they are the angels who support our visible world.

The Mutable Signs

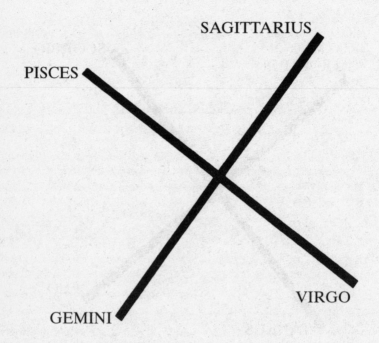

Mutable people are versatile, sensitive, intelligent, ner vous, and deeply curious about life. They are the translators of all energy. They often carry out or complete tasks initiated by others. Combinations of these signs have highly developed minds; they are imaginative and jumpy and think and talk a lot. At worst their lives are a Tower of Babel. At best they are adaptable and ready creatures who can assimilate one kind of experience and enjoy it while anticipating coming changes.

THE PLANETS
OF THE SOLAR SYSTEM

This section describes the planets of the solar system. In astrology, both the Sun and the Moon are considered to be planets. Because of the Moon's influence in our day-to-day lives, the Moon is described in a separate section following this one.

The Planets and the Signs They Rule

The signs of the Zodiac are linked to the planets in the following way. Each sign is governed or ruled by one or more planets. No matter where the planets are located in the sky at any given moment, they still rule their respective signs, and when they travel through the signs they rule, they have special dignity and their effects are stronger.

Following is a list of the planets and the signs they rule. After looking at the list, read the definitions of the planets and see if you can determine how the planet ruling *your* Sun sign has affected your life.

SIGNS	RULING PLANETS
Aries	Mars, Pluto
Taurus	Venus
Gemini	Mercury
Cancer	Moon
Leo	Sun
Virgo	Mercury
Libra	Venus
Scorpio	Mars, Pluto
Sagittarius	Jupiter
Capricorn	Saturn
Aquarius	Saturn, Uranus
Pisces	Jupiter, Neptune

Characteristics of the Planets

The following pages give the meaning and characteristics of the planets of the solar system. They all travel around the Sun at different speeds and different distances. Taken with the Sun, they all distribute individual intelligence and ability throughout the entire chart.

The planets modify the influence of the Sun in a chart according to their own particular natures, strengths, and positions. Their positions must be calculated for each year and day, and their function and expression in a horoscope will change as they move from one area of the Zodiac to another.

We start with a description of the sun.

THE SUN

SUN

This is the center of existence. Around this flaming sphere all the planets revolve in endless orbits. Our star is constantly sending out its beams of light and energy without which no life on Earth would be possible. In astrology it symbolizes everything we are trying to become, the center around which all of our activity in life will always revolve. It is the symbol of our basic nature and describes the natural and constant thread that runs through everything that we do from birth to death on this planet.

To early astrologers, the Sun seemed to be another planet because it crossed the heavens every day, just like the rest of the bodies in the sky.

It is the only star near enough to be seen well—it is, in fact, a dwarf star. Approximately 860,000 miles in diameter, it is about ten times as wide as the giant planet Jupiter. The next nearest star is nearly 300,000 times as far away, and if the Sun were located as far away as most of the bright stars, it would be too faint to be seen without a telescope.

Everything in the horoscope ultimately revolves around this singular body. Although other forces may be prominent in the charts of some individuals, still the Sun is the total nucleus of being and symbolizes the complete potential of every human being alive. It is vitality and the life force. Your whole essence comes from the position of the Sun.

You are always trying to express the Sun according to its position by house and sign. Possibility for all development is found in the Sun, and it marks the fundamental character of your personal radiations all around you.

It is the symbol of strength, vigor, wisdom, dignity, ardor, and generosity, and the ability for a person to function as a mature individual. It is also a creative force in society. It is consciousness of the gift of life.

The underdeveloped solar nature is arrogant, pushy, undependable, and proud, and is constantly using force.

MERCURY

Mercury is the planet closest to the Sun. It races around our star, gathering information and translating it to the rest of the system. Mercury represents your capacity to understand the desires of your own will and to translate those desires into action.

In other words it is the planet of mind and the power of communication. Through Mercury we develop an ability to think, write, speak, and observe—to become aware of the world around us. It colors our attitudes and vision of the world, as well as our capacity to communicate our inner responses to the outside world. Some people who have serious disabilities in their power of verbal communication have often wrongly been described as people lacking intelligence.

Although this planet (and its position in the horoscope) indicates your power to communicate your thoughts and perceptions to the world, intelligence is something deeper. Intelligence is distributed throughout all the planets. It is the relationship of the planets to each other that truly describes what we call intelligence. Mercury rules speaking, language, mathematics, draft and design, students, messengers, young people, offices, teachers, and any pursuits where the mind of man has wings.

VENUS

Venus is beauty. It symbolizes the harmony and radiance of a rare and elusive quality: beauty itself. It is refinement and delicacy, softness and charm. In astrology it indicates grace, balance, and the aesthetic sense. Where Venus is we see beauty, a gentle drawing in of energy and the need for satisfaction and completion. It is a special touch that finishes off rough edges. It is sensitivity, and affection, and it is always the place for that other elusive phenomenon: love. Venus describes our sense of what is beautiful and loving. Poorly developed, it is vulgar, tasteless, and self-indulgent. But its ideal is the flame of spiritual love—Aphrodite, goddess of love, and the sweetness and power of personal beauty.

MARS

Mars is raw, crude energy. The planet next to Earth but outward from the Sun is a fiery red sphere that charges through the horoscope with force and fury. It represents the way you reach out for new adventure and new experience. It is energy and drive, initiative, courage, and daring. It is the power to start something and see it through. It can be thoughtless, cruel and wild, angry and hostile, causing cuts, burns, scalds, and wounds. It can stab its way through a chart, or it can be the symbol of healthy spirited adventure, well-channeled constructive power to begin and keep up the drive. If you have trouble starting things, if you lack the get-up-and-go to start the ball rolling, if you lack aggressiveness and self-confidence, chances are there's another planet influencing your Mars. Mars rules soldiers, butchers, surgeons, salesmen—any field that requires daring, bold skill, operational technique, or self-promotion.

JUPITER

This is the largest planet of the solar system. Scientists have recently learned that Jupiter reflects more light than it receives from the Sun. In a sense it is like a star itself. In astrology it rules good luck and good cheer, health, wealth, optimism, happiness, success, and joy. It is the symbol of opportunity and always opens the way for new possibilities in your life. It rules exuberance, enthusiasm, wisdom, knowledge, generosity, and all forms of expansion in general. It rules actors, statesmen, clerics, professional people, religion, publishing, and the distribution of many people over large areas.

Sometimes Jupiter makes you think you deserve everything, and you become sloppy, wasteful, careless and rude, prodigal and lawless, in the illusion that nothing can ever go wrong. Then there is the danger of overconfidence, exaggeration, undependability, and overindulgence.

Jupiter is the minimization of limitation and the emphasis on spirituality and potential. It is the thirst for knowledge and higher learning.

SATURN

Saturn circles our system in dark splendor with its mysterious rings, forcing us to be awakened to what ever we have neglected in the past. It will present real puzzles and problems to be solved, causing delays, obstacles, and hindrances. By doing so, Saturn stirs our own sensitivity to those areas where we are laziest.

Here we must patiently develop *method*, and only through painstaking effort can our ends be achieved. It brings order to a horoscope and imposes reason just where we are feeling least reasonable. By creating limitations and boundary, Saturn shows the consequences of being human and demands that we accept the changing cycles inevitable in human life. Saturn rules time, old age, and sobriety. It can bring depression, gloom, jealousy, and greed, or serious acceptance of responsibilities out of which success will develop. With Saturn there is nothing to do but face facts. It rules laborers, stones, granite, rocks, and crystals of all kinds.

THE OUTER PLANETS:
URANUS, NEPTUNE, PLUTO

Uranus, Neptune, Pluto are the outer planets. They liberate human beings from cultural conditioning, and in that sense are the lawbreakers. In early times it was thought that Saturn was the last planet of the system—the outer limit beyond which we could never go. The discovery of the next three planets ushered in new phases of human history, revolution, and technology.

URANUS

Uranus rules unexpected change, upheaval, revolution. It is the symbol of total independence and asserts the freedom of an individual from all restriction and restraint. It is a breakthrough planet and indicates talent, originality, and genius in a horoscope. It usually causes last-minute reversals and changes of plan, unwanted separations, accidents, catastrophes, and eccentric behavior. It can add irrational rebelliousness and perverse bohemianism to a personality or a streak of unaffected brilliance in science and art. It rules technology, aviation, and all forms of electrical and electronic advancement. It governs great leaps forward and topsy-turvy situations, and *always* turns things around at the last minute. Its effects are difficult to predict, since it rules sudden last-minute decisions and events that come like lightning out of the blue.

NEPTUNE

Neptune dissolves existing reality the way the sea erodes the cliffs beside it. Its effects are subtle like the ringing of a buoy's bell in the fog. It suggests a reality higher than definition can usually describe. It awakens a sense of higher responsibility often causing guilt, worry, anxieties, or delusions. Neptune is associated with all forms of escape and can make things seem a certain way so convincingly that you are absolutely sure of something that eventually turns out to be quite different.

It is the planet of illusion and therefore governs the invisible realms that lie beyond our ordinary minds, beyond our simple factual ability to prove what is "real." Treachery, deceit, disillusionment, and disappointment are linked to Neptune. It describes a vague reality that promises eternity and the divine, yet in a manner so complex that we cannot really fathom it at all. At its worst Neptune is a cheap intoxicant; at its best it is the poetry, music, and inspiration of the higher planes of spiritual love. It has dominion over movies, photographs, and much of the arts.

PLUTO

Pluto lies at the outpost of our system and therefore rules finality in a horoscope—the final closing of chapters in your life, the passing of major milestones and points of development from which there is no return. It is a final wipeout, a closeout, an evacuation. It is a distant, subtle but powerful catalyst in all transformations that occur. It creates, destroys, then re creates. Sometimes Pluto starts its influence with a minor event or insignificant incident that might even go unnoticed. Slowly but surely, little by little, everything changes, until at last there has been a total transformation in the area of your life where Pluto has been operating. It rules mass thinking and the trends that society first rejects, then adopts, and finally outgrows.

Pluto rules the dead and the underworld—all the powerful forces of creation and destruction that go on all the time beneath, around, and above us. It can bring a lust for power with strong obsessions.

It is the planet that rules the metamorphosis of the caterpillar into a butterfly, for it symbolizes the capacity to change totally and forever a person's lifestyle, way of thought, and behavior.

THE MOON IN EACH SIGN

The Moon is the nearest planet to the Earth. It exerts more observable influence on us from day to day than any other planet. The effect is very personal, very intimate, and if we are not aware of how it works it can make us quite unstable in our ideas. And the annoying thing is that at these times we often see our own instability but can do nothing about it. A knowledge of what can be expected may help considerably. We can then be prepared to stand strong against the Moon's negative influences and use its positive ones to help us to get ahead. Who has not heard of going with the tide?

The Moon reflects, has no light of its own. It reflects the Sun—the life giver—in the form of vital movement. The Moon controls the tides, the blood rhythm, the movement of sap in trees and plants. Its nature is inconstancy and change so it signifies our moods, our superficial behavior—walking, talking, and especially thinking. Being a true reflector of other forces, the Moon is cold, watery like the surface of a still lake, brilliant and scintillating at times, but easily ruffled and disturbed by the winds of change.

The Moon takes about 27⅓ days to make a complete transit of the Zodiac. It spends just over 2¼ days in each sign. During that time it reflects the qualities, energies, and characteristics of the sign and, to a degree, the planet which rules the sign. When the Moon in its transit occupies a sign incompatible with our own birth sign, we can expect to feel a vague uneasiness, perhaps a touch of irritableness. We should not be discouraged nor let the feeling get us down, or, worse still, allow ourselves to take the discomfort out on others. Try to remember that the Moon has to change signs within 55 hours and, provided you are not physically ill, your mood will probably change with it. It is amazing how frequently depression lifts with the shift in the Moon's position. And, of course, when the Moon is transiting a sign compatible or sympathetic to yours, you will probably feel some sort of stimulation or just be plain happy to be alive.

In the horoscope, the Moon is such a powerful indicator that competent astrologers often use the sign it occupied at birth as the birth sign of the person. This is done particularly when the Sun is on the cusp, or edge, of two signs. Most experienced astrologers, however, coordinate both Sun and Moon signs by reading and confirming from one to the other and secure a far more accurate and personalized analysis.

For these reasons, the Moon tables which follow this section (see pages 86–92) are of great importance to the individual. They show the days and the exact times the Moon will enter each sign of the Zodiac for the year. Remember, you have to adjust the indicated times to local time. The corrections, already calculated for most of the main cities, are at the beginning of the tables. What follows now is a guide to the influences that will be reflected to the Earth by the Moon while it transits each of the twelve signs. The influence is at its peak about 26 hours after the Moon enters a sign. As you read the daily forecast, check the Moon sign for any given day and glance back at this guide.

MOON IN ARIES

This is a time for action, for reaching out beyond the usual self-imposed limitations and faint-hearted cautions. If you have plans in your head or on your desk, put them into practice. New ventures, applications, new jobs, new starts of any kind—all have a good chance of success. This is the period when original and dynamic impulses are being reflected onto Earth. Such energies are extremely vital and favor the pursuit of pleasure and adventure in practically every form. Sick people should feel an improvement. Those who are well will probably find themselves exuding confidence and optimism. People fond of physical exercise should find their bodies growing with tone and well-being. Boldness, strength, determination should characterize most of your activities with a readiness to face up to old challenges. Yesterday's problems may seem petty and exaggerated—so deal with them. Strike out alone. Self-reliance will attract others to you. This is a good time for making friends. Business and marriage partners are more likely to be impressed with the man and woman of action. Opposition will be overcome or thrown aside with much less effort than usual. CAUTION: Be dominant but not domineering.

MOON IN TAURUS

The spontaneous, action-packed person of yesterday gives way to the cautious, diligent, hardworking "thinker." In this period ideas will probably be concentrated on ways of improving finances. A great deal of time may be spent figuring out and going over schemes and plans. It is the right time to be careful with detail.

People will find themselves working longer than usual at their desks. Or devoting more time to serious thought about the future. A strong desire to put order into business and financial arrangements may cause extra work. Loved ones may complain of being neglected and may fail to appreciate that your efforts are for their ultimate benefit. Your desire for system may extend to criticism of arrangements in the home and lead to minor upsets. Health may be affected through overwork. Try to secure a reasonable amount of rest and relaxation, although the tendency will be to "keep going" despite good advice. Work done conscientiously in this period should result in a solid contribution to your future security. CAUTION: Try not to be as serious with people as the work you are engaged in.

MOON IN GEMINI
The humdrum of routine and too much work should suddenly end. You are likely to find yourself in an expansive, quicksilver world of change and self-expression. Urges to write, to paint, to experience the freedom of some sort of artistic outpouring, may be very strong. Take full advantage of them. You may find yourself finishing something you began and put aside long ago. Or embarking on something new which could easily be prompted by a chance meeting, a new acquaintance, or even an advertisement. There may be a yearning for a change of scenery, the feeling to visit another country (not too far away), or at least to get away for a few days. This may result in short, quick journeys. Or, if you are planning a single visit, there may be some unexpected changes or detours on the way. Familiar activities will seem to give little satisfaction unless they contain a fresh element of excitement or expectation. The inclination will be toward untried pursuits, particularly those that allow you to express your inner nature. The accent is on new faces, new places. CAUTION: Do not be too quick to commit yourself emotionally.

MOON IN CANCER
Feelings of uncertainty and vague insecurity are likely to cause problems while the Moon is in Cancer. Thoughts may turn frequently to the warmth of the home and the comfort of loved ones. Nostalgic impulses could cause you to bring out old photographs and letters and reflect on the days when your life seemed to be much more rewarding and less demanding. The love and understanding of parents and family may be important, and, if it is not forthcoming, you may have to fight against bouts of self-pity. The cordiality of friends and the thought of good times with them that are sure to be repeated will help to restore you to a happier frame

of mind. The desire to be alone may follow minor setbacks or re-buffs at this time, but solitude is unlikely to help. Better to get on the telephone or visit someone. This period often causes peculiar dreams and upsurges of imaginative thinking which can be help-ful to authors of occult and mystical works. Preoccupation with the personal world of simple human needs can overshadow any mate-rial strivings. CAUTION: Do not spend too much time thinking—seek the company of loved ones or close friends.

MOON IN LEO
New horizons of exciting and rather extravagant activity open up. This is the time for exhilarating entertainment, glamorous and lav-ish parties, and expensive shopping sprees. Any merrymaking that relies upon your generosity as a host has every chance of being a spectacular success. You should find yourself right in the center of the fun, either as the life of the party or simply as a person whom happy people like to be with. Romance thrives in this heady atmo-sphere and friendships are likely to explode unexpectedly into seri-ous attachments. Children and younger people should be attracted to you and you may find yourself organizing a picnic or a visit to a fun-fair, the movies, or the beach. The sunny company and vitality of youthful companions should help you to find some unsuspected energy. In career, you could find an opening for promotion or ad-vancement. This should be the time to make a direct approach. The period favors those engaged in original research. CAUTION: Bask in popularity, not in flattery.

MOON IN VIRGO
Off comes the party cap and out steps the busy, practical worker. He wants to get his personal affairs straight, to rearrange them, if necessary, for more efficiency, so he will have more time for more work. He clears up his correspondence, pays outstanding bills, makes numerous phone calls. He is likely to make inquiries, or sign up for some new insurance and put money into gilt-edged investment. Thoughts probably revolve around the need for future security—to tie up loose ends and clear the decks. There may be a tendency to be "finicky," to interfere in the routine of others, particularly friends and family members. The motive may be a genuine desire to help with suggestions for updating or streamlining their affairs, but these will probably not be welcomed. Sympathy may be felt for less fortunate sections of the community and a flurry of some sort of voluntary ser-vice is likely. This may be accompanied by strong feelings of respon-sibility on several fronts and health may suffer from extra efforts made. CAUTION: Everyone may not want your help or advice.

MOON IN LIBRA

These are days of harmony and agreement and you should find yourself at peace with most others. Relationships tend to be smooth and sweet-flowing. Friends may become closer and bonds deepen in mutual understanding. Hopes will be shared. Progress by cooperation could be the secret of success in every sphere. In business, established partnerships may flourish and new ones get off to a good start. Acquaintances could discover similar interests that lead to congenial discussions and rewarding exchanges of some sort. Love, as a unifying force, reaches its optimum. Marriage partners should find accord. Those who wed at this time face the prospect of a happy union. Cooperation and tolerance are felt to be stronger than dissension and impatience. The argumentative are not quite so loud in their bellowings, nor as inflexible in their attitudes. In the home, there should be a greater recognition of the other point of view and a readiness to put the wishes of the group before selfish insistence. This is a favorable time to join an art group. CAUTION: Do not be too independent—let others help you if they want to.

MOON IN SCORPIO

Driving impulses to make money and to economize are likely to cause upsets all around. No area of expenditure is likely to be spared the ax, including the household budget. This is a time when the desire to cut down on extravagance can become near fanatical. Care must be exercised to try to keep the aim in reasonable perspective. Others may not feel the same urgent need to save and may retaliate. There is a danger that possessions of sentimental value will be sold to realize cash for investment. Buying and selling of stock for quick profit is also likely. The attention turns to organizing, reorganizing, tidying up at home and at work. Neglected jobs could suddenly be done with great bursts of energy. The desire for solitude may intervene. Self-searching thoughts could disturb. The sense of invisible and mysterious energies in play could cause some excitability. The reassurance of loves ones may help. CAUTION: Be kind to the people you love.

MOON IN SAGITTARIUS

These are days when you are likely to be stirred and elevated by discussions and reflections of a religious and philosophical nature. Ideas of faraway places may cause unusual response and excitement. A decision may be made to visit someone overseas, perhaps a person whose influence was important to your earlier character development. There could be a strong resolution to get away from present intellectual patterns, to learn new subjects, and to meet more interesting people. The superficial may be rejected in all its forms. An impatience with old ideas and unimaginative contacts could lead to a change of companions and interests. There may be an upsurge of religious feeling and metaphysical inquiry. Even a new insight into the significance of astrology and other occult studies is likely under the curious stimulus of the Moon in Sagittarius. Physically, you may express this need for fundamental change by spending more time outdoors: sports, gardening, long walks appeal. CAUTION: Try to channel any restlessness into worthwhile study.

MOON IN CAPRICORN
Life in these hours may seem to pivot around the importance of gaining prestige and honor in the career, as well as maintaining a spotless reputation. Ambitious urges may be excessive and could be accompanied by quite acquisitive drives for money. Effort should be directed along strictly ethical lines where there is no possibility of reproach or scandal. All endeavors are likely to be characterized by great earnestness, and an air of authority and purpose which should impress those who are looking for leadership or reliability. The desire to conform to accepted standards may extend to sharp criticism of family members. Frivolity and unconventional actions are unlikely to amuse while the Moon is in Capricorn. Moderation and seriousness are the orders of the day. Achievement and recognition in this period could come through community work or organizing for the benefit of some amateur group. CAUTION: Dignity and esteem are not always self-awarded.

MOON IN AQUARIUS
Moon in Aquarius is in the second last sign of the Zodiac where ideas can become disturbingly fine and subtle. The result is often a mental "no-man's land" where imagination cannot be trusted with the same certitude as other times. The dangers for the individual are the extremes of optimism and pessimism. Unless the imagination is held in check, situations are likely to be misread, and rosy conclusions drawn where they do not exist. Consequences for the unwary can be costly in career and business. Best to think twice and not speak or act until you think again. Pessimism can be a cruel self-inflicted penalty for delusion at this time. Between the two extremes are strange areas of self-deception which, for example, can make the selfish person think he is actually being generous. Eerie dreams which resemble the reality and even seem to continue into the waking state are also possible. CAUTION: Look for the fact and not just for the image in your mind.

MOON IN PISCES

Everything seems to come to the surface now. Memory may be crystal clear, throwing up long-forgotten information which could be valuable in the career or business. Flashes of clairvoyance and intuition are possible along with sudden realizations of one's own nature, which may be used for self-improvement. A talent, never before suspected, may be discovered. Qualities not evident before in friends and marriage partners are likely to be noticed. As this is a period in which the truth seems to emerge, the discovery of false characteristics is likely to lead to disenchantment or a shift in attachments. However, when qualities are accepted, it should lead to happiness and deeper feeling. Surprise solutions could bob up for old problems. There may be a public announcement of the solving of a crime or mystery. People with secrets may find someone has "guessed" correctly. The secrets of the soul or the inner self also tend to reveal themselves. Religious and philosophical groups may make some interesting discoveries. CAUTION: Not a time for activities that depend on secrecy.

NOTE: When you read your daily forecasts, use the Moon Sign Dates that are provided in the following section of Moon Tables. Then you may want to glance back here for the Moon's influence in a given sign.

MOON TABLES

Atlanta, Boston, Detroit, Miami, Washington, Montreal,
Ottawa, Quebec, Bogota, Havana, Lima, Santiago...... Same time

Chicago, New Orleans, Houston, Winnipeg, Churchill,
Mexico City .... Deduct 1 hour

Albuquerque, Denver, Phoenix, El Paso, Edmonton,
Helena .... Deduct 2 hours

Los Angeles, San Francisco, Reno, Portland,
Seattle, Vancouver .... Deduct 3 hours

Honolulu, Anchorage, Fairbanks, Kodiak .... Deduct 5 hours

Nome, Samoa, Tonga, Midway .... Deduct 6 hours

Halifax, Bermuda, San Juan, Caracas, La Paz,
Barbados .... Add 1 hour

St. John's, Brasilia, Rio de Janeiro, Sao Paulo,
Buenos Aires, Montevideo .... Add 2 hours

Azores, Cape Verde Islands .... Add 3 hours

Canary Islands, Madeira, Reykjavik .... Add 4 hours

London, Paris, Amsterdam, Madrid, Lisbon,
Gibraltar, Belfast, Raba .... Add 5 hours

Frankfurt, Rome, Oslo, Stockholm, Prague,
Belgrade .... Add 6 hours

Bucharest, Beirut, Tel Aviv, Athens, Istanbul, Cairo,
Alexandria, Cape Town, Johannesburg .... Add 7 hours

Moscow, Leningrad, Baghdad, Dhahran,
Addis Ababa, Nairobi, Teheran, Zanzibar .... Add 8 hours

Bombay, Calcutta, Sri Lanka .... Add 10½

Hong Kong, Shanghai, Manila, Peking, Perth .... Add 13 hours

Tokyo, Okinawa, Darwin, Pusan .... Add 14 hours

Sydney, Melbourne, Port Moresby, Guam .... Add 15 hours

Auckland, Wellington, Suva, Wake .... Add 17 hours

2012 MOON SIGN DATES—
NEW YORK TIME

JANUARY		FEBRUARY		MARCH	
Day Moon Enters		Day Moon Enters		Day Moon Enters	
1. Aries		1. Gemini	2:16 pm	1. Gemini	
2. Taurus	5:17 pm	2. Gemini		2. Cancer	10:09 am
3. Taurus		3. Gemini		3. Cancer	
4. Taurus		4. Cancer	1:05 am	4. Leo	6:19 pm
5. Gemini	5:45 am	5. Cancer		5. Leo	
6. Gemini		6. Leo	8:25 am	6. Virgo	10:28 pm
7. Cancer	4:06 pm	7. Leo		7. Virgo	
8. Cancer		8. Virgo	12:33 pm	8. Libra	11:51 pm
9. Leo	11:36 pm	9. Virgo		9. Libra	
10. Leo		10. Libra	2:55 pm	10. Libra	
11. Leo		11. Libra		11. Scorp.	12:25 am
12. Virgo	4:45 am	12. Scorp.	5:02 pm	12. Scorp.	
13. Virgo		13. Scorp.		13. Sagitt.	1:55 am
14. Libra	9:29 am	14. Sagitt.	7:57 pm	14. Sagitt.	
15. Libra		15. Sagitt.		15. Capric	5:25 am
16. Scorp.	12:35 pm	16. Sagitt.		16. Capric.	
17. Scorp.		17. Capric.	12:04 am	17. Aquar.	11:13 am
18. Sagitt.	2:30 pm	18. Capric.		18. Aquar.	
19. Sagitt.		19. Aquar.	5:29 am	19. Pisces	7:06 pm
20. Capric.	5:41 pm	20. Aquar.		20. Pisces	
21. Capric.		21. Pisces	12:32 pm	21. Pisces	
22. Aquar.	9:54 pm	22. Pisces		22. Aries	4:58 am
23. Aquar.		23. Aries	9:49 pm	23. Aries	
24. Aquar.		24. Aries		24. Taurus	4:44 pm
25. Pisces	4:12 am	25. Aries		25. Taurus	
26. Pisces		26. Taurus	9:31 am	26. Taurus	
27. Aries	2:29 pm	27. Taurus		27. Gemini	5:44 am
28. Aries		28. Gemini	10:28 pm	28. Gemini	
29. Aries		29. Gemini		29. Cancer	6:06 pm
30. Taurus	1:29 am			30. Cancer	
31. Taurus				31. Cancer	

Daylight saving time to be considered where applicable.

2012 MOON SIGN DATES—
NEW YORK TIME

APRIL		MAY		JUNE	
Day Moon Enters		**Day Moon Enters**		**Day Moon Enters**	
1. Leo		1. Virgo		1. Scorp.	7:32 am
2. Leo		2. Libra	9:05 pm	2. Scorp.	
3. Virgo	8:54 am	3. Libra		3. Sagitt.	7:33 am
4. Virgo		4. Scorp.	9:21 pm	4. Sagitt.	
5. Libra	10:33 am	5. Scorp.		5. Capric.	7:32 am
6. Libra		6. Sagitt.	8:40 pm	6. Capric.	
7. Scorp.	10:19 am	7. Sagitt.		7. Aquar.	9:18 am
8. Scorp.		8. Capric.	9:01 pm	8. Aquar.	
9. Sagitt.	10:13 am	9. Capric.		9. Pisces	2:23 pm
10. Sagitt.		10. Capric.		10. Pisces	
11. Capric.	12:03 pm	11. Aquar.	12:04 am	11. Aries	11:22 am
12. Capric.		12. Aquar.		12. Aries	
13. Aquar.	4:49 pm	13. Pisces	6:43 am	13. Aries	
14. Aquar.		14. Pisces		14. Taurus	11:23 am
15. Aquar.		15. Aries	4:47 pm	15. Taurus	
16. Pisces	12:39 am	16. Aries		16. Taurus	
17. Pisces		17. Aries		17. Gemini	12:25 am
18. Aries	11:00 am	18. Taurus	5:04 am	18. Gemini	
19. Aries		19. Taurus		19. Cancer	12:35 pm
20. Taurus	11:06 pm	20. Gemini	6:06 pm	20. Cancer	
21. Taurus		21. Gemini		21. Leo	10:48 pm
22. Taurus		22. Gemini		22. Leo	
23. Gemini	12:06 pm	23. Cancer	6:32 am	23. Leo	
24. Gemini		24. Cancer		24. Virgo	6:44 am
25. Gemini		25. Leo	5:12 pm	25. Virgo	
26. Cancer	12:43 am	26. Leo		26. Libra	12:16 pm
27. Cancer		27. Leo		27. Libra	
28. Leo	11:12 am	28. Virgo	1:07 am	28. Scorp.	3:33 pm
29. Leo		29. Virgo		29. Scorp.	
30. Virgo	6:03 pm	30. Libra	5:47 am	30. Sagitt.	5:05 pm
		31. Libra			

Daylight saving time to be considered where applicable.

2012 MOON SIGN DATES—
NEW YORK TIME

JULY Day Moon Enters	AUGUST Day Moon Enters	SEPTEMBER Day Moon Enters
1. Sagitt.	1. Aquar. 4:57 am	1. Pisces
2. Capric. 5:52 pm	2. Aquar.	2. Aries 12:38 am
3. Capric.	3. Pisces 8:59 am	3. Aries
4. Aquar. 7:27 pm	4. Pisces	4. Taurus 10:42 am
5. Aquar.	5. Aries 4:00 pm	5. Taurus
6. Pisces 11:30 pm	6. Aries	6. Gemini 11:11 pm
7. Pisces	7. Aries	7. Gemini
8. Pisces	8. Taurus 2:29 am	8. Gemini
9. Aries 7:15 am	9. Taurus	9. Cancer 11:50 am
10. Aries	10. Gemini 3:12 pm	10. Cancer
11. Taurus 6:32 pm	11. Gemini	11. Leo 10:02 pm
12. Taurus	12. Gemini	12. Leo
13. Taurus	13. Cancer 3:29 am	13. Leo
14. Gemini 7:28 am	14. Cancer	14. Virgo 4:32 am
15. Gemini	15. Leo 1:06 pm	15. Virgo
16. Cancer 7:32 pm	16. Leo	16. Libra 7:56 am
17. Cancer	17. Virgo 7:34 pm	17. Libra
18. Cancer	18. Virgo	18. Scorp. 9:47 am
19. Leo 5:14 am	19. Libra 11:46 pm	19. Scorp.
20. Leo	20. Libra	20. Sagitt. 11:35 am
21. Virgo 12:25 pm	21. Libra	21. Sagitt.
22. Virgo	22. Scorp. 2:55 am	22. Capric. 2:22 pm
23. Libra 5:39 pm	23. Scorp.	23. Capric.
24. Libra	24. Sagitt. 5:51 am	24. Aquar. 6:34 pm
25. Scorp. 9:30 pm	25. Sagitt.	25. Aquar.
26. Scorp.	26. Capric. 9:00 am	26. Aquar.
27. Scorp.	27. Capric.	27. Pisces 12:25 am
28. Sagitt. 12:19 am	28. Aquar. 12:40 pm	28. Pisces
29. Sagitt.	29. Aquar.	29. Aries 8:15 am
30. Capric. 2:30 am	30. Pisces 5:32 pm	30. Aries
31. Capric.	31. Pisces	

Daylight saving time to be considered where applicable.

2012 MOON SIGN DATES—
NEW YORK TIME

OCTOBER Day Moon Enters		NOVEMBER Day Moon Enters		DECEMBER Day Moon Enters	
1. Taurus	6:27 pm	1. Gemini		1. Cancer	
2. Taurus		2. Gemini		2. Leo	8:58 pm
3. Taurus		3. Cancer	2:44 am	3. Leo	
4. Gemini	6:48 am	4. Cancer		4. Leo	
5. Gemini		5. Leo	2:40 pm	5. Virgo	6:53 am
6. Cancer	7:46 pm	6. Leo		6. Virgo	
7. Cancer		7. Virgo	11:36 pm	7. Libra	1:36 pm
8. Cancer		8. Virgo		8. Libra	
9. Leo	6:56 am	9. Virgo		9. Scorp.	4:52 pm
10. Leo		10. Libra	4:36 am	10. Scorp.	
11. Virgo	2:25 pm	11. Libra		11. Sagitt.	5:23 pm
12. Virgo		12. Scorp.	6:11 am	12. Sagitt.	
13. Libra	6:03 pm	13. Scorp.		13. Capric.	4:44 pm
14. Libra		14. Sagitt.	5:53 am	14. Capric.	
15. Scorp.	7:07 pm	15. Sagitt.		15. Aquar.	4:54 pm
16. Scorp.		16. Capric.	5:36 am	16. Aquar.	
17. Sagitt.	7:27 pm	17. Capric.		17. Pisces	7:49 pm
18. Sagitt.		18. Aquar.	7:11 am	18. Pisces	
19. Capric.	8:42 pm	19. Aquar.		19. Pisces	
20. Capric.		20. Pisces	11:56 am	20. Aries	2:44 am
21. Capric.		21. Pisces		21. Aries	
22. Aquar.	12:03 am	22. Aries	8:13 pm	22. Taurus	1:26 pm
23. Aquar.		23. Aries		23. Taurus	
24. Pisces	6:01 am	24. Aries		24. Taurus	
25. Pisces		25. Taurus	7:19 am	25. Gemini	2:14 am
26. Aries	2:32 pm	26. Taurus		26. Gemini	
27. Aries		27. Gemini	7:59 am	27. Cancer	3:08 pm
28. Aries		28. Gemini		28. Cancer	
29. Taurus	1:16 am	29. Gemini		29. Cancer	
30. Taurus		30. Cancer	8:56 am	30. Leo	2:46 am
31. Gemini	1:41 pm			31. Leo	

Daylight saving time to be considered where applicable.

2012 PHASES OF THE MOON—
NEW YORK TIME

New Moon	First Quarter	Full Moon	Last Quarter
Dec. 24 ('11)	Jan. 1	Jan. 9	Jan. 16
Jan. 23	Jan. 31	Feb. 7	Feb. 14
Feb. 21	Feb. 29	March 8	March 14
March 22	March 30	April 6	April 13
April 21	April 29	May 5	May 12
May 20	May 28	June 4	June 11
June 19	June 26	July 3	July 10
July 19	July 26	August 2	August 9
August 17	August 24	August 31	Sept. 8
Sept. 15	Sept. 22	Sept. 30	Oct. 8
Oct. 15	Oct. 21	Oct. 29	Nov. 6
Nov. 13	Nov. 20.	Nov. 28	Dec. 6
Dec. 13	Dec. 20	Dec. 28	Jan. 4 ('13)

Each phase of the Moon lasts approximately seven to eight days, during which the Moon's shape gradually changes as it comes out of one phase and goes into the next.

There will be a solar eclipse during the New Moon phase on May 20 and November 13.

There will be a lunar eclipse during the Full Moon phase on June 4 and November 28.

2012 FISHING GUIDE

	Good	Best
January	4-6-13-14-19-23	8-16-26
February	4-5-14-23-29	2-11-13-27
March	4-5-12-13-21-22	1-3-10-24-31
April	6-15-18-19-27-28	1-7-9-25
May	6-15-21-24-25-31	3-12-16-22
June	3-8-11-12-21-22-29-30	2-4-13-20-26
July	5-8-9-19-27	4-18-24-26
August	6-14-15-20-21-23	2-5-10-22
September	2-11-12-17-20-28-29	1-4-16-19-25
October	4-9-17-26-28-31	2-6-8-15-25
November	5-12-13-23-28	1-4-14-22-26
December	3-11-20-24-28-29	2-10-13-19

2012 PLANTING GUIDE

	Aboveground Crops	Root Crops
January	9-12-16-22-27	3-8-14-21
February	4-8-12-21-23	2-6-10-17
March	3-8-13-16-30	12-16-26
April	1-4-8-17	6-12-22
May	1-6-15-24-29	4-11-20-21
June	2-11-21-25	1-6-16-27
July	8-18-22-26	4-13-24-31
August	5-14-19-23	1-10-21-27
September	1-11-15-19	6-17-23-24
October	8-13-17-25	3-4-15-21
November	4-9-13-22	1-11-17-26
December	2-6-10-19-29	8-15-24-25

	Pruning	Weeds and Pests
January	1-18-31	2-6-10-23
February	3-4-15	7-8-29
March	14-23-24	1-5-18
April	10-20-21	2-15-25
May	8-17-18	13-22-27
June	4-13-14	9-18-23
July	1-11-29	6-16-20
August	7-25-26	3-12-29
September	3-4-22	8-13-26
October	1-2-19-20	6-10-23
November	15-24-25	2-7-19-29
December	12-13-22-23	1-4-17-22

MOON'S INFLUENCE OVER PLANTS

Centuries ago it was established that seeds planted when the Moon is in signs and phases called Fruitful will produce more growth than seeds planed when the Moon is in a Barren sign.
Fruitful Signs: Taurus, Cancer, Libra, Scorpio, Capricorn, Pisces
Barren Signs: Aries, Gemini, Leo, Virgo, Sagittarius, Aquarius
Dry Signs: Aries, Gemini, Sagittarius, Aquarius

Activity	Moon In
Mow lawn, trim plants	**Fruitful sign:** 1st & 2nd quarter
Plant flowers	**Fruitful sign:** 2nd quarter; best in Cancer and Libra
Prune	**Fruitful sign:** 3rd & 4th quarter
Destroy pests; spray	**Barren sign:** 4th quarter
Harvest potatoes, root crops	**Dry sign:** 3rd & 4th quarter; Taurus, Leo, and Aquarius

MOON'S INFLUENCE OVER YOUR HEALTH

ARIES	Head, brain, face, upper jaw
TAURUS	Throat, neck, lower jaw
GEMINI	Hands, arms, lungs, shoulders, ner vous system
CANCER	Esophagus, stomach, breasts, womb, liver
LEO	Heart, spine
VIRGO	Intestines, liver
LIBRA	Kidneys, lower back
SCORPIO	Sex and eliminative organs
SAGITTARIUS	Hips, thighs, liver
CAPRICORN	Skin, bones, teeth, knees
AQUARIUS	Circulatory system, lower legs
PISCES	Feet, tone of being

Try to avoid work being done on that part of the body when the Moon is in the sign governing that part.

MOON'S INFLUENCE OVER DAILY AFFAIRS

The Moon makes a complete transit of the Zodiac every 27 days 7 hours and 43 minutes. In making this transit the Moon forms different aspects with the planets and consequently has favorable or unfavorable bearings on affairs and events for persons according to the sign of the Zodiac under which they were born.

When the Moon is in conjunction with the Sun it is called a New Moon; when the Moon and Sun are in opposition it is called a Full Moon. From New Moon to Full Moon, first and second quarter—which takes about two weeks—the Moon is increasing or waxing. From Full Moon to New Moon, third and fourth quarter, the Moon is decreasing or waning.

Activity	Moon In
Business: buying and selling new, requiring public support	Sagittarius, Aries, Gemini, Virgo 1st and 2nd quarter
meant to be kept quiet	3rd and 4th quarter
Investigation	3rd and 4th quarter
Signing documents	1st & 2nd quarter, Cancer, Scorpio, Pisces
Advertising	2nd quarter, Sagittarius
Journeys and trips	1st & 2nd quarter, Gemini, Virgo
Renting offices, etc.	Taurus, Leo, Scorpio, Aquarius
Painting of house/apartment	3rd & 4th quarter, Taurus, Scorpio, Aquarius
Decorating	Gemini, Libra, Aquarius
Buying clothes and accessories	Taurus, Virgo
Beauty salon or barber shop visit	1st & 2nd quarter, Taurus, Leo, Libra, Scorpio, Aquarius
Weddings	1st & 2nd quarter

Sagittarius

SAGITTARIUS

Character Analysis

People born under this ninth sign of the Zodiac are quite often self-reliant and intelligent. Generally, they are quite philosophical in their outlook on life. They know how to make practical use of their imagination.

There is seldom anything narrow about a Sagittarius man or woman. He or she is generally very tolerant and considerate. They would never consciously do anything that would hurt another's feelings. They are gifted with a good sense of humor and believe in being honest in relationships with others. At times Sagittarius is a little short of tact. They are so intent on telling the truth that sometimes they can be blunt.

Nevertheless, Sagittarius men and women mean well, and people who enjoy a relationship with them are often willing to overlook this flaw. Sagittarius may even tell people true things about themselves that they do not wish to hear. At times this can cause a strain in the relationship. Sagittarius often wishes that others were as forthright and honest as he or she is—no matter what the consequences.

Sagittarius men and women are positive and optimistic and love life. They often help others to snap out of an ill mood. Their joie de vivre is often infectious. People enjoy being around Sagittarius because they are almost always in a good mood.

Quite often people born under the sign of Sagittarius are fond of the outdoors. They enjoy sporting events and often excel in them. Like the Archer, the zodiacal symbol of the sign, Sagittarius men and women are fond of animals, especially horses and dogs.

Generally, the Archer is healthy—in mind and in body. They have pluck. They enjoy the simple things of life. Fresh air and good comradeship are important to them. On the other hand, they are fond of developing their minds. Many Sagittarius cannot read or study enough. They like to keep abreast of things. They are interested in theater and the arts in general. Some of them are quite religious. Some choose a religious life.

Because they are outgoing for the most part, they sometimes come in touch with situations that others are never confronted with. In the long run this tends to make their life experiences quite rich and varied. They are well-balanced. They like to be active. And they enjoy using their intellects.

It is important to the person born under this sign that justice prevails. They dislike seeing anyone treated unfairly. If Sagittarius feels that the old laws are out of date or unrealistic, he or she will fight to have them changed. At times they can be true rebels. It is important to the Archer that law is carried out impartially. In matters of law, they often excel.

Sagittarius are almost always fond of travel. It seems to be imbedded in their natures. At times, they feel impelled to get away from familiar surroundings and people. Faraway places have a magical attraction for someone born under this sign. They enjoy reading about foreign lands and strange customs.

Many people who are Sagittarius are not terribly fond of living in big cities; they prefer the quiet and greenery of the countryside. Of all the signs of the Zodiac the sign of Sagittarius is closest to mother nature. They can usually build a trusting relationship with animals. They respect wildlife in all its forms.

Sagittarius is quite clever in conversation. He or she has a definite way with words. They like a good argument. They know how to phrase things exactly. Their sense of humor often has a cheerful effect on their manner of speech. They are seldom without a joke.

At times, the Sagittarius wit is apt to hurt someone's feelings, but this is never intentional. A slip of the tongue sometimes gets the Archer into social difficulties. As a result, there can be argumentative and angry scenes. But Sagittarius men and women cool down quickly. They are not given to holding grudges. They are willing to forgive and forget.

On the whole, Sagittarius is good-natured and fun-loving. They find it easy to take up with all sorts of people. In most cases, their social circle is large. People enjoy their company and their parties. Many friends share the Sagittarius interest in the outdoor life as well as intellectual pursuits.

Sagittarius sometimes can be impulsive. They are not afraid of risk. On the contrary, they can be foolhardy in the way they court danger. But Sagittarius men and women are very sporting in all they that do. If they should wind up the loser, they will not waste time grieving about it. They are fairly optimistic—they believe in good luck.

Health

Often people born under the sign of Sagittarius are quite athletic. They are healthy-looking—quite striking in a robust way. Often they are rather tall and well-built. They are enthusiastic people and like being active or involved. Exercise and sports may interest them a great deal.

Sagittarius cannot stand not being active. They have to be on the go. As they grow older, they seem to increase in strength and physical ability. At times they may have worries, but they never allow them to affect humor or health.

It is important to Sagittarius men and women to remain physically sound. They are usually very physically fit, but their nervous system may be somewhat sensitive. Too much activity—even while they find action attractive—may put a severe strain on them after a time. The Archer should try to concentrate their energies on as few objects as possible. However, usually they have many projects scattered here and there, and can be easily exhausted.

At times, illnesses fall upon the Archer suddenly or strangely. Some Sagittarius are accident-prone. They are not afraid of taking risks and as a result are sometimes careless in the way they do things. Injuries often come to them by way of sports or other vigorous activities.

Sometimes men and women of this sign try to ignore signs of illness—especially if they are engaged in some activity that has captured their interest. This results in a severe setback at times.

In later life, Sagittarius sometimes suffers from stomach disorders. High blood pressure is another ailment that might affect them. They should also be on guard for signs of arthritis and sciatica. In spite of these possible dangers, the average Sagittarius manages to stay quite youthful and alert through their many interests and pastimes.

Occupation

Sagittarius is someone who can be relied upon in a work situation. They are loyal and dependable. They are energetic workers, anxious to please superiors. They are forward-looking by nature and enjoy working in modern surroundings and toward progressive goals.

Challenges do not frighten Sagittarius. They are flexible and can work in confining situations even though they may not enjoy it. Work that gives them a chance to move around and meet new people is well suited to their character. If they have to stay in one locale, they become sad and ill-humored. They can take orders but they would rather be in a situation where they do not have to. They are difficult to please at times, and may hop from job to job before feeling that it is really time to settle down. Sagittarius do their best work when they are allowed to work on their own.

Sagittarius individuals are interested in expressing themselves in the work they do. If they occupy a position that does not allow them to be creative, they will seek outside activities. Such hobbies or pastimes give them a chance to develop and broaden their talents.

Some Sagittarius do well in the field of journalism. Others make good teachers and public speakers. They are generally quite flexible and would do well in many different positions. Some excel as foreign ministers or in music. Others do well in government work or in publishing.

Men and women born under this ninth sign are often more intelligent than the average person. The cultivated Sagittarius knows how to employ intellectual gifts to their best advantage. In politics and religion, Sagittarius often displays brilliance.

The Sagittarius man or woman is pleasant to work with. They are considerate of colleagues and would do nothing that might upset the working relationship. Because they are so self-reliant, they often inspire teammates. Sagittarius likes to work with detail. Their ideas are both practical and idealistic. Sagittarius is curious by nature and is always looking for ways of expanding their knowledge.

Sagittarius are almost always generous. They rarely refuse someone in need, but are always willing to share what they have. Whether they are up or down, Sagittarius can always be relied upon to help someone in dire straits. Their attitude toward life may be happy-go-lucky in general. They are difficult to depress no matter what the situation. They are optimistic and forward-looking. Money always seems to fall into their hands.

The average Sagittarius is interested in expansion and promotion. Sometimes these concerns weaken their projects rather than strengthen them. Also, the average Sagittarius is more interested in contentment and joy than in material gain. However, they will do their best to make the most of any profit that comes their way.

When Sagittarius does get hooked on a venture, he or she is often willing to take risks to secure a profit. In the long run they are successful. They have a flair for carrying off business deals. It is the cultivated Sagittarius who prepares in advance for any business contingency. In that way he or she can bring knowledge and experience to bear on their professional and financial interests.

Home and Family

Not all Sagittarius are very interested in home life. Many of them set great store in being mobile. Their activities outside the home may attract them more than those inside the home. Not exactly homebodies, Sagittarius, however, can adjust themselves to a stable domestic life if they put their minds to it.

People born under this sign are not keen on luxuries and other displays of wealth. They prefer the simple things. Anyone entering their home should be able to discern this. They are generally neat. They like a place that has plenty of space—not too cluttered with imposing furniture.

Even when they settle down, Sagittarius men and women like to keep a small corner of their life just for themselves. Independence is important to them. If necessary, they will insist upon it, no matter what the situation. They like a certain amount of beauty in the home, but they may not be too interested in keeping things looking nice. Their interests lead them elsewhere. Housekeeping may bore them to distraction. When forced to stick to a domestic routine, they can become somewhat disagreeable.

Children bring Sagittarius men and women a great deal of happiness. They are fond of family life. Friends generally drop in any old time to visit for they know they will always be welcomed and properly entertained. The Archer's love for their fellow man is well known.

The Sagittarius parent may be bewildered at first by a newborn baby. They may worry about holding such a tiny tot for fear of injuring the little one. Although some Sagittarius may be clumsy, they do have a natural touch with small children and should not worry about handling them properly. As soon as the infant begins to grow up and develop a definite personality, Sagittarius can relax and relate. There is always a strong tie between children and the Sagittarius parent.

Children are especially drawn to Sagittarius because they seem to understand them better than other adults.

One is apt to find children born under this sign a little restless and disorganized at times. They are usually quite independent in their ways and may ask for quite a bit of freedom while still young. They don't like being fussed over by adults. They like to feel that their parents believe in them and trust them on their own.

Social Relationships

Sagittarius enjoys having people around. It is not difficult for them to make friends. They are very sociable by nature. Most of the friends they make they keep for life.

Sagittarius men and women are broad-minded, so they have all sorts of pals and casual acquaintances. They appreciate people for their good qualities, however few a person might have. Sagittarius are not quick to judge and are usually very forgiving. They are not impressed by what a friend has in the way of material goods.

Sagittarius men and women are generally quite popular. They are much in demand socially. People like their easy disposition and good humor. Their friendship is valued by others. Quite often in spite of their chumminess, Sagittarius is rather serious. Light conversation may be somewhat difficult for them.

Sagittarius men and women believe in speaking their minds, in saying what they feel. Yet at times, they can appear quiet and retiring. It all depends on their mood. Some people feel that there are two sides to the Sagittarius personality. This characteristic is reflected in the zodiacal symbol for the sign—a double symbol: the hunter and the horse intertwined, denoting two different natures.

It may be difficult for some people to get to know a Sagittarius man or woman. In some instances Sagittarius employ silence as a sort of protection. When people pierce through, however, and will not leave him or her in peace, Sagittarius can become quite angry.

On the whole, Sagittarius is kind and considerate. Their nature is gentle and unassuming. With the wrong person, though, they can become somewhat disagreeable. They do become angry, but they cool down quickly and are willing to let bygones be bygones. Sagittarius individuals never hold a grudge against anyone.

Companionship and harmony in all social relationships is necessary for Sagittarius. They are willing to make some sacrifices for it. Any partner, friend, or mate must be a good listener. There are times when Sagittarius feel it necessary to pour their hearts out. They are willing to listen to someone's problems and want the same considerate treatment in return.

A partner, friend, or lover should also be able to take an interest in any hobbies, pastimes, or sports a Sagittarius wants to pursue. If not, Sagittarius men and women will be tempted to go their own way even more so than their nature dictates.

Sagittarius individuals do not beat around the bush. They do say what they mean. Being direct is one of their strongest qualities. Sometimes it pays off, sometimes it doesn't. They often forget that the one they love may be very sensitive and can take offhand remarks personally.

Sagittarius has a tendency to be too blunt and to reveal secrets, innocently or otherwise, that hurt people's feelings. A friend or partner may not be able to overlook this flaw or may not be able to correct it either in a subtle or direct way. When making jokes or casual comments, Sagittarius sometimes strikes a sensitive chord in a companion, which can result in a serious misunderstanding.

But the cultivated Sagittarius learns the boundaries of social behavior. They know when not to go too far. Understanding a partner's viewpoint is the first step toward assuring a good relationship down the road.

Love and Marriage

Sagittarius individuals are faithful to their loved ones. They are affectionate and not at all possessive. Love is important for them spiritually as well as physically. For some Sagittarius, romance is a chance to escape reality—a chance for adventure.

Quite often a mate or lover finds it difficult to keep up with Sagittarius—they are so active and energetic. When Sagittarius men and women fall in love, however, they are quite easy to handle.

Sagittarius do like having freedom. They will make concessions in a steady relationship. Still there will be a part of themselves that they keep from others. He or she is very intent on preserving their individual rights, no matter what sort of relationship they are engaged in. Sagittarius ideals are generally high, and they are important. Sagittarius is looking for someone with similar standards, not someone too lax or too conventional.

In love, Sagittarius men and women may be a bit childlike at times. As a result of this they are apt to encounter various disappointments before they find the one meant for them. At times he or she says things they really shouldn't, and this causes the end of a romantic relationship.

Men and women born under this sign may have many love affairs before they feel ready to settle down with just one person. If the person they love does not exactly measure up to their standards, they are apt to overlook this—depending on how strong their love is—and accept the person for what that person is.

On the whole, Sagittarius men and women are not envious. They are willing to allow a partner needed freedoms—within reason. Sagittarius does this so they will not have to jeopardize their own liberties. Live and let live could easily be their motto. If their ideals and freedom are threatened, Sagittarius fights hard to protect what they believe is just and fair.

They do not want to make any mistakes in love, so they take their time when choosing someone to settle down with. They are direct and positive when they meet the right one. They do not waste time.

The average Sagittarius may be a bit altar-shy. It may take a bit of convincing before Sagittarius agree that married life is right for them. This is generally because they do not want to lose their freedom. Sagittarius is an active person who enjoys being around a lot of other people. Sitting quietly at home does not interest them at all. At times it may seem that he or she wants to have things their own way, even in marriage. It may take some doing to get Sagittarius to realize that in marriage, as in other things, give-and-take plays a great role.

Romance and the Sagittarius Woman

The Sagittarius woman is kind and gentle. Most of the time she is very considerate of others and enjoys being of help in some way to her friends. She can be quite active and, as a result, be rather difficult to catch. On the whole, she is optimistic and friendly. She believes in looking on the bright side of things. She knows how to make the best of situations that others feel are not worth salvaging. She has plenty of pluck.

Men generally like her because of her easygoing manner. Quite often she becomes friends with a man before venturing on to romance. There is something about her that makes her more of a companion than a lover. The woman Archer can best be described as sporting and broad-minded.

She is almost never possessive. She enjoys her own freedom too much to want to make demands on that of another person.

She is always youthful in her disposition. She may seem naive or guileless at times. Generally it takes her longer really to mature than it does others. She tends to be impulsive and may easily jump from one thing to another. If she has an unfortunate experience in love early in life, she may shy away from fast or intimate contacts for a while. She is usually very popular. Not all the men who are attracted to her see her as a possible lover, but more as a friend or companion.

The woman born under the sign of the Archer generally believes in true love. She may have several romances before she decides to settle down. For her there is no particular rush. She is willing to have a long romantic relationship with the man she loves before making marriage plans.

The Sagittarius woman is often the outdoors type and has a strong liking for animals—especially dogs and horses. Quite often she excels in sports. She is not generally someone who is content to stay at home and cook and take care of the house. She would rather be out attending to her other interests. When she does household work, however, she does it well.

She makes a good companion as well as a wife. She usually enjoys participating with her husband in his various interests and affairs. Her sunny disposition often brightens up the dull moments of a love affair.

At times her temper may flare, but she is herself again after a few moments. She would never butt into her husband's business affairs, but she does enjoy being asked for her opinion from time to time. Generally she is up to date on all that her husband is doing and can offer him some pretty sound advice.

The Sagittarius woman is seldom jealous of her husband's interest in other people—even if some of them are of the opposite sex. If she has no reason to doubt his love, she never questions it.

She makes a loving and sympathetic mother. She knows all the sports news and probably has the latest board game to play with her children. Her cheerful manner makes her an invaluable playmate and encouraging guide.

Romance and the Sagittarius Man

The Sagittarius man is often an adventurer. He likes taking chances in love as well as in life. He may hop around quite a bit—from one romance to another—before really thinking about settling down. Many men born under this sign feel that marriage would mean the end of their freedom, so they avoid it as much as possible. Whenever a romance becomes too serious, they move on.

Many Sagittarius men are impulsive in love. Early marriages for some often end unpleasantly. A male Archer is not a very mature person, even at an age when most others are. He takes a bit more time. He may not always make a wise choice in a love partner.

He is affectionate and loving but not at all possessive. Because he is rather lighthearted in love, he sometimes gets into trouble.

Most Sagittarius men find romance an exciting adventure. They make attentive lovers and are never cool or indifferent. Love should also have a bit of fun in it for him too. He likes to keep things light and gay. Romance without humor can at times be difficult for him to accept. The woman he loves should also be a good sport. She should have as open and fun-loving a disposition as he has if she is to understand him properly.

He wants his mate to share his interest in the outdoor life and animals. If she is good at sports, she is likely to win his heart. The average Sagittarius generally has an interest in athletics of various sorts—from bicycling to baseball.

His mate must also be a good intellectual companion, someone who can easily discuss those matters which interest him. Physical love is important to him—but so is spiritual love. A good romance will contain these in balance.

His sense of humor may sometimes seem a little unkind to someone who is not used to being laughed at. He enjoys playing jokes now and again. It is the child in his nature that remains a part of his character even when he grows old and gray.

He is not a homebody. He is responsible, however, and will do what is necessary to keep a home together. Still and all, the best wife for him is one who can manage household matters single-handedly if need be.

He loves the children, especially as they grow older and begin to take on definite personalities.

Woman—Man

SAGITTARIUS WOMAN
ARIES MAN

In some ways, the Aries man resembles a wandering mountain sheep seeking high land. He has an insatiable thirst for knowledge. He's ambitious and is apt to have his finger in many pies. He can do with a woman like you—someone attractive, quick-witted, and smart.

He is not interested in a clinging vine for a mate. He wants someone who is there when he needs her, someone who listens and understands what he says, someone who can give advice if he should ever need it, which is not likely to be often.

The Aries man wants a woman who will look good on his arm without hanging on it too heavily. He is looking for a woman who has both feet on the ground and yet is mysterious and enticing, a kind of domestic Helen of Troy whose face or fine dinner can launch a thousand business deals if need be. That woman he's in search of sounds a little like you, doesn't she? If the shoe fits, put it on. You won't regret it.

The Aries man makes a good husband. He is faithful and attentive. He is an affectionate man. He'll make you feel needed and loved. Love is a serious matter for the Aries man. He does not believe in flirting or playing the field—especially after he's found the woman of his dreams. He'll expect you to be as constant in your affection as he is in his. He'll expect you to be one hundred percent his. He won't put up with any nonsense while romancing you.

The Aries man may be pretty progressive and modern about many things. However, when it comes to pants wearing, he's downright conventional: it's strictly male attire. The best role you can take in the relationship is a supporting one. He's the boss and that's that. Once you have learned to accept that, you'll find the going easy.

The Aries man, with his endless energy and drive, likes to relax in the comfort of his home at the end of the day. The good homemaker can be sure of holding his love. He'll watch a sports match with you from his favorite armchair. If you see to it that everything in the house is where he expects to find it, you'll have no difficulty keeping the relationship on an even keel.

Life and love with an Aries man may be just the medicine you need. He'll be a good provider. He'll spoil you if he's financially able.

The Aries father is young at heart and will spoil children every chance he gets. So naturally the kids will take to him like ducks to water. His quick mind and energetic behavior appeal to the young. His ability to jump from one thing to another will delight the kids and keep them active. You will have to introduce some rules of the game so that the children learn how to start things properly and finish them before running off elsewhere.

SAGITTARIUS WOMAN
TAURUS MAN

If you've got your heart set on a man born under the sign of Taurus, you'll have to learn the art of being patient. Taurus take their time about everything—even love.

The steady and deliberate Taurus man is a little slow on the draw. It may take him quite a while before he gets around to popping that question. For the woman who doesn't mind twiddling her thumbs, the waiting and anticipating almost always pays off in the end. Taurus men want to make sure that every step they take is a good one, particularly if they feel that the path they're on is one that leads to the altar.

If you are in the mood for a whirlwind romance, you had better cast your net in shallower waters. Moreover, most Taurus prefer to do the angling themselves. They are not keen on a woman taking the lead. Once she does, they might drop her like a dead fish. If you let yourself get caught in his net, you'll find that he's fallen for you—hook, line, and sinker.

The Taurus man is fond of a comfortable home life. It is very important to him. If you keep those home fires burning you will have no trouble keeping that flame in your Taurus mate's heart aglow. You have a talent for homemaking; use it. Your taste in furnishings is excellent. You know how to make a house come to life with colors and decorations.

Taurus, the strong, steady, and protective Bull, may not be your idea of a man on the move. Still he's reliable. Perhaps he could be the anchor for your dreams and plans. He could help you to acquire a more balanced outlook and approach to your life. If you're given to impulsiveness, he could help you to curb it. He's the man who is always there when you need him.

When you tie the knot with a man born under Taurus, you can put away fears about creditors pounding on the front door. Taurus are practical about everything including bill paying. When he carries you over that threshold, you can be certain that the entire house is paid for, not only the doorsill.

As a wife, you won't have to worry about putting aside your many interests for the sake of back-breaking house chores. Your Taurus husband will see to it that you have all the latest time-saving appliances and comforts.

The Taurus father has much love and affection for the children, and he has no trouble demonstrating his warmth. Yet he does not believe in spoiling the kids. The Taurus father believes that children have a place, and they should know their place at all times. He is an excellent disciplinarian and will see to it that the youngsters grow up to be polite, obedient, and respectful. You will provide mirth and fun to balance things out.

SAGITTARIUS WOMAN
GEMINI MAN

If opposites attract, as the notion goes, then Gemini and Sagittarius should be swell together. The fact that you two are astrologically related—being zodiacal partners as well as zodiacal opposites—does not automatically guarantee that you will understand each other, at least at first. Gemini is an air sign, you are a fire sign, so the initial contact between you should be warm and breezy.

The Gemini man is quite a catch. Many a woman has set her cap for him and failed to bag him. Generally, Gemini men are intelligent, witty, and outgoing. Many of them tend to be versatile.

On the other hand, some of them seem to lack that sort of common sense that you set so much store in. Their tendency to start a half-dozen projects, then toss them up in the air out of boredom may do nothing more than exasperate you.

One thing that causes a Twin's mind and affection to wander is a bore. But it is unlikely that the active Sagittarius woman would ever allow herself to be accused of dullness. The Gemini man who has caught your heart will admire you for your ideas and intellect—perhaps even more than for your athletic talents and good looks.

A strong-willed woman could easily fill the role of rudder for her Gemini's ship-without-a-sail. The intelligent Gemini is often aware of his shortcomings and doesn't mind if someone with better bearings gives him a shove in the right direction—when it's needed. The average Gemini doesn't have serious ego hang-ups and will even accept a well-deserved chewing out from his mate or girlfriend gracefully.

A successful and serious-minded Gemini could make you a very happy woman, perhaps, if you gave him half the chance. Although he may give you the impression that he has a hole in his head, the Gemini man generally has a good head on his shoulders and can make efficient use of it when he wants to. Some of them, who have learned the art of being steadfast, have risen to great heights in their professions.

Once you convince yourself that not all people born under the sign of the Twins are witless grasshoppers, you won't mind dating a few—to test your newborn conviction. If you do wind up walking down the aisle with one, accept the fact that married life with him will mean your taking the bitter with the sweet.

Life with a Gemini man can be more fun than a barrel of clowns. You'll never be allowed to experience a dull moment. But don't leave money matters to him, or you'll both wind up behind the eight ball.

Gemini men are always attractive to the opposite sex. You'll perhaps have to allow him an occasional harmless flirt. It will seldom amount to more than that if you're his ideal mate.

Gemini is your zodiacal mate, as well as your zodiacal opposite, so the Gemini-Sagittarius couple will make delightful parents together. Airy Gemini will create a very open, experimental environment for the kids. He loves them so much, he sometimes lets them do what they want. You will keep the kids in line and prevent them from running the household. But you and your Gemini mate's combined sense of humor is infectious, so the youngsters will naturally come to see the fun and funny sides of life.

SAGITTARIUS WOMAN
CANCER MAN

Chances are you won't hit it off too well with the man born under Cancer if your plans concern love. But then, Cupid has been known to do some pretty unlikely things. The Cancer man is very sensitive—thin-skinned and occasionally moody. You've got to keep on your toes—and not step on his—if you're determined to make a go of the relationship.

The Cancer man may be lacking in some of the qualities you seek in a man. But when it comes to being faithful and being a good provider, he's hard to beat.

The perceptive woman will not mistake the Crab's quietness for sullenness or his thriftiness for penny-pinching. In some respects, he is like that wise old owl out on a limb. He may look like he's dozing but actually he hasn't missed a thing.

Cancers possess a well of knowledge about human behavior. They can come across with some pretty helpful advice to those in trouble or in need. He can certainly guide you in making investments both in time and money. He may not say much, but he's always got his wits about him.

The Crab may not be the match or catch for a woman like you. At times, you are likely to find him downright dull. True to his sign, he can be fairly cranky and crabby when handled the wrong way. He is perhaps more sensitive than he should be.

If you're smarter than your Cancer friend, be smart enough not to let him know. Never give him the idea that you think he's a little short on brainpower. It would send him scurrying back into his shell. And all that ground lost in the relationship will perhaps never be recovered.

The Crab is most content at home. Once settled down for the night or the weekend, wild horses couldn't drag him any farther than the gatepost—that is, unless those wild horses were dispatched by his mother.

The Crab is sometimes a Momma's boy. If his mate does not put her foot down, he will see to it that his mother always comes first. No self-respecting wife would ever allow herself to play second fiddle, even if it's to her mother-in-law. With a little bit of tact, however, she'll find that slipping into that number-one position is as easy as pie (that legendary one his mother used to bake).

If you pamper your Cancer man, you'll find that mother turns up less and less, at the front door and in conversations.

Cancers make proud, patient, and protective fathers. But they can be a little too protective. Their sheltering instincts can interfere with a youngster's natural inclination to test the waters outside the home. Still, the Cancer father doesn't want to see his kids learning about life the hard way from the streets. Your qualities of optimism and encouragement and your knowledge of right and wrong will guide the youngsters along the way.

SAGITTARIUS WOMAN
LEO MAN

For the woman who enjoys being swept off her feet in a romantic whirlwind fashion, Leo is the sign of such love. When the Lion puts his mind to romancing, he doesn't stint. It's all wining and dining and dancing till the wee hours of the morning.

Leo is all heart and knows how to make his woman feel like a woman. The woman in constant search of a man she can look up to need go no farther: Leo is ten-feet tall—in spirit if not in stature. He's a man not only in full control of his faculties but in full control of just about any situation he finds himself in. Leo is a winner.

The Leo man may not look like Tarzan, but he knows how to roar and beat his chest if he has to. The woman who has had her fill of weak-kneed men finds in a Leo someone she can at last lean upon. He can support you not only physically but spiritually as well. He's good at giving advice that pays off.

Leos are direct people. They don't believe in wasting time or effort. They almost never make unwise investments.

Many Leos rise to the top of their professions. Through example, they often prove to be a source of great inspiration to others.

Although he's a ladies' man, Leo is very particular about his ladies. His standards are high when it comes to love interests. The idealistic and cultivated woman should have no trouble keeping her balance on the pedestal the Lion sets her on.

Leo believes that romance should be played on a fair give-and-take basis. He won't stand for any monkey business in a love relationship. It's all or nothing.

You'll find him a frank, off-the-shoulder person. He generally says what is on his mind.

If you decide upon a Leo man for a mate, you must be prepared to stand behind him full force. He expects it—and usually deserves it. He's the head of the house and can handle that position without a hitch. He knows how to go about breadwinning and, if he has his way (and most Leos do have their own way), he'll see to it that you'll have all the luxuries you crave and the comforts you need.

It's unlikely that the romance in your marriage will ever die out. Lions need love like flowers need sunshine. They're ever amorous and generally expect similar attention and affection from their mates. Leos are fond of going out on the town. They love to give parties, as well as to go to them. Because you, too, love to throw a party, you and your Leo mate will be the most popular host and hostess in town.

Leo fathers have a tendency to spoil the children—up to a point. That point is reached when the children become the center of attention, and Leo feels neglected. Then the Leo father becomes strict and insists that his rules be followed. You will have your hands full pampering both your Leo mate and the children. As long as he comes first in your affections, the family will be creative and joyful.

SAGITTARIUS WOMAN
VIRGO MAN

Although the Virgo man may be a bit of a fussbudget at times, his seriousness and dedication to common sense may help you to overlook his tendency to be too critical about minor things.

Virgo men are often quiet, respectable types who set great store in conservative behavior and levelheadedness. He'll admire you for your practicality and tenacity, perhaps even more than for your good looks. He's seldom bowled over by a glamour-puss. When he gets his courage up, he turns to a serious and reliable girl for romance.

The Virgo man will be far from a Valentino while dating. In fact, you may wind up making all the passes. Once he does get his motor running, however, he can be a warm and wonderful fellow—to the right lover.

He's gradual about love. Chances are your romance with him will start out looking like an ordinary friendship. Once he's sure you're no fly-by-night flirt and have no plans of taking him for a ride, he'll open up and rain sunshine all over your heart.

Virgo men tend to marry late in life. Virgo believes in holding out until he's met the right woman. He may not have many names in his little black book; in fact, he may not even have a black book. He's not interested in playing the field; leave that to men of the more flamboyant signs. The Virgo man is so particular that he may remain romantically inactive for a long period. His woman has to be perfect or it's no go.

If you find yourself feeling weak-kneed for a Virgo, do your best to convince him that perfect is not so important when it comes to love. Help him to realize that he's missing out on a great deal by not considering the near perfect or whatever it is you consider yourself to be. With your surefire perseverance, you will most likely be able to make him listen to reason and he'll wind up reciprocating your romantic interests.

The Virgo man is no block of ice. He'll respond to what he feels to be the right feminine flame. Once your love life with a Virgo man starts to bubble, don't give it a chance to fall flat. You may never have a second chance at winning his heart.

If you should ever break up with him, forget about patching it up. He'd prefer to let the pieces lie scattered. Once married, though, he'll stay that way—even if it hurts. He's too conscientious to try to back out of a legal deal of any sort.

The Virgo man is as neat as a pin. He's thumbs down on sloppy housekeeping. Keep everything bright, neat, and shiny. That goes for the children, too, at least by the time he gets home.

The Virgo father appreciates good manners, courtesy, and cleanliness from the children. He will instill a sense of order in the household, and he expects youngsters to respect his wishes. He can become very worried about scrapes, bruises, and all sorts of minor mishaps when the kids go out to play. Your easygoing faith in the children's safety will counteract Virgo's tendency to fuss and fret over them.

SAGITTARIUS WOMAN
LIBRA MAN

If there's a Libra in your life, you are most likely a very happy woman. Men born under this sign have a way with women. You'll always feel at ease in a Libra's company. You can be yourself when you're with him.

The Libra man can be moody at times. His moodiness is often puzzling. One moment he comes on hard and strong with declarations of his love, the next moment you find that he's left you like yesterday's mashed potatoes. He'll come back, though, don't worry. Libras are like that. Deep down inside he really knows what he wants even though he may not appear to.

You'll appreciate his admiration of beauty and harmony. If you're dressed to the teeth and never looked lovelier, you'll get a ready compliment—and one that's really deserved. Libras don't indulge in idle flattery. If they don't like something, they are tactful enough to remain silent.

Libras will go to great lengths to preserve peace and harmony—they will even tell a fat lie if necessary. They don't like showdowns or disagreeable confrontations. The frank woman is all for getting whatever is bothering her off her chest and out into the open, even if it comes out all wrong. To the Libra, making a clean breast of everything seems like sheer folly sometimes.

You may lose your patience while waiting for your Libra friend to make up his mind. It takes him ages sometimes to make a decision. He weighs both sides carefully before committing himself to anything. You seldom dillydally, at least about small things. So it's likely that you will find it difficult to see eye-to-eye with a hesitating Libra when it comes to decision-making methods.

All in all, though, he is kind, considerate, and fair. He is interested in the real truth. He'll try to balance everything out until he has all the correct answers. It's not difficult for him to see both sides of a story.

He's a peace-loving man. Even a rough-and-tumble sports event, and certainly a violent one, will make Libra shudder.

Libras are not show-offs. Generally, they are well-balanced, modest people. Honest, wholesome, and affectionate, they are serious about every love encounter they have. If Libra should find that the woman he's dating is not really suited to him, he will end the relationship in such a tactful manner that no hard feelings will come about.

The Libra father is patient and fair. He can be firm without exercising undue strictness or discipline. Although he can be a harsh judge at times, with the youngsters he will radiate sweetness and light in the hope that they will grow up to imitate his gentle manner. To balance the essential refinement the children will acquire from their Libra father, you will teach them a few rough-and-ready ways to enjoy recreation.

SAGITTARIUS WOMAN
SCORPIO MAN

Scorpio shares at least one trait in common with Sagittarius. You both are blunt. But Scorpio, who can be vengeful and vindictive, intends an insult as an insult, not just a thoughtless comment. Many find Scorpio's sting a fate worse than death. When his anger breaks loose, you better clear out of the vicinity.

The average Scorpio may strike you as a brute. He'll stick pins into the balloons of your plans and dreams if they don't line up with what he thinks is right. If you do anything to irritate him—just anything—you'll wish you hadn't. He'll give you a sounding out that would make you pack your bags and go back to Mother—if you were that kind of woman.

The Scorpio man hates being tied down to home life. He would rather be out on the battlefield of life, belting away at whatever he feels is a just and worthy cause, instead of staying home nestled in a comfortable armchair with the evening paper. If you have a strong homemaking streak, don't keep those home fires burning too brightly too long; you may just run out of firewood.

As passionate as he is in business affairs and politics, the Scorpio man still has plenty of fire and light stored away for the pursuit of romance and lovemaking.

Most women are easily attracted to him—perhaps you are no exception. Those who allow a man born under this sign to sweep them off their feet quickly find that they're dealing with a pepper pot of seething excitement. The Scorpio man is passionate with a capital P, you can be sure of that. When you two meet on the playing field of love, Scorpio will be much more intense and competitive than you.

If you can match his intensity and adapt to his mood swings, you are fair game. If you're the kind of woman who can keep a stiff upper lip, take it on the chin, turn a deaf ear, and all of that, because you feel you are still under his love spell in spite of everything—lots of luck.

If you have decided to take the bitter with the sweet, prepare yourself for a lot of ups and downs. Chances are you won't have as much time for your own affairs and interests as you'd like. The Scorpio's love of power may cause you to be at his constant beck and call.

Scorpios like fathering large families. He is proud of his children, but often he fails to live up to his responsibilities as a parent. In spite of the extremes in his personality, the Scorpio man is able to transform the conflicting characteristics within himself when he becomes a father. When he takes his fatherly duties seriously, he is a powerful teacher. He believes in preparing his children for the hard knocks life sometimes delivers. He is adept with difficult youngsters because he knows how to tap the best in each child.

SAGITTARIUS WOMAN
SAGITTARIUS MAN

The woman who has set her cap for a man born under the sign of Sagittarius may have to apply an awful amount of strategy before she can get him to drop down on bended knee. Although some Sagittarius may be marriage-shy, they're not ones to skitter away from romance. A high-spirited woman may find a relationship with a Sagittarius—whether a fling or the real thing—a very enjoyable experience.

As you know, Sagittarius are bright, happy, and healthy people. You all have a strong sense of fair play. You all are a source of inspiration to others. You're full of ideas and drive.

You'll be taken by the Sagittarius man's infectious grin and his lighthearted friendly nature. If you do wind up being the woman in his life, you'll find that he's apt to treat you more like a buddy than the love of his life. It's just his way. Sagittarius are often chummy instead of romantic.

You'll admire his broad-mindedness in most matters—including those of the heart. If, while dating you, he claims that he still wants to play the field, he'll expect you to enjoy the same liberty. Once he's promised to love, honor, and obey, however, he does just that. Marriage for him, once he's taken that big step, is very serious business.

A woman who has a keen imagination and a great love of freedom will not be disappointed if she does tie up with the Archer. The Sagittarius man is often quick-witted. Men of this sign have a genuine interest in equality. They hate prejudice and injustice.

If he does insist on a night out with the boys once a week, he won't scowl if you decide to let him shift for himself in the kitchen once a week while you pursue some of your own interests. He believes in fairness.

He's not much of a homebody. Quite often he's occupied with

faraway places either in his dreams or in reality. He enjoys—just as you do—being on the go or on the move. He's got ants in his pants and refuses to sit still for long stretches at a time. Humdrum routine, especially at home, bores him. So the two of you will probably go out a lot or throw lots of parties at home.

He likes surprising people. He'll take great pride in showing you off to his friends. He'll always be a considerate mate; he will never embarrass or disappoint you intentionally.

He's very tolerant when it comes to friends, and you'll most likely spend a lot of time entertaining people—which suits you party animals royally.

The Sagittarius father, unlike you, may be bewildered and made utterly nervous by a newborn. He will dote on any infant son or daughter from a safe distance because he can be clumsy and frightened handling the tiny tot. The Sagittarius dad usually becomes comfortable with youngsters once they have passed through the baby stage. As soon as they are old enough to walk and talk, he will encourage each and every visible sign of talent and skill.

SAGITTARIUS WOMAN
CAPRICORN MAN

A with-it woman like you is likely to find the average Capricorn man a bit of a drag. The man born under this sign is often a closed up person and difficult to get to know. Even if you do get to know him, you may not find him very interesting.

In romance, Capricorn men are a little on the rusty side. You'll probably have to make all the passes.

You may find his plodding manner irritating and his conservative, traditional ways downright maddening. He's not one to take a chance on anything. If it was good enough for his father, it's good enough for him. Capricorn can be habit-bound. He follows a way that is tried and true.

Whenever adventure rears its tantalizing head, the Goat will turn the other way. Unlike you, he is not prone to taking risks.

He may be just as ambitious as you are, perhaps even more so. But his ways of accomplishing his aims are more subterranean than yours. He operates from the background a good deal of the time. At a gathering you may never even notice him. But he's there, taking everything in, sizing everyone up, planning his next careful move.

Although Capricorns may be intellectual to a degree, it is not generally the kind of intelligence you appreciate. He may not be as quick or as bright as you. It may take him ages to understand a joke, and you love jokes.

If you do decide to take up with a man born under the sign of the Goat, you ought to be pretty good in the cheering up department.

The Capricorn man often acts as though he's constantly being followed by a cloud of gloom.

The Capricorn man is most himself when in the comfort and privacy of his own home. The security possible within four walls can make him a happy man. He'll spend as much time as he can at home. If he is loaded down with extra work, he'll bring it home instead of finishing it up at the office.

You'll most likely find yourself frequently confronted by his relatives. Family is very important to the Capricorn—his family that is. They had better take an important place in your life, too, if you want to keep your home a happy one.

Although his caution in most matters may all but drive you up the wall, you'll find that his concerned way with money is justified most of the time. He'll plan everything right down to the last penny.

The Capricorn father is a dutiful parent and takes a lifelong interest in seeing that his children make something of themselves. He may not understand their hopes and dreams because he often tries to put his head on their shoulders. The Capricorn father believes that there are certain goals to be achieved, and there is a traditional path to achieving them. He can be quite a scold if the youngsters break the rules. Your easygoing, joyful manner will moderate Capricorn's rigid approach and will make things fun again for the children.

SAGITTARIUS WOMAN
AQUARIUS MAN

Aquarius individuals love everybody—even their worst enemies sometimes. Through your love relationship with an Aquarius you'll find yourself running into all sorts of people, ranging from near genius to downright insane—and they're all friends of his.

As a rule, Aquarius are extremely friendly and open. Of all the signs, they are perhaps the most tolerant. In the thinking department, they are often miles ahead of others.

You'll most likely find your relationship with this man a challenging one. Your high respect for intelligence and imagination may be reason enough for you to set your heart on a Water Bearer. You'll find that you can learn a lot from him.

In the holding-hands phase of your romance, you may find that your Water Bearer friend has cold feet. Aquarius take quite a bit of warming up before they are ready to come across with that first goodnight kiss. More than likely, he'll just want to be your pal in the beginning. For him, that's an important first step in any relationship—love included.

The poetry and flowers stage—if it ever comes—will come later. Aquarius is all heart. Still, when it comes to tying himself down to one person and for keeps, he is almost always sure to hesitate.

He may even try to get out of it if you breathe down his neck too heavily.

The Aquarius man is no Romeo, and he wouldn't want to be. The kind of love life he's looking for is one that's made up mainly of companionship. He may not be very romantic, but still the memory of his first romance will always hold an important position in his heart. So in a way he is like Romeo after all. Some Aquarius wind up marrying their childhood sweethearts.

You won't find it difficult to look up to a man born under the sign of the Water Bearer, but you may find the challenge of trying to keep up with him dizzying. He can pierce through the most complicated problem as if it were simple math. You may find him a little too lofty and high-minded. But don't judge him too harshly if that's the case. He's way ahead of his time.

If you marry this man, he'll stay true to you. Don't think that once the honeymoon is over, you'll be chained to the kitchen sink forever. Your Aquarius husband will encourage you to keep active in your own interests and affairs. You'll most likely have a minor tiff now and again but never anything serious.

The Aquarius father has an almost intuitive understanding of children. He sees them as individuals in their own right, not as extensions of himself or as beings who are supposed to take a certain place in the world. He can talk to the kids on a variety of subjects, and his knowledge can be awe-inspiring. Your dedication to learning and your desire to educate the children will be bolstered by your Aquarius mate. And your love of sports and games, the fun physical activities in life, will balance the airy Aquarius intellectualism.

SAGITTARIUS WOMAN
PISCES MAN

The man born under Pisces is quite a dreamer. Sometimes he's so wrapped up in his dreams that he's difficult to reach. To the average, active woman, he may seem a little passive.

He's easygoing most of the time. He seems to take things in his stride. He'll entertain all kinds of views and opinions from just about everyone, nodding or smiling vaguely, giving the impression that he's with them one hundred percent while that may not be the case at all. His attitude may be why bother when he's confronted with someone wrong who thinks he's right. The Pisces man will seldom speak his mind if he thinks he'll be rigidly opposed.

The Pisces man is oversensitive at times. He's afraid of getting his feelings hurt. He'll sometimes imagine a personal affront when none's been made. Chances are you'll find this complex of his maddening. At times you may feel like giving him a swift kick where it hurts the most. It wouldn't do any good, though. It would just add fuel to the fire of his complex.

One thing you'll admire about this man is his concern for people who are sickly or troubled. He'll make his shoulder available to anyone in the mood for a good cry. He can listen to one hard-luck story after another without seeming to tire. When his advice is asked, he is capable of coming across with some words of wisdom. He often knows what is bothering someone before that person is aware of it. It's almost intuitive with Pisces.

Still, at the end of the day, this man will want some peace and quiet. If you've got a problem when he comes home, don't unload it in his lap. If you do, you are apt to find him short-tempered. He's a good listener but he can only take so much.

Pisces are not aimless although they may seem so at times. The positive sort of Pisces man is quite often successful in his profession and is likely to wind up rich and influential. Material gain, however, is never a direct goal for a man born under this sign.

The weaker Pisces are usually content to stay on the level where they find themselves. They won't complain too much if the roof leaks or if the fence is in need of repair.

Because of their seemingly laissez-faire manner, people under the sign of the Fishes—needless to say—are immensely popular with children. For tots the Pisces father plays the double role of confidant and playmate. It will never enter the mind of a Pisces to discipline a child, no matter how spoiled or incorrigible that child becomes.

Man—Woman

SAGITTARIUS MAN
ARIES WOMAN

The Aries woman is quite a charmer. When she tugs at the strings of your heart, you'll know it. She's a woman who's in search of a knight in shining armor. She is a very particular person with very high ideals. She won't accept anyone but the man of her dreams.

The Aries woman never plays around with passion. She means business when it comes to love.

Don't get the idea that she's a dewy-eyed damsel. She isn't. In fact, she can be practical and to the point when she wants to be. She's a dame with plenty of drive and ambition.

With an Aries woman behind you, you can go far in life. She knows how to help her man get ahead. She's full of wise advice; you only have to ask. The Aries woman has a keen business sense. Many of them become successful career women. There is nothing passive or retiring about her. She is equipped with a good brain and she knows how to use it.

Your union with her could be something strong, secure, and romantic. If both of you have your sights fixed in the same direction, there is almost nothing that you could not accomplish.

The Aries woman is proud and capable of being quite jealous. While you're with her, never cast your eye in another woman's direction. It could spell disaster for your relationship. The Aries woman won't put up with romantic nonsense when her heart is at stake.

If the Aries woman backs you up in your business affairs, you can be sure of succeeding. However, if she only is interested in advancing her own career and puts her interests before yours, she can be sure to rock the boat. It will put a strain on the relationship. The overambitious Aries woman can be a pain in the neck and make you forget you were in love with her once.

The cultivated Aries woman makes a wonderful wife and mother. She has a natural talent for homemaking. With a pot of paint and some wallpaper, she can transform the dreariest domicile into an abode of beauty and snug comfort. The perfect hostess—even when friends just happen by—she knows how to make guests feel at home.

You'll also admire your Aries because she knows how to stand on her own two feet. Hers is an independent nature. She won't break down and cry when things go wrong, but will pick herself up and try to patch up matters.

The Aries woman makes a fine, affectionate mother. Although she is not keen on burdensome responsibilities, like you she relishes the joy that children bring. The Aries woman is skilled at juggling both career and motherhood, so her kids will never feel that she is an absentee parent. In fact, as the youngsters grow older, they might want some of the liberation that is so important to her. One of your roles is to encourage the children's quest for independence.

SAGITTARIUS MAN
TAURUS WOMAN

The woman born under the sign of Taurus may lack a little of the sparkle and bubble you often like to find in a woman. The Taurus woman is generally down to earth and never flighty. It's important to her that she keep both feet flat on the ground. She is not fond of bounding all over the place, especially if she's under the impression that there's no profit in it.

On the other hand, if you hit it off with a Taurus woman, you won't be disappointed in the romance area. The Taurus woman is all woman and proud of it, too. She can be very devoted and loving once she decides that her relationship with you is no fly-by-night romance. Basically, she's a passionate person. In sex, she's direct and to the point. If she really loves you, she'll let you know she's yours—and without reservations.

Better not flirt with other women once you've committed yourself to her. She's capable of being very jealous and possessive.

She'll stick by you through thick and thin. It's almost certain that if the going ever gets rough, she won't go running home to her mother. She can adjust to the hard times just as graciously as she can to the good times.

Taurus are, on the whole, pretty even-tempered. They like to be treated with kindness. Beautiful things and aesthetic objects make them feel loved and treasured.

You may find her a little slow and deliberate. She likes to be safe and sure about everything. Let her plod along if she likes. Don't coax her, but just let her take her own sweet time. Everything she does is done thoroughly and, generally, without mistakes.

Don't deride her for being a slowpoke. It could lead to a tirade of insults that could put even your blunt manner to shame. The Taurus woman doesn't anger readily but when prodded often enough, she's capable of letting loose with a cyclone of ill will. If you treat her with kindness and consideration, you'll have no cause for complaint.

The Taurus woman loves doing things for her man. She's a whiz in the kitchen and can whip up feasts fit for a king if she thinks they'll be royally appreciated. She may not fully understand you, but she'll adore you and be faithful to you if she feels you're worthy of it.

The Taurus woman makes a wonderful mother. She knows how to keep her children loved, cuddled, and warm. She may have some difficult times with them when they reach adolescence, and start to rebel against her strictness. You can inject a sense of adventure even in the most mundane of household responsibilities, so you will moderate your Taurus mate's insistence on discipline.

SAGITTARIUS MAN
GEMINI WOMAN

You may find a romance with a woman born under the sign of the Twins a many-splendored thing. In her you can find the intellectual companionship you often look for in a friend or mate.

Gemini, your astrological mate, can appreciate your aims and desires because she travels pretty much the same road as you do intellectually. At least she will travel part of the way. She may share your interests, but she will lack your tenacity.

She suffers from itchy feet. She can be here, there, all over the place and at the same time, or so it would seem. Her eagerness to move around may make you dizzy. Still, you'll enjoy and appreciate her liveliness and mental agility.

Geminis have sparkling personalities. You'll be attracted by her warmth and grace. While she's on your arm, you'll probably notice that many male eyes are drawn to her. She may even return a gaze or two, but don't let that worry you. All women born under this sign have nothing against a harmless flirt once in a while. They enjoy this sort of attention. If Gemini feels she is already spoken for, however, she will never let such attention get out of hand.

Although she may not be as handy as you'd like in the kitchen, you'll never go hungry for a filling and tasty meal. The Gemini woman is always in a rush. She won't feel like she's cheating by breaking out the instant mashed potatoes or the frozen peas. She may not be much of a good cook but she is clever. With a dash of this and a suggestion of that, she can make an uninteresting TV dinner taste like a gourmet meal.

Then, again, maybe you've struck it rich and have a Gemini lover or mate who finds complicated recipes a challenge to her intellect. If so, you'll find every meal an experiment—a tantalizing and mouth-watering surprise.

When you're beating your brains out over the Sunday crossword puzzle and find yourself stuck, just ask your Gemini partner. She'll give you all the right answers without batting an eyelash.

Like you, she loves all kinds of people. You may even find that you're a bit more particular than she. Often all that a Gemini requires is that her friends be interesting—and stay interesting. One thing she's not able to abide is a dullard.

Leave the party organizing to your Gemini sweetheart or mate, and you'll never have a chance to know a dull moment. She'll bring out the swinger in you if you give her half the chance.

The Gemini mother has a youthful streak that guides her in bringing up children through the various stages. She enjoys her kids, which can be the most sincere form of love. Like you—and like them—the Gemini mother is often restless, adventurous, and easily bored. She will never complain about the children's fleeting interests because she understands how they will change as they mature. Gemini-Sagittarius parents, being true zodiacal mates as well as zodiacal opposites, can encourage variety and experience in life so the kids really get to know what the world is like.

SAGITTARIUS MAN
CANCER WOMAN

If you fall in love with a Cancer woman, be prepared for anything. Cancer is sometimes difficult to understand when it comes to love. In one hour, she can unravel a whole gamut of emotions that will leave you in a tizzy. She'll undoubtedly keep you guessing.

You may find her a little too uncertain and sensitive for your liking. You'll most likely spend a good deal of time encouraging her, helping her to erase her foolish fears. Tell her she's a living doll a dozen times a day, and you'll be well loved in return.

Be careful of the jokes you make when in her company. Don't let any of them revolve around her, her personal interests, or her family. If you do, you'll most likely reduce her to tears. She can't stand being made fun of. It will take bushels of roses and tons of chocolates—not to mention the apologies—to get her to come back out of her shell.

In matters of money managing, she may not easily come around to your way of thinking. Money will never burn a hole in her pocket. You may get the notion that your Cancer sweetheart or mate is a direct descendent of Scrooge. If she has her way, she'll hang onto that first dollar you earned. She's not only that way with money, but with everything right on up from bakery string to jelly jars. She's a saver. She never throws anything away, no matter how trivial.

Once she returns your love, you'll find you have an affectionate, self-sacrificing, and devoted woman for life. Her love for you will never alter unless you want it to. She'll put you high upon a pedestal and will do everything—even if it's against your will—to keep you up there.

Cancer women love home life. For them, marriage is an easy step. They're domestic with a capital D. The Cancer woman will do her best to make your home comfortable and cozy. She, herself, is more at ease at home than anywhere else. She makes an excellent hostess. The best in her comes out when she is in her own environment, one she has created to meet her own and her family's needs.

Cancer women make the best mothers. Each will consider every complaint of her child a major catastrophe. With her, children always come first. If you're lucky, you'll run a close second. You'll perhaps see her as too devoted to the children. You may have a hard time convincing her that her apron strings are a little too tight.

SAGITTARIUS MAN
LEO WOMAN

If you can manage a woman who likes to kick up her heels every now and again, then the Lioness was made for you. You'll have to learn to put away jealous fears when you take up with a woman born under the sign of Leo. She's often the kind that makes heads turn and tongues wag. You don't have to believe any of what you hear. It's most likely jealous gossip or wishful thinking.

The Leo woman has more than a fair share of grace and glamour. She knows it, and she knows how to put it to good use. Needless to say, other women in her vicinity turn green with envy and will try anything to put her out of the running.

If she's captured your heart and fancy, woo her full force—if your intention is eventually to win her. Shower her with expensive gifts and promise her the moon, if you're in a position to go that far. Then you'll find her resistance beginning to weaken. It's not that she's such a difficult cookie. She'll probably pamper you once she's decided you're the man for her. But she does enjoy a lot of attention. What's more, she feels she's entitled to it. Her mild arrogance, however, is becoming.

The Leo woman knows how to transform the crime of excessive pride into a very charming misdemeanor. It sweeps most men—or rather, all men—right off their feet. Those who do not succumb to her leonine charm are few and far between.

If you've got an important business deal to clinch and you have doubts as to whether you can bring it off as you should, take your Leo mate along to the business luncheon. It will be a cinch that you'll have that contract—lock, stock, and barrel—in your pocket before the meeting is over. She won't have to say or do anything, just be there at your side. The grouchiest oil magnate can be transformed into a gushing, obedient schoolboy if there's a Leo woman in the room.

If you're rich and want to see to it that you stay that way, don't give your Leo spouse a free hand with the charge accounts and credit cards. When it comes to spending, Leo tends to overdo. If you're poor, you have no worries because the luxury-loving Leo will most likely never recognize your existence—let alone consent to marry you.

A Leo mother can be so proud of her children that she is sometimes blind to their faults. Yet when she wants them to learn and take their rightful place in the social scheme of things, the Leo mother can be strict. She is a patient teacher, lovingly explaining the rules the youngsters are expected to follow. Easygoing and friendly, like you are, she loves to pal around with the kids and show them off on every occasion. Your family will be a bundle of joy.

SAGITTARIUS MAN
VIRGO WOMAN

The Virgo woman may be a little too difficult for you to understand at first. Her waters run deep. Even when you think you know her, don't take any bets on it. She's capable of keeping things hidden in the deep recesses of her womanly soul—things she'll only release when she's sure that you're the man she's been looking for.

It may take her some time to come around to this decision. Virgo women are finicky about almost everything. Everything has to be letter-perfect before they're satisfied. Many of them have the idea that the only people who can do things right are Virgos.

Nothing offends a Virgo woman more than slovenly dress, sloppy character, or a careless display of affection. Make sure your tie is not crooked and that your shoes sport a bright shine before you go calling on this lady. The typical Sagittarius male should keep the off-color jokes for the locker room. She'll have none of that. Take her arm when crossing the street. Don't rush the romance. Trying to corner her in the back of a cab may be one way of striking out. Never criticize the way she looks. In fact, the best policy would be to agree with her as much as possible.

Still, there's just so much a man can take. All those dos and don'ts you'll have to observe if you want to get to first base with a Virgo may be just a little too much to ask of you. After a few dates, you may come to the conclusion that she just isn't worth all that trouble.

However, the Virgo woman is mysterious enough, generally speaking, to keep her men running back for more. Chances are you'll be intrigued by her airs and graces.

If lovemaking means a lot to you, you'll be disappointed at first in the cool ways of your Virgo partner. However, under her glacial facade there lies a hot cauldron of seething excitement. If you're patient and artful in your romantic approach, you'll find that all that caution was well worth the trouble. When Virgos love, they don't stint. It's all or nothing as far as they're concerned. Once they're convinced that they love you, they go all the way, tossing all cares to the wind.

One thing a Virgo woman can't stand in love is hypocrisy. They don't give a hoot about what the neighbors say if their hearts tell them to go ahead. They're very concerned with human truths. So if their hearts stumble upon another fancy, they will be true to that new heartthrob and leave you standing in the rain.

The Virgo woman is honest to her heart and will be as true to you as you are with her, generally. Do her wrong once, however, and it's farewell.

The Virgo mother has high expectations for her children, and she will strive to bring out the very best in them. They usually turn out just as she hoped, despite her anxiety about health and hygiene, safety and good sense. You must step in and ease her fears when she tries to restrict the kids at play or at school. The Virgo mother is more tender than strict, though, and the children will sense her unconditional love for them.

SAGITTARIUS MAN
LIBRA WOMAN

You'll probably find that the woman born under the sign of Libra is worth more than her weight in gold. She's a woman after your own heart.

With her, you'll always come first—make no mistake about that. She'll always be behind you 100 percent, no matter what you do. When you ask her advice about almost anything, you are likely to get a very balanced and realistic opinion. She is good at thinking things out and never lets her emotions run away with her when clear logic is called for.

As a homemaker she is hard to beat. She is very concerned with harmony and balance. You can be sure she'll make your house a joy to live in. She'll see to it that the home is tastefully furnished and decorated. A Libra cannot stand filth or disarray or noise. Anything that does not radiate harmony, in fact, runs against her orderly grain.

She is chock-full of charm and womanly ways. She can sweep just about any man off his feet with one winning smile. When it comes to using her brains, she can outthink almost anyone and, sometimes, with half the effort. She is diplomatic enough, though, never to let this become glaringly apparent. She may even turn the conversation around so that you think you were the one who did all the brainwork. She couldn't care less, really, just as long as you wind up doing what is right.

The Libra woman will put you up on a pretty high pedestal. You are her man and her idol. She'll leave all the decision making, large or small, up to you. She's not interested in running things and will only offer her assistance if she feels you really need it.

Some find her approach to reason masculine. However, in the areas of love and affection the Libra woman is all woman. She'll literally shower you with love and kisses during your romance with her. She doesn't believe in holding out. You shouldn't, either, if you want to hang onto her.

She is the kind of lover who likes to snuggle up to you in front of the fire on chilly autumn nights, the kind who will bring you breakfast in bed on Sunday. She'll be very thoughtful about anything that concerns you. If anyone dares suggest you're not the grandest guy in the world, she'll give that person what-for. She'll defend you till her dying breath. The Libra woman will be everything you want her to be.

The Libra mother will create a harmonious household in which young family members can grow up as equals. She will foster an environment that is sensitive to their needs. The Libra mother understands that children need both guidance and encouragement. With your enthusiastic input, the youngsters will never lack for anything that could make their lives easier and richer.

SAGITTARIUS MAN
SCORPIO WOMAN

The Scorpio woman can be a whirlwind of passion, perhaps too much passion to suit you casual types. When her temper flies, you'd better lock up the family heirlooms and take cover. When she chooses to be sweet, you're overcome with joy. When she uses sarcasm, she can shock even a blunt Sagittarius.

The Scorpio woman can be as hot as a tamale or as cool as a cucumber, but whatever mood she's in, she's in it for real. She does not believe in posing or putting on airs.

The Scorpio woman is often sultry and seductive. Her femme fatale charme can pierce through the hardest of hearts like a laser ray. She may not look like Mata Hari (quite often Scorpios resemble the tomboy next door) but once she's fixed you with her tantalizing eyes, you're a goner.

Life with the Scorpio woman will not be all smiles and smooth sailing. When prompted, she can unleash a gale of venom. Generally, she'll have the good grace to keep family battles within the walls of your home. When company visits, she's apt to give the impression that married life with you is one great big joyride. It's just one of her ways of expressing her loyalty to you, at least in front of others. She may fight you tooth and nail in the confines of your living room, but at a party or during an evening out, she'll hang onto your arm and have stars in her eyes.

Scorpio women are good at keeping secrets. She may even keep a few buried from you if she feels like it.

Never cross her up on even the smallest thing. When it comes to revenge, she's an eye-for-an-eye woman. She's not one for forgiveness, especially if she feels she's been wronged unfairly. You'd be well-advised not to give her any cause to be jealous, either. When the Scorpio woman sees green, your life will be made far from rosy. Once she's put you in the doghouse, you can be sure that you're going to stay there awhile.

You may find life with a Scorpio woman too draining. Although she may be full of extreme moods, it's quite likely that she's not the kind of woman you'd like to spend the rest of your natural life with. You'd prefer someone gentler and not so hot-tempered, someone who can take the highs with the lows and not complain, someone who is flexible and understanding. A woman born under Scorpio can be heavenly, but she can also be the very devil when she chooses.

The Scorpio mother is protective yet encouraging. The opposites within her nature mirror the very contradictions of life itself. Under her skillful guidance, the children learn how to cope with extremes and grow up to become many-faceted individuals.

SAGITTARIUS MAN
SAGITTARIUS WOMAN

You are in sync with your zodiacal sister born under the sign of Sagittarius. This good-natured gal is full of bounce and good cheer. Her sunny disposition seems almost permanent and can be relied upon even on the rainiest of days.

Women born under the sign of the Archer are almost never malicious. If ever they seem to be, it is only seeming. Sagittarius are often a little short on tact and say literally anything that comes into their heads, no matter what the occasion is. Sometimes the words that tumble out of their mouths seem downright cutting and cruel.

Still, no matter what the Sagittarius woman says, she means well. Lover or spouse, she is quite capable of losing some of your friends through a careless slip of the lip.

On the other hand, you will appreciate her honesty and good intentions. To you, qualities of this sort play an important part in life. With a little patience and practice, you can probably help cure your Sagittarius partner of her loose tongue. In most cases, you both will have to use better judgment, and you both will have to practice what you preach.

Chances are, she'll be the outdoors type of woman who likes sports, recreation, and exercise. Long hikes, fishing trips, and white-water canoeing will most likely appeal to her. She's a busy person. No one could ever call her a slouch. She sets great store in mobility. She won't sit still for one minute if she doesn't have to.

The Sagittarius woman is great company most of the time and, generally, lots of fun. Even if your buddies drop by for poker and beer, she won't have any trouble fitting in.

On the whole, she is a very kind and sympathetic woman. If she feels she's made a mistake, she'll be the first to call your attention to it. She's not afraid to own up to her own faults and shortcomings.

You might lose your patience with her once or twice. After she's seen how upset her shortsightedness or carelessness with money has made you, she'll do her best to straighten up.

The Sagittarius woman is not the kind who will pry into your business affairs. But she'll always be there, ready to offer advice if you need it.

The Sagittarius woman is seldom suspicious. Your word will almost always be good enough for her.

The Sagittarius mother is a wonderful and loving friend to her children. She is not afraid if a youngster learns some street smarts along the way. In fact, both of you Sagittarius parents may compete playfully in teaching the children all about the world from your various and combined experiences. You both will see to it that the kids get the best education and recreation money can buy.

SAGITTARIUS MAN
CAPRICORN WOMAN

If you are not a successful businessman or, at least, on your way to success, it's quite possible that a Capricorn woman will have no interest in entering your life. Generally, she is a very security-minded female. She'll see to it that she invests her time only in sure things.

Men who whittle away their time with one unsuccessful scheme or another seldom attract a Capricorn. Men who are interested in getting somewhere in life and keep their noses close to the grindstone quite often have a Capricorn woman behind them, helping them to get ahead.

Although she can be an opportunist and a social climber, she is not what you could call cruel or hard-hearted. Beneath that cool, seemingly calculating exterior, there is a warm and desirable woman. She happens to think that it is just as easy to fall in love with a rich or ambitious man as it is with a poor or lazy one. She's practical.

The Capricorn woman may be interested in rising to the top, but she'll never be aggressive about it. She'll seldom step on someone's feet or nudge competitors away with her elbows. She's quiet about her desires. She sits, waits, and watches. When an opening or opportunity does appear, she'll latch onto it.

For an on-the-move man, an ambitious Capricorn wife or lover can be quite an asset. She can probably give you some very good advice about business matters. When you invite the boss and his wife for dinner, she'll charm them both and make you look good.

The Capricorn woman is thorough in whatever she does: cooking, cleaning, making a success out of life. Capricorns are excellent hostesses as well as guests. Generally, they are very well-mannered and gracious, no matter what their backgrounds are. They seem to have a built-in sense of what is right. Crude behavior or a careless faux pas can offend them no end.

If you should marry a woman born under Capricorn, you need never worry about her going on a wild shopping spree. Capricorns are careful with every cent that comes into their hands. They understand the value of money better than most women and have no room in their lives for careless spending.

The Capricorn woman is usually very fond of family—her own, that is. With her, family ties run very deep. Don't make jokes about her relatives; she won't stand for it. You'd better check her family out before you get down on bended knee. After your marriage, you'll undoubtedly be seeing a lot of her relatives.

The Capricorn mother is very ambitious for her children. She wants them to have every advantage and to benefit from things she perhaps lacked as a child. She will train her youngsters to be polite and kind and to honor traditional codes of conduct.

SAGITTARIUS MAN
AQUARIUS WOMAN

If you find that you've fallen head over heels for a woman born under the sign of the Water Bearer, you'd better fasten your safety belt. It may take you quite a while actually to discover what this woman is like. Even then, you may have nothing to go on but a string of vague hunches.

Aquarius is like a rainbow, full of bright and shining hues. She's like no other woman you've ever known. There is something elusive about her—something delightfully mysterious. You'll most likely never be able to put your finger on it. It's nothing calculated, either. Aquarius do not believe in phony charm.

There will never be a dull moment in your life with this Water Bearer woman. She seems to radiate adventure and magic. She'll most likely be the most open-minded and tolerant woman you've ever met. She has a strong dislike for injustice and prejudice. Narrow-mindedness runs against her grain.

She is very independent by nature and quite capable of shifting for herself if necessary. She may receive many proposals of marriage from all sorts of people without ever really taking them seriously. Marriage is a very big step for her; she wants to be sure she knows what she's getting into. If she thinks that it will seriously curb her independence and love of freedom, she might return the engagement ring—if indeed she's let the romance get that far.

The line between friendship and romance is a pretty fuzzy one for an Aquarius. It's not difficult for her to remain buddy-buddy with an ex-lover. She's tolerant, remember? So, if you should see her on the arm of an old love, don't jump to any hasty conclusions.

She's not a jealous person herself and doesn't expect you to be, either. You'll find her pretty much of a free spirit most of the time. Just when you think you know her inside out, you'll discover that you don't really know her at all, though.

She's a very sympathetic and warm person. She can be helpful to people in need of assistance and advice.

She'll seldom be suspicious even if she has every right to be. If she loves a man, she'll forgive him just about anything. If he allows himself a little fling, chances are she'll just turn her head the other way. Her tolerance does have its limits, however, and her man should never press his luck.

The Aquarius mother is bighearted and seldom refuses her children anything. Her open-minded attitude is easily transmitted to her youngsters. They have every chance of growing up as respectful and tolerant individuals who feel at ease anywhere. You will appreciate the lessons of justice and equality that your Aquarius mate teaches the children.

SAGITTARIUS MAN
PISCES WOMAN

Many a man dreams of an alluring Pisces woman. You're perhaps no exception. She's soft and cuddly and very domestic. She'll let you be the brains of the family; she's contented to play a behind-the-scenes role in order to help you achieve your goals. The illusion that you are the master of the household is the kind of magic that the Pisces woman is adept at creating.

She can be very ladylike and proper. Your business associates and friends will be dazzled by her warmth and femininity. Although she's a charmer, there is a lot more to her than just a pretty exterior. There is a brain ticking away behind that soft, womanly facade. You may never become aware of it—that is, until you're married to her. It's no cause for alarm, however; she'll most likely never use it against you, only to help you and possibly set you on a more successful path.

If she feels you're botching up your married life through careless behavior or if she feels you could be earning more money than you do, she'll tell you about it. But any wife would, really. She will never try to usurp your position as head and breadwinner of the family.

No one had better dare say one uncomplimentary word about you in her presence. It's likely to cause her to break into tears. Pisces women are usually very sensitive beings. Their reaction to adversity, frustration, or anger is just a plain, good, old-fashioned cry. They can weep buckets when inclined.

She can do wonders with a house. She is very fond of dramatic and beautiful things. There will always be plenty of fresh-cut flowers around the house. She will choose charming artwork and antiques, if they are affordable. She'll see to it that the house is decorated in a dazzling yet welcoming style.

She'll have an extra special dinner prepared for you when you come home from an important business meeting. Don't dwell on the boring details of the meeting, though. But if you need that grand vision, the big idea, to seal a contract or make a conquest, your Pisces woman is sure to confide a secret that will guarantee your success. She is canny and shrewd with money, and once you are on her wavelength you can manage the intricacies on your own.

Treat her with tenderness and generosity and your relationship will be an enjoyable one. She's most likely fond of chocolates. A bunch of beautiful flowers will never fail to make her eyes light up. See to it that you never forget her birthday or your anniversary. These things are very important to her. If you let them slip your mind, you'll send her into a crying fit that could last a considerable length of time.

If you are patient and kind, you can keep a Pisces woman happy for a lifetime. She, however, is not without her faults. Her sensitivity may get on your nerves after a while. You may find her lacking in practicality and good old-fashioned stoicism. You may even feel that she uses her tears as a method of getting her own way.

The Pisces mother has, as you do, great joy and utter faith in the children. She makes a strong, self-sacrificing mother through all the phases from infancy to young adulthood. She will teach her youngsters the value of service to the community while not letting them lose their individuality.

SAGITTARIUS
LUCKY NUMBERS 2012

Lucky numbers and astrology can be linked through the movements of the Moon. Each phase of the thirteen Moon cycles vibrates with a sequence of numbers for your Sign of the Zodiac over the course of the year. Using your lucky numbers is a fun system that connects you with tradition.

New Moon	First Quarter	Full Moon	Last Quarter
Dec. 24 ('11) **3257**	Jan. 1 **9408**	Jan. 9 **3665**	Jan. 16 **2357**
Jan. 23 **8482**	Jan. 31 **9670**	Feb. 7 **6359**	Feb. 14 **9474**
Feb. 21 **8253**	Feb. 29 **9146**	March 8 **8830**	March 14 **7172**
March 22 **5752**	March 30 **3680**	April 6 **1593**	April 13 **3947**
April 21 **5289**	April 29 **3572**	May 5 **5696**	May 12 **6142**
May 20 **8982**	May 28 **4618**	June 4 **0859**	June 11 **9317**
June 19 **8281**	June 26 **3725**	July 3 **3269**	July 10 **9745**
July 19 **5813**	July 26 **2614**	August 2 **9586**	August 9 **6347**
August 17 **7926**	August 24 **0085**	August 31 **4317**	Sept. 8 **7824**
Sept. 15 **4618**	Sept. 22 **8560**	Sept. 30 **7289**	Oct. 8 **9357**
Oct. 15 **7269**	Oct. 21 **6147**	Oct. 29 **5236**	Nov. 6 **6815**
Nov. 13 **5939**	Nov. 20 **4718**	Nov. 28 **2692**	Dec. 6 **2480**
Dec. 13 **3637**	Dec. 20 **1841**	Dec. 28 **3579**	Jan. 4 ('13) **9482**

SAGITTARIUS
YEARLY FORECAST 2012

*Forecast for 2012 Concerning Business
and Financial Affairs, Job Prospects,
Travel, Health, Romance and Marriage
for Persons Born with the Sun
in the Zodiacal Sign of Sagittarius.
November 23–December 20.*

For those born under the influence of the Sun in the zodiacal sign of Sagittarius, ruled by Jupiter, the planet of wisdom and good fortune, 2012 offers the opportunity to develop your creative potential and find a far more honest and satisfying level of existence in your daily life. There is the promise of many opportunities to expand your horizons, develop your potential, and find happiness. But along with opportunity come challenges that will test your commitment and abilities, especially in regard to your long-range goals. Many aspects of your current life may come under the microscope as restlessness and dissatisfaction cause you to take a long hard look at where you are heading and what you hope to achieve. Many of you will discover, after being forced to do some intensive soul searching, that you need to alter your direction and find the one the fulfills what you personally desire the most. Don't be afraid to make changes. If you ensure that you have given plenty of thought to your decisions before taking action, you should be sure of success.

From January 25 until April 15, Mars, the ruler of energy and action, turns retrograde in the sign of Virgo, which represents your sector of career and long-term direction. During this time, you can experience an increase in competition and conflict. What you had thought would be an excellent career for you may now lose its enjoyment. You may come to question whether you have chosen a field that doesn't suit your abilities and temperament. On the other hand, you could enjoy the challenge but should watch that your jousting for position doesn't turn into a war and create enemies among colleagues you may need in your climb to the top. Be ready to take as well as give, and don't stubbornly grasp at what's not worth fighting for. You are more likely to find your position by re-positioning rather than by siege. Once this period passes, you will know more about what you wish to achieve. A single-minded commitment will be rewarded with success and recognition.

Expansive Jupiter, your ruling planet, is in Taurus, your sector of daily work and well-being, for the first six months of the year. With Jupiter here the possibility of achieving success in your career is enhanced. During this transit of Jupiter in Taurus, you can find much joy in your work. Do not be afraid to change your course if you find your present career is unsatisfying. Even if you have to start at the bottom, you will take a pride in your work and be recognized for your usefulness and ability, which in itself will bring rewards. You are able to handle the details required to do a good job, making others aware of your skills. In this environment, improvements to your working conditions are likely. In addition, the more integrity and honesty you bring to your services, the more payback you will receive. In some cases, the loss of one job paves the way for the discovery of another that is more in line with what you really want to do.

With Pluto now resident in Capricorn and your sector of money and values, you do need to pay more attention to your finances. In particular, it is important to consider your attitude and attachment to money matters. With this position of Pluto, a desire for wealth can bring out the beast in you. Be wary of going to any lengths to obtain money, whether it be ruthless or underhanded. You do need to be concerned over any obsession over money. If your self-worth is tied up in how much money you have, you can experience rock bottom. This will teach you to find an internal sense of self-worth and gain an inner strength that is not contingent on the external world. Here you may decide to switch to an occupation or business that pays less but offers greater satisfaction and fulfillment in other ways.

From July onward, business interests and propositions can pick up. If you are working on establishing a business of your own, spend the first half of the year in preparation to ensure that you have covered all your bases. This will establish your legal and financial position so that you can swing into operation after June.

Venus, which rules money and business as well as love, turns retrograde in Gemini, your opposite as well as partnership sign and sector of relationships, from May 16 to June 28. During this retrograde period, there can be involvement with legal matters that can prove to be unprofitable. Business plans also can be held up with costly delays and setbacks. On the positive side, it is a good time to complete preparations before venturing into new projects and for reviewing financial matters from the past. Then you can evaluate the pros and cons of future actions and establish a better way of balancing your finances and budget.

After July, Jupiter moves into Gemini and your sector of relationship. This passage should bode well for any business partnerships that may be in the pipeline. But you do need to have a legally binding agreement in place to ensure each person's security and establish a stable base from which to start business proceedings. Investment could be a risky business at any time during the year. If you are interested in doing so, however, the second half of the year should be profitable as long as you receive advice from a professional.

With Saturn in Libra and your sector of associates, hopes, and wishes, you probably will find that working with other people can be tedious at times. Be prepared to express your ideas instead of stepping back and accepting a weak deal. You will be much more willing to shoulder any extra responsibilities that come your way. Under the transit of Saturn in Libra, you may be offered a job promotion or get elected to an office in a club. Either or both can take you closer to reaching your hopes and wishes.

There is a restless mood to this year, which will give Archers even more cause to seek out travel and excitement. August and September are very favorable times to set sail. But be aware that if you are planning to head off during July, be prepared for holdups and delays with flights and your itinerary. And ensure you have adequate travel insurance to cover lost luggage or theft along the way. There is an indication that you will be mixing with people from different cultures and walks of life. Your horizons will broaden and your mind will open to new ideas and concepts. These influences can act as a catalyst to encourage you toward a spiritual or philosophical search for more meaning and understanding of the world and within your own life. Some Archers could marry while overseas, bringing a new language and culture into your home and daily life. There is also a possibility that you may travel overseas on a spiritual journey in an attempt to nourish your health and well-being.

Health is likely to prosper in the first half of the year while Jupiter is resident in your sector of health. Medical procedures or programs, if necessary, are more apt to be successful at this time. There may be an inclination to put on weight, however, if you don't watch your sweet tooth and avoid any tendency toward indulgence. With Neptune moving through Pisces and your sector of home, there may be a possibility that you will take some time from work to recuperate. This should be a successful process as long as you do what is required, especially with regard to diet and exercise. You do need to contain your emotions when dealing with the problems you encounter. Emotions are probably the biggest stumbling block you will encounter to detract from your natural healing abilities in many areas. You are being called on to face up to your past and put any pain and childhood problems behind you. As you do, you can live in the present in a peaceful and contented state. If you find that problems centered around your home keep bringing you down, start counseling with a recommended specialist. You need to become conscious of childhood complexes that are like weak foundations that sabotage your good intentions. Spiritual practices are also recommended. Yoga and meditation are very effective at bringing peace of mind and acceptance, releasing the pain and fears from the past.

Romance for the Archer is likely to take on a quite different aspect than ever before, bringing change and excitement into your life. If you are dating, you will be attracted to people who are weird, unusual, independent, and maybe even a bit shocking. There could be a great difference in ages, or the person can just be someone you would have never considered dating before. For Sagittarius who may be restless or dissatisfied with an existing relationship, unless you can find some way of breathing new life into it, you may start to look elsewhere for love and romance. There is the possibility that endings can come suddenly, which could be the result of an irrational impulse. Be wise concerning with whom you fall into bed and be discriminating about spontaneous behavior with a new partner. Remember how painful it might be if the shoe were on the other foot and you discovered that your lover or spouse was cheating. If there is a bad affair, determine to make a clean and nondestructive end to it as soon as possible. It would be awkward to end up involving friends and family in an embarrassing situation. There could be many short relationships for single Sagittarius. Regardless of their meaning for you, they may pull you out of a rut or introduce you to different adventures, marking a new chapter in your life.

Couples can suddenly get the urge to tie the knot and decide on the spur of the moment. Such a spontaneous event may last or not, depending on the couple. Marriage is a very family- orientated celebration, and consideration should be given to parents who would like to enjoy the ceremony as well. From July on, couples are more likely to establish or solidify a significant partnership, suggesting that marriage, especially in the second half of the year, is a possibility. Avoid marriage plans in May and June and avoid problems in intimacy. During these months, Venus, the planet of love, is retrograde. When it comes to children, there can be a few surprises also. Lives can be changed forever by becoming a parent for the first time. A baby might be unexpected, so precautions will need to be taken if you don't wish to become a parent. Children could become rebellious or disruptive and demand that you take a new and different approach to your parenting. If they are growing older, they could demand that you relinquish your hold on them so that they can be free to find their own identity. Try to find the right balance. You can allow them greater autonomy while being there for them and setting the limits they still require.

Overall, this year looks positive. There is a wealth of opportunity to grow in creative self-expression and self-knowledge if you are willing to give yourself the time needed for introspection and self-understanding. Above all, be willing to gain help from professionals in all areas of life, including financial, psychological, educational, business, and marriage. When you do, you will be able to succeed even in times of adversity. Be prepared to complete projects from the past. Be ready as well to attend to any festering resentments in an honest and loving manner so that any damaged personal relationships can be salvaged and mended. Love is there for those of you seeking it along with the opportunity to build and sustain a family life and profession that will give you lifelong satisfaction.

SAGITTARIUS
DAILY FORECAST

January–December 2012

JANUARY

1. SUNDAY. Fulfilling. Happy New Year! Not only is it a new year, but a new and exciting reality is dawning for the Archer. The planetary influences are asking you to shrug off your fears about expressing who you really are so you can obtain the sense of freedom that you so dearly seek. You can enjoy a very special and warm connection with someone. Whether this is with a family member, a friend, or lover, your appreciation of what they bring to your life is marked. This is an auspicious phase for your love life. If you are partnered, you will feel more romantic than usual. Or you could be socializing with longtime pals when a good friend might confess their love and create some intriguing moments.

2. MONDAY. Cautious. Many possibilities are available to you now. But you need to develop your powers of discrimination if you are to choose successfully. Respond both intellectually and emotionally to the world around you, and you will not remain divided. Small annoyances that arise within your relationships might be reminders of an underlying problem. Be honest with yourself and stop blaming others if you want to resolve this problem once and for all. Luck in money matters promises the chance of a successful business deal, satisfactory contract negotiations, or a joint investment that is likely to bring rewards. A creative project can get the go-ahead. Don't be shy to put your talents on show.

3. TUESDAY. Uplifting. A romantic interlude will reinforce an optimistic frame of mind. Take a leap of faith and allow your inspirations to lead you. When you do, you can turn out some very creative work. Delightful surprises await you, so don't hesitate to put yourself out there among others. Speculation can be profitable if you do your homework first. Try not to involve friends in your financial ventures, especially if you are really looking for support. If you are not one hundred percent sure, then do more research rather than drag others into an enterprise. Relationship difficulties or any feelings of being out of your depth can be helped with therapy, giving you new insights into old problems.

4. WEDNESDAY. Practical. Stick to your original plans and don't let others persuade you to do otherwise. Do one task at a time, and you won't have any trouble getting on top of your workload. In fact, Sagittarius might be in line for a pay increase or promotion at this time. You can lift the spirits of those around you at the moment. Be aware that a particular coworker may need your moral support. Suggest a walk together during the lunch break. The exercise and fresh air can be an important way to help ease their stress levels. A nosey neighbor could be a real nuisance. But if you don't give them a lot of thought and be kind and friendly, they may end up being a very valuable friend and ally.

5. THURSDAY. Emotional. Be extrasensitive to your partner's feelings. This extends to business partners and your friends as well. The key is to stop worrying about what you want to say and to listen to what others have to say. This can help you get ahead in many ways. Instead of telling others what you think, put your thoughts down on paper. This visual technique can give you fresh insights. Some of you might even start writing a book, one that could receive a publishing offer in the near future. This evening is starred for spending time and connecting with those important people in your life. Be open to love and be willing to bare your soul, as greater intimacy is sure to be the result.

6. FRIDAY. Uneven. An uneasy sense that you should be doing something else, but you don't know what, can encroach on enjoyment of the day. Check in with your loved ones and ensure that all is okay. At least you will have that assurance. A legal situation could threaten to worsen. Before making any further decisions, you need to talk with a professional. Whatever you do, don't be tempted to take the law into your own hands. The results are not likely to be pleasant. Be prepared to compromise and share your load; then watch the pressures and problems ease. The evening brings loving and creative thoughts. Plan to share a meal with your lover and enjoy the heightened intimacy between you.

7. SATURDAY. Edgy. Internal pressure is strong as the Moon and Mercury clash. Watch your tongue, for you may hurt someone's feelings if you aren't careful. It probably seems that everyone is getting on your nerves, so take a step back and try to be more objective. If things do get heated, go for a walk and enjoy the fresh air. There is nothing wrong with walking away from an argument. Be especially careful not to let the pressures of the outside world keep you from putting a serious effort into your closest relationships and making the necessary changes. Sagittarius parents may have to cancel your own plans to help your child cope with changes in their friendships or sports. Make sure you are their number-one fan.

8. SUNDAY. Nurturing. Think laterally, and you might come up with some great ideas at work. If you are planning to go into business for yourself, now is the time to talk to your financial adviser about a loan to get you started. A friend in the know can also be a great help. Don't hesitate to talk to them about your ideas. Jobseekers may find an opening in the career of your choice. Should you have competition for the job, a persistent effort will pay off. A celebration can put you in the limelight and boost your ego. But don't let too much of the good things go to your head. Otherwise you could turn positive effort into a public display and ruin your reputation. Be moderate with food and drink.

9. MONDAY. Private. Keep your secrets to yourself and eliminate the possibility of someone stealing your ideas. This is a time for research and reflection rather than action. Be content to ensure that you have covered all your bases. If you have to handle money on behalf of others, make sure you leave a satisfactory paper trail and avoid any doubts over your actions. This is especially necessary when it comes to keeping your tax records. It can make all the difference in the amount you will end up paying. Consciously practice moderation today. It may be all too easy to go overboard and give into temptation. If you must practice romantic interludes, make sure they are safe ones.

10. TUESDAY. Impulsive. Either you or those around you may be given to an outburst of feeling. This is the time to practice forgiveness and compassion. A sudden attraction has the potential to lead to a one-night stand. You will need to keep your eyes open and tend to your boundaries when it comes to romance. Unexpected surprises can bring opportunities if you hold true to your dreams and don't get swept along with the excitement of others. Financial concerns can be charged with emotion. If you are attempting to sort out a property settlement, today is not a good time to enter into discussions. In preparation for any negotiations, you would be wiser to seek advice on your rights and obligations to clarify your position.

11. WEDNESDAY. Beneficial. Be aware of your finances when planning a new venture. Your ideas and desires are likely to outweigh the practicalities at the moment. This is a great time to push for a promotion or apply for the job of your dreams. Seize the moment with whatever good fortune comes your way, and you won't miss a great opportunity. Of course, you may daydream your way through the day. If you do, you could find that by nightfall you have traveled to many distant places and done and said lots of things you could only do in your wildest dreams. A distant contact might call with a business proposition. It is definitely worth considering. Have faith in yourself and you can overcome difficulties.

12. THURSDAY. Insightful. There are a lot of positive influences on offer today. It is up to you to know what to go with and what to let pass. Be aware of your own values, and you won't get talked into doing or accepting something that you really don't want. In fact, this is a good time to speak up for what you believe in. You never know what can happen. The boss might notice your spunk and single you out for a promotion or pay increase. Job seekers could be in luck today. No matter how daunting an interview might seem, be enthusiastic, and you are bound to succeed. Do not neglect your loved ones though. Someone may need your love and support. If you can spare the time, it will make all the difference for the future.

13. FRIDAY. Dogmatic. The tendency to hear only what you want to hear may apply to all and sundry today. This can make it very hard to reach agreement on anything. Practice compassion and patience. Through understanding those around you, you might gain valuable insight into yourself. You may feel that your family and other members of the community are relying on you to hold everything together. This situation is likely to put you under a lot of pressure. Instead of becoming resentful, be proud that they believe in you and are asking for your help and support. Make sure you get all the small jobs done and out of the way early. Then you will have a clear run to tackle something that you really want to do.

14. SATURDAY. Productive. Venus, the planet of love, moves into Pisces and your fourth house of personal security, inspiring an inner need for harmonious and artistic expression. Plans to beautify your home can go ahead now. If you have some friends who would be willing to give you a hand, you can have a lot of fun doing it. Singles might get a surprise invitation from a friend who wants to be more than friends. Be open to allowing this relationship to grow rather than only looking for the physical side of love. Listen to advice from an old friend regardless of how much it might be contrary to your own ideas. They do have an objective perspective as well as your best interests at heart.

15. SUNDAY. Favorable. Loving vibes continue. Take it easy and please yourself. Be aware, however, that you do need to show your respect for an elderly associate or family member to ensure their valuable support. An employment opportunity can come your way, but you will have to act quickly if you are interested. This chance could be gone as quickly as it appeared. Social gatherings in your home are starred, inclining you to redecorate or refurbish to present a beautiful home to your guests. Some of you are likely to become interested in purchasing your own home. Visiting properties for sale might be on your agenda this afternoon. Dress up no matter what you do, as the chances of running into someone gorgeous are likely.

16. MONDAY. Changeable. Don't put anything important off until later in the day. Likely as not, you probably won't get around to it. It is especially important if you have a meeting with a challenging client or a pushy employer. The sooner you get these encounters behind you the better chance you have of coming out on top. One of your associates or partners might let you down in a deal. So if you need assistance, make sure you have backup to ensure your success. Some of you may be heading off on a journey or saying goodbye to a close friend. The tendency to block your emotions can cause more pain. Allow your tears to flow. Don't worry about what other people think, and you can enjoy the whole process of pleasure and pain. Time alone would be beneficial tonight.

17. TUESDAY. Fruitful. Whether you want to or not, you are likely to mull over past situations and regret missed opportunities. Don't be too hard on yourself, or you might miss a present-day opportunity. Practice being in the moment and enjoy the spontaneity that this can afford. You have a good balance between the intuitive and rational sides of your behavior at the moment. Your attitude suggests acting on an impulse could turn out to be exactly the right thing for you to do. A friend may have a hot tip for an investment. You would be wise to take notice, as you can stand to make an unexpected profit right now. This is a good time to pick up the pieces of an old romance and make a new beginning.

18. WEDNESDAY. Imaginative. Be kind to yourself today and don't take on anything extra that will tax you physically. You are much more likely to enjoy reading an inspiring book, thinking about creating something artistic, or enjoying the beauty of the natural world. If you are concerned for the health of another, do some research before you start worrying them. You will want to give the person some solutions rather than simply adding to their worries. If you are feeling like giving of yourself, consider getting involved in a volunteer organization. In addition to expressing your compassion, you can enjoy the emotional reward of helping others. Don't be surprised if your phone starts ringing this evening and a problem gets solved.

19. THURSDAY. Magnetic. This is a wonderful day to express your thoughts and feelings to the important people in your life. You can find that others will appreciate your unique and special qualities. There are particularly strong cooperative vibes. So if you need to get something done, now is the time to call on others for beneficial assistance. One of your friends might be experiencing a difficult emotional situation. Even though you might find it hard to express your emotional support, do so anyway. It will be good for both of you and add another dimension to your life experience. Not to mention your support will strengthen the bonds toward each other. Don't be afraid to try something new and surprise yourself.

20. FRIDAY. Problematic. Your temper may be especially active today, although you aren't likely to lash out unless provoked. A wonderful way to use this energy is to allow for spontaneity in your life. Ignore stale routines and let the day unfold exactly as the universe would have it. If you find yourself up against a disagreeable person, change your scenery and leave them with it, as there is probably nothing you can do to change their mood. Prioritize your day before you leave home and you will be well prepared when surprises can threaten to side-track your thoughts. A romantic interlude could surprise you. Be prepared to let this person grow on you and there is the possibility it could become a life-long love affair.

21. SATURDAY. Valuable. The Sun is now in Aquarius, illuminating your communications sector for the next few weeks. This cycle suggests busyness and movement. You are exploring and searching now, making connections and paying attention to your immediate environment. Siblings, neighbors, close relatives, friends and coworkers may play a more important role in your life during this cycle. If you are feeling vulnerable or insecure, try throwing yourself wholeheartedly into your work or plans and watch your mood stabilize. Take a practical approach to all things, and don't let another talk you into doing anything that doesn't suit you. A shopping trip could turn up something collectible or a real bargain.

22. SUNDAY. Energetic. Consciousness of a goal or objective can make this a good day for organizing plans. As the Moon harmonizes with Mars you will find the assertiveness and self-confidence to move forward into problematic areas, which are then likely to dissolve into more productive situations. Planetary energies point to a love for indulgence, so watch your spending. If you are out socializing or planning to travel, you could spend on a whim and end up on a tight budget. Dietary extravagances can also expand the waistline or compromise your health. Now is the time to be practical. Practice moderation, and you will enjoy whatever you are doing. Overseas working contacts are highlighted as is Internet dating.

23. MONDAY. Advantageous. This morning's New Moon in Aquarius suggests it is a favorable time for learning something new. It is also a time when you will feel at ease in social situations, take care of the details of daily life, and develop a mental rapport with others. Over the coming month it is a good time for taking tests, especially driving tests, writing letters, making phone calls, and getting on top of all your paperwork. An offer of a promotion could mean having to take up extra study. Don't worry about putting yourself under pressure at this time, You should find the pressure enhances your performance more than it inhibits it. If you are suffering from a nervous disorder, meditation may be your best medicine.

24. TUESDAY. Informative. Don't let your daydreams slip past and disappear into the ether of your unconscious. Get out your journal and start writing them down. Don't let any aspect slip through your consciousness, and you will begin to know yourself better. Expand on your daily activities. When you do, you are bound to uncover talents and abilities you never knew you had. Some of you may be training for a new job and should listen to fellow employees who have been working on the job before you. You will learn some valuable information to enhance your performance and chance of promotion. A roommate might give notice and leave you worrying about making the rent. Another will likely appear without much bother.

25. WEDNESDAY. Domestic. With the Moon moving through your fourth house of home and family, you will be ready for a quiet retreat. Avoid crowded places and unpleasant people in favor of environments and companions that make you feel cozy and warm.

There may be some personal difficulties to work through in a significant relationship. Be assured that unconditional love can help you sort out any problems. Fill your environment with pleasant music, fresh flowers, and scented candles and allow your mind to drift off, leaving all daily annoyances far behind. Your artistic side is strong now. It is the perfect time to shop for your home or implement a home beautification project to help enhance an inner sense of belonging.

26. THURSDAY. Intriguing. Although the harmonious vibes seem to pervade all situations, look deeper to understand what is really going on. There is bound to be much that is left unsaid that really needs to be addressed while the harmonious vibes are conducive to a positive result. Watch indulgence and laziness so that you don't let a beneficial opportunity slip through your fingers. This is not a good time to branch out into a business of your own. Give a little more time to research and talk with friends and relatives who have experience in this area. Double-check your budget also, as you may have over- or underestimated an important cost. Make the most of the loving vibes with your family this evening.

27. FRIDAY. Stressful. Anticipation can cause unnecessary worries, so try to concentrate on the present. Worrying about a future event won't change the outcome, but a positive attitude will. Someone who you are relying on may unexpectedly let you down, putting you into a depressed mood. Consider that the person may have a good excuse for their actions and may be feeling just as bad as you are. Since your power to motivate others is strong, don't pass up an opportunity to coach your colleagues. Romance can heat up later in the day with someone new moving into your orb of influence. As your popularity increases don't be surprised if you have more than one romantic hopeful to choose from.

28. SATURDAY. Empowering. Pleasure is a nutrient necessary for spiritual and emotional health, so focus on love, laughter, and life today. Mercury joins the Sun in Aquarius and enhances your ability to multitask successfully. Catch up with neighbors and siblings if possible. Some interesting and valuable gossip could come your way. Intensity and passion play a role in your romance and friendships. But it would not be wise to let a passionate whim override good sense. Watch any tendency to speculate with your savings. You aren't likely to be happy with the results if you indulge in any risky financial ventures. There is enough opportunity for fun and excitement without taking risks with your money or your heart.

29. SUNDAY. Manageable. Juggling your social life with your responsibilities can get out of hand if you are not careful. Your penchant for putting a positive face on a situation might lead you to underestimate the effort needed. Be kind to yourself and avoid making commitments on this day of rest and relaxation. Team sports can become intense and encourage your competitive side. Avoid letting your desire for victory turn into an unfriendly battle. Be very aware that sometimes words or actions expressed in the heat of the moment might linger way past the memory of whatever instigated them. If you are celebrating a happy event, remember to take some photos to add to your family album.

30. MONDAY. Expansive. Employment prospects are bound to be on the rise now. Job seekers may find more than one opening to apply for, doubling your possibility for success. If aches and pains have been a less than welcome addition in recent weeks, perhaps this has more to do with everyday stresses and work demands than you have realized. Some gentle stretching can help. Or if you are an advocate of tai chi or yoga, these exercises would prove very helpful. The Internet is a valuable source of information. If you have any queries regarding your health or work opportunities, this is the best medium for research and advice. Then you can further use scholarly works to fine-tune your facts.

31. TUESDAY. Irritating. All sorts of annoyances can put you off your game. Try not to let the behavior of others disrupt your concentration, and you will have a much more fulfilling day. Independent thinking may not be encouraged in your workplace. If, however, you think there is something amiss in a project, then follow it up. The credit that you will earn for discovering the problem is well worth taking the risk. A health and safety matter may also be a problem. You will be better off sticking with the side of safety than risking an injury, even if it means upsetting your superiors. Once they realize that fixing the problem may save them a lot of money in compensation, their attitude should change considerably.

FEBRUARY

1. WEDNESDAY. Steady. With your ruling planet Jupiter, the planet of expansion, moving through your house of work, you do need to be sensible about what you can and can't do. Your optimistic attitude might encourage you to think you can do everything, but your body may not agree. Don't rush. Above all, don't try to please everybody, and you will still get enough work finished while maintaining your energy levels. If you don't, you are likely to suffer from burnout and be of no use to anybody, least of all yourself. This goes for your social calendar also. You know what they say about burning the candle at both ends. A niggling health problem could be the result of diet, so reduce stress and watch what you eat.

2. THURSDAY. Harmonious. Healing old wounds between you and those you are closest to is favored today. Let your communication be open and loving, and grievances can emerge into the light and finally be forgiven. Cooperate with people in authority, and you will be rewarded for your efforts. A home renovation or beautification project could put your savings in the red. If, however, you feel that the added advantages of these improvements could boost your income or work potential, then you may have to take a risk. Don't rush into anything though, as the intuitive fire signs are inclined to act spontaneously without thinking things through. Get professional advice on financial matters if possible.

3. FRIDAY. Challenging. Be extrasensitive to your partner's feelings today. This attitude should extend to your business partners and best friends as well. The key is to stop worrying about what you want to say and listen to what others have to say. Attention to others can help you get ahead in many ways. Keep in mind that you cannot change the way others behave, but you can alter and control your own reactions. Archers looking to buy property could unexpectedly find what you are looking for. But make sure your partner and others in your family feel the same way you do before you make an offer. Business negotiations may not be totally honest. Exaggerations or omissions that would make a difference to your decision may be lurking in the fine print.

4. SATURDAY. Possessive. As the Moon opposes Pluto in your sector of money and values, you are not going to want to share with anyone you don't trust or like. On the other hand, you might come up against someone who wants something that you possess. Ensure that you have adequate security around your home and car for your own protection and peace of mind. Mysterious Neptune slips into Pisces and your sector of home and family, making you much more sensitive to the environment in which you live. Be very careful that when offering to help a family member you are doing so for the right reasons. You might find you are sacrificing your own needs and end up feeling resentful and disillusioned.

5. SUNDAY. Restless. Although you may have a smorgasbord of social entertainment to choose from, you might prefer a more private and intimate pastime. Partnered Archers should beware of your roving eye when out with your loved one. Even if you are simply appreciating beauty for its own sake, jealous feelings will come into play. No matter how casual your setting, emotional encounters with others can highlight moods and feelings quite different from the usual. This is a good time to clear up a misunderstanding, especially if you have been having problems over shared resources. You could be more inclined to be possessive and jealous, so try to be self-aware when pointing the finger at another.

6. MONDAY. Uplifting. Travel and education come to the fore as the Moon shines in Leo. Think about broadening your horizons by starting to plan an overseas vacation. If you have a head full of dreams, instead of wishing and hoping, start acting. All you need to do is put one foot in front of the other, and you might be surprised where you end up. Overcome self-imposed limits by stretching the boundaries little bit by little bit. Distant business connections could bring contact with an offer to branch out into a new business on your own. Check out all your possibilities for financial assistance and extra training, and you may be able to pull it off. Any plans for self-improvement should be successful.

7. TUESDAY. Hectic. Today's Full Moon in Leo suggests it is time to break out of the rut you are in and enjoy a sense of freedom. You won't want to be pinned down to a schedule or told what to do. So don't put yourself in a position of having to disappoint anybody. Leave your plans flexible. Opportunities in love are just around the corner. If you are already playing the dance of courtship, make sure you get together in an intimate setting this evening. Sagittarius already in a relationship should make this evening special because the time is ripe to experience the closeness and warmth of family living. One thing you might need to take extra care with is a tendency toward overindulgence.

8. WEDNESDAY. Refreshing. An overpowering mood for love and creativity can affect your slant on the day's events. Be wary of donning those rose-colored glasses that make everything look so dreamy but which never materializes. Be sure to channel your energies into creative work and study, and you will achieve good results. If you find your mood a little depressed, visit an art gallery, go to an adventure movie, or take a walk in a local nature spot. Now watch your inspiration surge. You can achieve quite a lot so long as you are clear about what you want. Should you have any doubts, listen to your heart for trustworthy signals. An unexpected invitation from a friend or neighbor could be life changing.

9. THURSDAY. Empowering. Sometimes we can see the obstacles that prevent us from getting ahead; at other times we can't. The strange dynamic now is that you can start to uncover more of the inner obstacles that have been stopping you. Or if anyone has been doing their best to hold you back, you can start to liberate yourself from their negative hold. Important transformations beckon, but you do need to be brave. Career matters could seem to slow and cause frustration to you and your superiors. Don't take this personally. Regardless of how you feel inside, act with confidence and ease. Others will see you as having control of the situation. Act right and your feelings will follow suit your actions.

10. FRIDAY. Unexpected. Tension is in the air and will upset the usual flow. Practice relaxation techniques to give you an edge over your competition, and you can finish the day successfully. Watch any urges to act impulsively, as nothing will be quite as it seems now. You don't want to damage your reputation through associations with dubious organizations or disreputable individuals. Venus, the planet of love, is in Pisces and your house of love and is connecting with excitable Uranus. This phase brings a strong possibility that single Archers might receive a surprise invitation from an admirer. Or you may simply run into a gorgeous stranger and find yourself in an intimate and delightful conversation.

11. SATURDAY. Pleasurable. Whatever you have a passion for, be it the arts, yoga, or ecological causes, your interest can peak. Your desires may see you joining together with other people who share your interest. If you attend a gathering, rally, or workshop you are likely to receive a burst of energy and enthusiasm for social change or for improving the environment around you. Sports Archers will enjoy club activities and might get involved in the politics of club regulations or get caught up in an exciting fund-raising event. Your interest in learning is sharp. You might pick up some new techniques and approaches to an activity you enjoy that can put you ahead of your competitors in the near future.

12. SUNDAY. Fulfilling. If you find that you feel out of your league when mixing with a new social group, try not to show it. This is more likely an inner feeling that has nothing to do with your real abilities. Instead, watch and learn from the people you admire and would like to imitate. Such a person could very well take you under their wing and give you the benefit of their experience. Check out what is going on in your local community and get involved if possible. You stand to enjoy new experiences and opportunities for spiritual growth at the moment. If you are feeling a bit down or depressed, call a friend and suggest mixing with others. There is nothing better than companionship to cheer you up.

13. MONDAY. Reflective. Guard your solitude and privacy today, and you will enjoy whatever you have in front of you. Don't think twice about postponing an appointment or meeting if you need to gain more clarity. If a health issue is worrying you, don't accept just one diagnosis without obtaining a second opinion and doing your own research. There are many different therapies available these days, and some offer cheap and safe alternatives to the more expensive pharmaceuticals. Keep out of the limelight at work. You may miss some juicy gossip, but you will also avoid being the subject of it. Get advice on any financial problems you have. There is likely to be help available when you look in the right place.

14. TUESDAY. Problematic. No matter how you feel this morning, just keep plodding along. The sooner you get on top of your chores the better you will feel and the better the day will turn out. An important ingredient is relaxation. Following your schedule in a slow and steady manner will be the most satisfactory approach. If you practice yoga and meditation, these exercises are especially important now in aiding peace of mind and clarity. If you haven't tried these, consider enrolling in a class in these tried and true age-old spiritual practices. You might also think about going on a retreat. With Mercury and Neptune together, extra energy put into clarifying your thoughts, such as writing them down to create a visual picture, can be helpful.

15. WEDNESDAY. Excellent. With the Moon now in Sagittarius, Archer's personal magnetism will be high, bringing people and opportunities your way. Try not to take on too much and be especially careful not to people please. Instead, for optimal achievement, be aware of your intentions and alert to the moment for action. Focus on advancing your personal talents by getting extra training or practice, as your abilities will come to the fore now. Romance is another area that may broaden your sphere of influence and introduce you to new and untried avenues of self-expression. Plan to wine and dine your your closest loved one and make them feel loved and appreciated for all the wonderful things they do for you.

16. THURSDAY. Beneficial. Spontaneous opportunities for fun and laughter will bring your talents and creativity to the fore.

Focus on personal appeal and update your appearance with some new fashions and a new hairdo. Sagittarius people are so often caught up in understanding the way of the world and other people's behavior that you sometimes don't concentrate enough energy on your personal issues. For young Archers, a class in self-development and awareness would be beneficial. For those older, training in creative pursuits that interest you would be very rewarding. Anything that bolsters your self-confidence and gives you more tools to get out in the world and become part of the community will take you far.

17. FRIDAY. Uncertain. Evaluate your motives and ensure that you act with integrity. It is very easy to think that the end justifies the means. But this attitude won't build self-worth and self-respect. A colleague may try to help you, but you may not be pleased with their methods. It would be better to risk their displeasure than suffer the consequences. If you have a drawer full of bank statements and bills, organize them and straighten out any problems. Not only will it be strangely cathartic, but it will reveal exactly where you are financially. It may be tedious, but it is better than having that vague worry that something is amiss. If you are in the red, cut out all unnecessary spending and use cash rather than your credit cards.

18. SATURDAY. Reassuring. Use today's energies to get ahead in life. Unemployed Archers can discover opportunities for work or study toward the job of your dreams. A close friend might have powerful contacts that they can connect you with. Don't be shy about accepting any invitations to meet and mix with influential people. Romantic Archers could find that today's invitations draw you into a circle of very attractive and inspiring people, filling your head with all sorts of dreams of love and success. Try not to hold on too closely to your cherished ideas and opinions. Some of your values could be in for a shakeup. Homely pursuits can take precedence over socializing later on. Cooking up exotic dishes or chatting on the Internet will offer enjoyment.

19. SUNDAY. Promising. The Sun is now in Pisces and will be spotlighting your house of home and family for the next few weeks. Besides spending more time tending to domestic affairs, the focus will be on cultivating and nourishing the inner foundations that support you and your growth. This is a time to do what you can to build trust in your family life and a strong foundation within yourself. Accomplishing this can mean that regardless of what you meet in the outside world over the next month, you will have a secure place to which you can return. Misunderstandings in all forms of communication are possible today. To avoid unpleasantness, be sure you are clear about your intentions and meaning before you speak or act.

20. MONDAY. Demanding. Annoyances can be because of laxity or impatience. If you are going to do anything at all, do it properly and save yourself any hassles. Since you can be good at working with other people, don't discount an offer to enter into a joint enterprise or project. What may seem like idle chatter with a friend or relative about the potential for success may merit further thought. Think about how you can complement each other's skills. Each of you may not bring all the same qualities to the situation, but working together you can be very successful. Unexpected delays or holdups to long-term plans could be encountered. Use this time to revise and update to be ready when things start to move again.

21. TUESDAY. Confusing. Don't push yourself too hard, and you won't make stupid mistakes. Today's New Moon joins Neptune in Pisces, adding a touch of divine discontent to your coming plans. Be kind to yourself and your loved ones by setting the scene for compassion and understanding over the coming month. Otherwise, all of you might end up working at cross-purposes and wondering why nothing eventuates. This aspect can make it easy to blame another without seeing one's own handiwork. Don't be too quick to judge another since you could really be judging yourself. Kindness is an important ingredient at this time. You might find yourself doing someone a favor and receive another's help in return.

22. WEDNESDAY. Sensitive. An overly emotional frame of mind appears to dominate you and those around you. Everyone could be inclined to take behavior and comments personally. This is the time to watch out for symptoms of impulsive buying. You cannot fill an emotional need with material things. It is important to be more creative and allow yourself to speak honestly about your feelings to your loved ones. A private conversation could be informative and insightful, giving you more confidence to express your own thoughts and desires than ever before. Archers who share a house with others may need to call a meeting so that each of you can talk about your needs and set up some rules and guidelines to gain more harmony.

23. THURSDAY. Tense. The abundance of planets in Pisces suggests there are many emotional undercurrents that can be confusing and conflicting. Get in touch with your own feelings, be honest about them, and then allow others to be responsible for their own emotions. This is the way to sidestep unnecessary hurt and resentment. Take some time to fine-tune and implement a practical budget for your household so that you can alleviate any pressure on the financial side of life. A good budget will allow for small rewards to encourage everyone to stick to it. Be prepared to work cooperatively with others, and you will achieve the best results. If you find yourself at loggerheads with anyone, stop and listen before speaking.

24. FRIDAY. Happy. A very active and positive day should be in order for Sagittarius. Your working day can get very busy and involve a variety of activities. These might include travel, public relations, educational activities, or promoting art, culture, and sports. Even a very menial task could absorb your interest and give you inspiration. Be ready for anything. Plan a vacation and enjoy traveling in your head while you search out all the possible destinations on the Internet. Great plans for the evening might involve shopping for an outfit or costume or organizing the entertainment. Sagittarius musicians who may have a gig tonight shouldn't try to practice all day. Getting out in the fresh air and possibly meeting someone interesting is a fine way to spend your time.

25. SATURDAY. Harmonious. With the Moon and Venus playing a romantic duet in your sector of love, you should get set for a fun time today. You will want to express yourself in a creative way. Enjoying a hobby, attending the theater, or visiting an art gallery could be exciting activities to put on your agenda. Take notice of your loved ones though. You don't want to get too wrapped up in your own fun and forget about a promise you have made. Sports enthusiasts could be involved in an important game and experience an attack of nerves before you play. Have a chat with a close friend or talk with another player, and your tension will melt away. Try not to get caught up with gambling or risky speculation. Keep your money in your own pocket.

26. SUNDAY. Practical. No matter what you are expecting today, you are sure to find that routine turns into the extraordinary. Little jobs can turn into large ones, or a quiet day at home might change when a crowd of friends knock at your door. Whatever the case, you can rely on your practical side to perform well and succeed in solving any problems that may arise. Study and research will attract your interest, leading you to spontaneously sign up for a course of study while viewing an interesting site on the Internet. A spiritual gathering could be informative and encourage you to be more honest with yourself and your loved ones. Warm feelings from your loved ones should also be supportive.

27. MONDAY. Helpful. Extra work pressures can force you to move faster and think less, which may be a blessing if you are worrying about money. Try not to let your finances rule your life. You would be wise to focus on those things you love that are in your life now. The practice of writing a thankful list each day can have a marvelous effect on your physical and spiritual health. If you have taken on more work, be sure to look out for your well-being. You can get fresh ingredients into your diet by creating salads instead of lunching on fast foods. Do some research to ensure that you get the valuable enzymes needed for maximum performance. If you feel stuck in a rut, start making small changes and watch how the ripple effect can change your life.

28. TUESDAY. Mixed. Today's trends point toward complications in communication. Often, people do not say what they think, but that is their problem. It won't do you any good to start wondering how other people think or judge you. Keep it simple and you can't go wrong. An old friend or family member may come back into your life after being away. Their presence can trigger thoughts and feelings you have forgotten about. Keep these to yourself, however, and you might discover a valuable insight into your inner drives and emotions. The universe is asking you to stop playing the victim and start taking responsibility for your own position in life. If somebody rubs you the wrong way, then move away. Those with whom you choose to mix is ultimately your choice.

29. WEDNESDAY. Interesting. While professional prospects look good, relationships may be problematic. If you want to sustain your involvement with someone close, be prepared to work hard at building that relationship. You don't want to have to choose between a career and a partner or lover. If a personal decision is weighing on your mind, just remember that change is good even though it may sometimes be painful. Socializing could be difficult, as everybody's moods are likely to be at odds with one another. Still, if you can compromise as much as possible, you could find yourself the life of the party. Or you might end up going home with everyone's most popular person. Spending time with your loved one will help heal any rifts between you. Make sure you listen as much as possible.

MARCH

1. THURSDAY. Testing. Juggling your home and your job can take you on a merry dance. Don't let a family member or a colleague get your back up to the point that you overreact, or you will be sorry later. You need to define yourself aside from family and career. Listen to your inner voice to help you find a sense of identity. Once you do, you will become impervious to the jibes of others. Try not to focus on the rational and sensible at the expense of feelings, warmth, and physical closeness. Take the time to understand the feelings of your partner. You may be taking them for granted now. If you have negative thoughts about others, make every effort to replace them with positive feelings. You can turn your whole world around if you really want to.

2. FRIDAY. Uncertain. Your acumen is likely to be sharper than usual, giving you the edge over your competition. You will be anxious to work your way around any obstacle and could very well fall into the trap of manipulation. Watch what you say and to whom you say it, as any dishonesty may be spotted. As Mercury joins erratic Uranus in Aries and your sector of love and friendship, you may experience restlessness and a need for variety in your love life. An attraction to intellectually stimulating people can lead you away from your usual crowd. But you need to be alert to characters who may just be fast-talkers waiting to take you for a ride. Keep your home and valuables secure also, and you won't have to make an insurance claim.

3. SATURDAY. Energetic. Although some complications are likely, you have the energy to overcome any obstacle that may arise in your path. Use your energy in a positive fashion and, in your best interests, recognize the difference between being assertive and being aggressive. Luck in investments may be possible as long as you stick to the ventures that you know enough about. If you are working today, you can make extra commissions and could be promoted for your problem-solving ability. Issues of trust are likely to surface. If you have been let down by your partner more than once, perhaps it is time to consider your alternatives. Loving someone does not oblige you to put up with their hurtful behavior.

4. SUNDAY. Mixed. Be selective about the company you keep. Remember the wise old saying that if you lie down with dogs you will rise up with fleas. This can work in reverse though. If you hang with successful and positive people, you too can be successful and positive. Be cautious about arguing with your lover and very careful of what you say. Your words can make the difference between making or breaking your relationship. A sixth sense about children and relationships could be strong, but wait before initiating any new actions. There is a spiritual aspect to the day's vibes that will be enhanced if you are at all interested in spiritual gatherings, yoga, or meditation. If you're not, grab a few moments for contemplation anyway.

5. MONDAY. Instructive. Venus, the planet of love, joins expansive Jupiter in Taurus and your sector of work, service, and health. This can suggest that you will take pleasure in developing and fine-tuning your talents, skills, and abilities. Venus will stay in this sector for the next four weeks. This is an excellent time to concentrate on improving the running of everyday affairs, issues of work and service, and attending to your health. Consider a change of diet and try to stick to the rule of fresher is better. You may find some exciting and tasty recipes from foreign cuisine. Look for those that are easy to prepare and add extra spice and flavor to your meals. Lose yourself in the housework. You will enjoy it.

6. TUESDAY. Revealing. As your sphere of opportunity broadens, you will have to choose what you do and don't want. Try not to let impulsive or obsessive desires get in the way of the things that your heart truly desires. Travel plans could be delayed because of a financial shortfall. Don't despair, however, you can save up the funds in no time if you are committed to your goal. Some of you may be planning a permanent move overseas for work or business reasons. Be sure to research the political and social structures of your destination before you go. That way you will be prepared and can avoid making silly but nevertheless serious mistakes. A foreign industrial dispute could cause delays, so be aware of what is going on.

7. WEDNESDAY. Productive. Linking your need for personal contentment with additonal success won't work at this time. Rather, be content and the success will follow later. Jot down a list of positives, and you will be amazed at how good your life really is. While Mars, the planet of action and energy, is moving retrograde in Virgo and your sector of career and ambition, it is the right time to reflect on how far you have come. You should also fine-tune your future direction to be ready when Mars moves forward in April. Good relations with coworkers can lead to after-work activities, which might include sports or chess and other strategy games. But make sure that you balance your time between home and work.

8. THURSDAY. Special. Take pride in who you are and how the world sees you today. Of course you aren't perfect, but no one else is either. Reflect on the good that you have done and dream of all the good you can still do. This is also a good time to spend with the parent who has influenced you the most throughout your lifetime.

Get their views on some of the instances in your childhood about which you may be a little confused. Take the time for a heart-to-heart talk. You are bound to learn a great deal of valuable information about your roots and who you really are. The Full Moon in Virgo lights up your sector of ambition but may also cause some dissatisfaction on the home front. Be sure to attend to your home responsibilities first.

9. FRIDAY. Stimulating. Although there is some tension in the air early on, the overall harmonious celestial patterns make this a great day for social activities. Archers involved in budding romances will find that today is perfect for love, so reach out to your lover or spouse. Partnerships of all kinds are favored. Be assured that spending time planning for the future with a like-minded friend or business associate will be productive. Let your individuality shine through in whatever you do. Right now, you can't help being innovative and different. Take up classes in music, dance, art, or craft and watch your talent flourish. Parents might want to encourage your child's creativity. But it is really you who should be creative and let them join in if they so desire.

10. SATURDAY. Responsible. Any membership fees you have could go through the roof. Take an honest look at your club or association and weigh the benefits that you receive through social activity and interaction. You might decide that it is worth going without other spending for a couple of weeks just to maintain the benefits. Be mindful to maintain a balance in all you do today. You might tend toward being more indulgent or obsessive than usual, bringing harm to your health, your diet, or your friendships. Practice humility, and you will find it easier to avoid overstepping the mark. A good friend could be going through a difficult period, causing you to cancel a cherished event so that you can give them the support they need.

11. SUNDAY. Renewing. Archers may find that you have overextended yourself in a heartfelt desire to save the world. It's time to step back and focus on your own needs. Since good fortune is working in your favor behind the scenes, have faith that all will turn out well. In the meantime, make an effort to rest your body and mind in preparation for busier times ahead. An intense and demanding romance could also take its toll on your normal routine of relaxation. Why not just relax together and enjoy the thrill and romance of a passionate and true love? Spiritual practices would be beneficial even if it's just getting out for a walk. Reveling in the fresh air among nature's wonders will refresh and renew you mentally and physically.

12. MONDAY. Disconcerting. You may be faced with challenges that seem insurmountable. But you are truly capable enough to meet and overcome them. Don't allow fear to stop you from aiming high. Instead, concentrate on the work in front of you at the present moment, and bit by bit over time you will notice your progress. Avoid a tendency to be your own worst enemy. It is often difficult for Sagittarius to stay in one place to get established. Take a cue from your steady Taurus friends by digging in your heels and staying where you are. Mercury, the planet of communication, goes retrograde today, which will cause misunderstandings and holdups in business dealings and investments. This influence will last until April 5..

13. TUESDAY. Pressured. There are many stresses and strains in your environment today. You may be tiptoeing around someone else's bad mood or trying to control a basically uncontrollable situation. Stop thinking about anything but what you are feeling and let everyone else do the same. If you are living with someone who won't allow you your personal freedom, then it is time for you to start thinking about whether or not to stay in this relationship. A superior in your workplace may seem less agreeable than usual. Their behavior might be caused by your own negative thoughts. It seems likely they have your best interests at heart. Search outside the box, and you will be surprised at what you find.

14. WEDNESDAY. Creative. Anything you set out to do should turn out well. You can proceed with confidence. The only thing holding you back is fear or insecurity, so make the effort to rise above self-doubt. It is possible that a false friend is in the picture. But this person will reveal their hand soon. If you have doubts about someone in your circle, play it safe and don't let them in on your secrets. Sagittarius could start to get itchy feet again and want to move to another neighborhood. Rather than move, consider enjoying different places and different activities in your own area. Keep in mind that when you move elsewhere, you are still taking yourself along. Change yourself and watch your interest and enjoyment return.

15. THURSDAY. Tricky. With the Moon making hard aspects to Pluto and Uranus you can expect the unexpected. Now is the time to batten down the hatches. Whether you find the enemy inside or out, you need to be clear about where you stand and what you want out of the situation. You can be a powerhouse at work, so keep your head down and push forward. If you have been frustrated or angry lately, channel this excess energy into achieving your goals. Even if you are unemployed, you can use today's aspects to get ahead in life. It will be a lot easier to understand that living well is the best revenge in life. Keep tabs on where your children go after school. They may not be telling you the whole truth about their activities.

16. FRIDAY. Ambitious. Today's focus is on your earth houses, making material goals and gains foremost in your mind. Inspired ideas on your part can get you started in the right direction, giving you the energy to begin work on a creative project. Your values and ethics are evident in the work you do, so choose your assignments with care. Work with joy and love in your heart and see how quickly you will prosper. Repairs may be necessary around your home If you are unsure about structure and plumbing, don't hesitate to get a professional. It is false economy to do a job you are unsure about. Proceeding on your own could cost you more in the long run when you uncover exactly what the problem is.

17. SATURDAY. Erratic. Use the morning hours to sort out your finances and your plans for the rest of the day. If you are planning a special gathering for later, it would be a good idea to call around and check that everybody is coming. There is an aspect to the day that suggests the unexpected. A few people could have forgotten all about your plans. Since communication is highlighted, you could meet some exceptional people and learn some interesting information. Archers are likely to have an important event that plays havoc with your nerves. Try going for a jog around the block to use up your excess energy and help calm your mind. Artists of all kinds can produce some stunning creations.

18. SUNDAY. Spirited. Good vibes are in the air today. You can expect plenty of social contact, with your phone ringing off the hook all day long. Single Archers should dress up for whatever you have planned, as there is likely to be a surprise romance waiting for you. Impulsive moods can lead to lots of fun and excitement. Still, it would be wise to keep tabs on the company you keep and stay away from risky ventures. Gossip sessions could get out of hand. Be cautious about what you say to whom, and you won't have to suffer any untoward consequences. A sudden onslaught of visitors is a good excuse to get into home entertaining. Make sure you have plenty of supplies in your cupboards to make your preferred impression.

19. MONDAY. Flexible. Get any important work done early so that you are free to deal with what may come along. Take note of authority figures, especially as they could be more particular than usual and make life hard for everybody. Don't be surprised if you also have to travel back and forth across town. Pack some soothing CDs to keep you calm while you're in traffic. Shopping trips might not get you any bargains. Sharp-talking salespeople can try to sell you items that are very tempting. Avoid coming home with more than you can afford. If you work in sales, you can make extra commission and impress your boss. A family member may need your support. Make sure you have your phone with you at all times.

20. TUESDAY. Motivating. Get set for a day full of ideas and fun. The Sun rolls into Aries today, joining mischievous Mercury and wacky Uranus to energize your sector of fun, lovers, and children. During this four-week period, some form of artistic expression is advised. The richness of your life is enhanced through hobbies, sporting events, and recreational pursuits. Romance and love will also be part of today's agenda. Archers in long-term relationships are particularly favored and can spark the fires of romance through shared enjoyment. The need to be at home with your loved ones could cause some dissatisfaction at work. It could be because one of your colleagues is giving you some troube. It might be time to start looking for a different job.

21. WEDNESDAY. Upsetting. No matter how important your own plans may be, you will be ready to help another. A family member could need you more than you need to finish your projects. Worries over your own performance could also cause anxiety. This is probably because of a lack of self-confidence. Only through facing your fears will you overcome this feeling. Sagittarius travelers may be experiencing a bout of homesickness. Take the time to call home. Hearing a familiar voice will make all the difference in alleviating your loneliness and will assure you of the well-being of your loved ones. Some of you may feel lonely in your own home. Consider getting out and joining a club or community group to help you form friendships and take your mind off your own woes.

22. THURSDAY. Sparkling. Your wit is sharp and your love of beauty and pleasure comes to the fore. With the New Moon in Aries joining savvy Mercury and impulsive Uranus, you can do anything and will probably even surprise yourself. Romance is starred. And whether you are single or partnered, this next lunar cycle suggests that you will spend more time and energy on this aspect of your life. This is the best time to start creative projects and put yourself forward for prominent positions. Since you will enjoy being noticed and performing, the dramatic arts might be a great outlet for your self-expression. This can be a passionate time for you during which you will feel bolder than usual.

23. FRIDAY. Bneficial. Although everything may seem fine, those around you might not respond in the way you expect. Be independent as much as possible, and you won't have to worry when someone lets you down. It may be time to start planning your next vacation. If you are not single, make sure you include the whole family in this process. You may think you know what your children would like, but if you ask them they may surprise you. Their ideas might be better than any you have thought up so far. Don't hesitate about enjoying a blind date. You might be pleasantly surprised with whom you meet. Strange things can happen, so banish your expectations and judgments. You are bound to learn something new.

24. SATURDAY. Intuitive. As Mercury, the ruler of your mind, slips back into Pisces and your sector of home and family, childhood memories and thoughts from the past may occupy much of your time. Keep an eye on the present though. The pace is likely to pick up, and you could receive a very exciting invitation from an unexpected source. A particular coworker can be overly friendly and apparently looking for your affections. Don't go along with anything just because you don't want to hurt their feelings. Use your sixth sense and listen to your heart first. Lessons in love often test our personal security. You can use this experience to test how strong or weak yours is at the moment.

25. SUNDAY. Gratifying. The simple pleasures in life should be enjoyed to the fullest now. Even for you the most mundane domestic chores can be enjoyable. If you focus on all those tasks that never get done, you can reach a wonderful sense of satisfaction by the afternoon. Also, your attention to detail is sharper than usual so that any repairs or paperwork won't seem as difficult as they usually do. Your busy schedule of late may be placing too much stress on your health and well-being. It is especially important that you eat your meals in a calm and relaxing environment so that your digestive system will obtain optimum nourishment. Make some changes to your dining area to make mealtimes that much more enjoyable.

26. MONDAY. Cooperative. As the Moon nestles in between Venus and Jupiter in your house of work, service, and health, you can expect good vibes among coworkers and an enjoyable day at the office. Romantic vibes could be flowing between you and another. Or perhaps a relationship is brewing between two of your other colleagues, giving you all much food for jokes and frivolity. The tendency to overindulge in food and drink is higher than usual. If you are dieting, now is the time to be extradiligent. Instead, feed your cravings for sweets with fruit. For extra vitamins, indulge in vegetable juices instead of soft drinks or alcoholic beverages. Gym enthusiasts should also be very careful not to overdo your exercise. You could pull a muscle or ligament.

27. TUESDAY. Uncertain. Pressures or stresses could come from dissatisfied colleagues or unfriendly authority figures. If your supervisor is giving you a hard time over production, be wary of biting back. Instead of making yourself worse off than before, simply do your best and leave it at that. Some of you might need to give your partner extra support while they find a new job. Increases in the cost of living probably added a burden to already stretched finances. This is the time to start talking to your angels to ask for their help and support. As your faith gets stronger, you will find that your life will improve. Remember that miracles do happen, and there's no reason for you to miss out. It is always better to love than be loved.

28. WEDNESDAY. Uneven. An up-and-down day appears likely. Just when you think you have it nailed, the rules of the game can change. Your lover may seem particularly possessive of you, questioning where you are going and what you are doing. This might not be intended as it seems. Give them that reassurance they are looking for and allow the trust to build naturally. Small compromises can go a long way, not just in loving relationships but in all areas of your life. Legal matters could come up against an unforeseen problem, causing you to rethink exactly what your next move should be. In today's celestial climate, you would be wise to err on the side of caution. Plan a romantic evening for two.

29. THURSDAY. Inspirational. Thanks to Neptune and Chiron in the realm of the Moon, your dreams may reflect your unconscious desires concerning your home and family. Take this opportunity to analyze the clues your subconscious mind is sending you. On the surface, most dreams make little sense. Look for the symbols or archetypes, and you should find the answers to many of your problems. Your inner restlessness can push you too hard to reach the gold at the end of the rainbow. Stop looking forward and start noticing what is around you right here and now. An opportunity for career advancement can come along out of the blue, so keep your eyes and ears open to what those around you are saying.

30. FRIDAY. Powerful. Caution is needed in all financial dealings. Make sure you are in possession of all of the relevant facts before entering any business negotiations. Otherwise you might lose your credibility or be taken for a ride. Joint finances are another area to watch. Ensure that your partner is in agreement before spending too much. If you are worried about your partner's spending habits, then sit them down and talk about it. If you are afraid of your partner's response, then you need to seek help and should probably reappraise what you are looking for within this relationship. Passion plays a large part in interactions at this time. The dance circuit can hold passionate delights for single Archers.

31. SATURDAY. Relaxing. Some of you may be feeling quite generous while other Archers could be the recipients of special gifts. Keep in mind that what you give or receive need not have any material value whatsoever. A spiritual gift of time or talent is often priceless, so consider this when looking for the perfect present. For advice on a personal problem. turn to an older friend who has been through it. They may have a very interesting take on your situation that will allow you to see your way clear to a resolution. Housework can be very enjoyable today. Share the tasks with your loved ones and enjoy talking about your week while you work. Don't hesitate to tell that special someone how you really feel.

APRIL

1. SUNDAY. Spontaneous. Let your inner urges have free rein and fun and laughter will follow. An inner restlessness will make anything that takes your mind off your present situation look like fun. Start planning your next overseas trip by exploring some exotic destinations on the Internet. Or check out the newspapers for a community event that may involve artistic or zany activities. A romantic attraction to foreigners could take you to a cultural event where you are sure to hook up with some interesting possibilities. Sagittarius parents should make the most of your parents and in-laws. Let your children reap the benefits of grandparents while you kick up your heels and escape the humdrum of routine.

2. MONDAY. Interesting. Minor disruptions in the family can be upsetting to your peace and harmony. Consider your own position, your attitudes and expectations, and finally whether you value yourself or others enough. If you can let go of blaming others and work on your own issues, you will find that peace will return. The more you look at yourself the better you can see your own self-imposed limits. Be aware that a whole new world of possibilities can open up once you let go of these inhibitions. Start a dream diary and explore your unconscious for more insights. An interest in philosophical or spiritual issues could be inspiring. Follow up on your interests and forget about everyone else.

3. TUESDAY. Aspiring. Your admiration for other people can give you the impetus to continue on your road to success. Start to recognize your own talents and abilities and get advice from these people you wish to emulate. Then, watch your position improve. Venus, the planet of love and harmony, moves into Gemini and your sector of partnerships today, where it will stay until August 8. This position of Venus is favorable for public relations and for establishing new partnerships. During this phase, you will experience increased mutual consideration and kindness in marital and other personal relationships. Your usual adventurous nature might become even more so, adding a thirst to meet new people and learn new things.

4. WEDNESDAY. Favorable. Try to find a healthy balance between your private life and your public life today. The pressures of the workplace can be overwhelming at times, and you really need to have time to relax. Some of you might be considering a plan to work from home. If so, be aware of what this can entail. You don't want to let the pressures of work remove what home life you do have. Chatty Mercury is now moving direct in Pisces, signaling a positive time to buy or sell a home, sign a rental agreement, or make a major purchase to improve living conditions. You may have been stressing over a contract or business dealings that have been held up. You can now breathe a sigh of relief because the matter should receive the go-ahead.

5. THURSDAY. Promising. The people whom you meet now may have a significant impact on your life. For the best outcomes, look for those who display optimism, generosity, and faith. Avoid people who are most obviously on power trips or who display an unhealthy drive for control and power. Your social life is likely to pick up a beat. But you do have to be careful not to neglect your loved ones in the process. Those you care about may not tell you how they feel and wind up harboring resentments. Public relations work would be right up your alley now. If you get the opportunity to take a representative role at work, it could be the start of a new direction in life. Love and romance are highly possible. Look your best to make an impression.

6. FRIDAY. Demanding. Watch your health today and don't push yourself too hard. You may be more sensitive to innuendos and undercurrents among those around you. This could confuse you about what you are feeling as opposed to what others are feeling. Try to take some time out during your breaks to stay in touch with yourself. The Full Moon is in Libra and your house of friends, hopes, and wishes. This could mean you are looking for validation from friends and through group activities. Be your own best friend by giving yourself a pat on the back for the things you know you do well. If called upon to perform a humanitarian gesture, you might be surprised at how much satisfaction you gain and how you can be inspired to volunteer more.

7. SATURDAY. Quiet. As the Moon glides into Scorpio and your house of solitude, you could be ready to take a break. These next two days are your lunar low cycle. Rest as much as possible and don't overdo anything. Surround yourself with pleasant people and stick to places where you feel comfortable. Some of you might be inspired to join a spiritual retreat at which you can take on meditation and yoga. Such practices will buoy your spirits. Enjoy tasks that you can do on your own and get in touch with your inner feelings. Then you can plan your next project or finish an old one. If you are concerned for the health of another, spend time with them to help them research a healthy course of action.

8. SUNDAY. Renewing. A friend from the past could suddenly contact you. If you are thinking that you should have hooked up with them years ago, don't fret over it. They are probably planning to renew the relationship now. You are likely to have friends and people around you who are happy to help. But it would be better for you to do as much for yourself as possible at this time. That way you will accomplish tasks the way you want them done without uncomfortable feelings getting in the way. Get out in nature if you can. The fresh air and the exercise will do you good and will give you inspiration for new ways of self-expression. Your sense of adventure would enjoy exploring new territory or just taking in a change of scenery.

9. MONDAY. Opportune. The Moon is in Sagittarius, illuminating your first house of personality, and strengthening and awakening your latent energies. Sexual energy reaches a peak during the next two days, so plan accordingly. If you're married, make time for your spouse. Single Archers may find this the best time of the month to make a play for someone in whom you are interested. This is a great time for a makeover. If you have the time for shopping, you might come across some funky gear that is priced right. Stay away from moody or depressed people, as their mood could rub off on you. And beware of power plays by control freaks at work. If you are feeling down, get a massage and enjoy pampering yourself.

10. TUESDAY. Helpful. Obstacles may stand in your path early in the day, making life seem like hard work. The trouble is that you are currently feeling the need to expand your horizons. But it appears difficult to get out of the smoothly worn ruts in your life. Persistence and optimism will pay off. Since it is really a matter of changing daily routines and habits, focus on one thing at a time. Later in the day, you will find traveling far smoother and easygoing. This is a good time to initiate a personal project that you have had on the drawing board and have been agonizing over whether it is good enough. Determine to get started. You will be surprised at how much fun it will be. Your popularity is on the rise, adding extra support.

11. WEDNESDAY. Exacting. Take it easy this morning and enjoy your morning ritual for a change. Be aware of how your lover or spouse is coping with life and give them your support. Try some hugs and loving words or simply listen to them complain for a while. You could be tempted to buy your loved one a gift to make them feel special. Be careful when it comes to spending money though. You may have the proverbial hole in your pocket. Speculation on the stock market could be attractive. Avoid investing in anything risky until you have thoroughly investigated and done your research. Disagreements among friends could make it hard to bite your tongue. You will be much happier with yourself in the long run if you do.

12. THURSDAY. Prosperous. With the Moon in your sector of money and in harmonious aspect with expansive Jupiter, you should do well in finance today. If a promotion is coming up within your company, this is the time to put yourself forward for the position. You have good support from superiors and coworkers, so don't hold yourself back. This is an excellent time to look into investing in a promising new company or starting a business of your own. It would be worthwhile to see a financial adviser to talk over all your options because you might not know of some that are available. If you are seeking financial support, call your bank. A talk with a banker may reveal an opportunity that you have missed up until now.

13. FRIDAY. Motivating. The need for security and income can interfere with the amount of time you want to spend on creative and recreational activities. Instead of the situation being a problem, it might motivate you to start looking at the different possibilities for work. You don't have to settle for what you have. Right now a change would be as good as a vacation for you. If a younger family member seems to have some excellent advice for you, don't discount anything they tell you. Check out your options for retraining as well. This is the time when you can enjoy learning something new. A sporting or social group could test your patience. If you are not getting your money's worth, look for something better.

14. SATURDAY. Constructive. Mars, the planet of action and energy, starts to move forward after a bimonthly period that may have caused you to experience stiff competition and not much reward for your efforts. A turnaround is now becoming a possibility if you corral your efforts and choose a single plan of operation. Believe in yourself now and follow words with deeds. Your actions will be the proof of the pudding as far as others are concerned. A touch of jealousy could mar your day when either you or your partner starts to resent other outside friendships or commitments. This feeling can be avoided if you determine to talk to each other and be sensitive to each other's needs. A nosey neighbor may surprise you.

15. SUNDAY. Trying. As the Sun grapples with stern Saturn it may be hard to express your inner urges without upsetting somebody or some situation. Stay committed to whatever you have planned. Even when you are experiencing the mundane, you will have opportunities to add your own zest and interest. Artists of all sorts could have an opportunity to put your work on display. You could find, however, that the rules and regulations are inhibiting your preferred effect. Be prepared to compromise, and you will get a lot farther than if you fly off the handle. A love affair may seem to be going wrong with emotional misunderstandings hampering real communication. Be honest and with a large dose of tact and diplomacy if you want to get over this hump.

16. MONDAY. Challenging. Use your intuition and brains rather than brawn if you want to succeed in your endeavors today. Somebody could be causing waves simply because they don't really know what they want and are dissatisfied with everything. Archers living in shared accommodations may decide to move because of a difficult situation. You would be wise to do so. With what you know now, you will be able to hunt out more suitable roommates easily. Try not to rush, no matter how late you may be, as there is a potential for accidents to occur. House hunters might be ready to sign a contract on a new home. But you will likely want to sleep on it before making a decision. What you think is fabulous now may not look that way tomorrow.

17. TUESDAY. Adaptable. Quick-witted Mercury moves back into Aries and your sector of fun, lovers, and children. Sagittarius lovers might want to start a family now but find that your elders are not in agreement. Consider all the implications, such as finances, security, and future potentials before you get carried away with the moment. Many decisions that are made over the next couple of days could turn out to be regrettable. You have a generous and kind nature and could be tempted to help a friend or colleague with accommodations. You do need to set out the boundaries very clearly before they move in though. You could live to regret your kind act. Set aside some time for romance this evening.

18. WEDNESDAY. Imaginative. Your thoughts and spoken words are strongly linked to your emotions today. It is important to keep tabs on your feelings and avoid any unfavorable blowups. If you feel that those around you are moodier than usual, try to keep an independent approach. Creative energy flows freely, which could bring unexpected and intriguing activities and opportunities your way. Romantic interludes could also be part of your day. Even if you are at work, you might be sending romantic messages or talking via the Internet. Parents should keep an eye on the children since they seem likely to get into mischief now. An opportunity to make money from a hobby or skill might take the pressure off your finances too.

19. THURSDAY. Surprising. Your sector of romance and children holds the spotlight as the Sun, Moon, Mercury, and Uranus are all in residence here. This mix equals high-voltage energy, giving you the courage and strength to tackle whatever comes your way. Dramatic actions are likely. These can extend from romantic hopefuls declaring their undying love to kids throwing tantrums. Use the energy in positive ways, especially with your children. Enroll them in sporting or artistic activities that will use up their energy in a creative way. Some of you might be tempted to join a theater group and strut your stuff on the stage. One thing is for certain, you won't get too nervous at having to stand up in front of a crowd.

20. FRIDAY. Practical. The shining Sun is now looking down at us from the earthy sign of Taurus and is putting your work and health in the spotlight. This is an excellent time to start a new diet and exercise regimen. At this point your enthusiasm and determination won't wane after the first day or so. You might enjoy joining a gym or a weight-watching group to enjoy making new friends and sharing your journey to better health. Job seekers can have success in finding a spot that offers plenty of opportunity for advancement. Even those of you already working might decide to change your vocation and begin reading the help-wanted ads. Make some time for relaxation this evening and enjoy an intimate moment or two with someone special.

21. SATURDAY. Revitalizing. A Taurus New Moon culminating well before dawn provides a practical overtone. You will be encouraged to finish your chores and even complete repairs around the house that you have been meaning to do for a long time. Students can start a new research project and easily focus on the small details now. Some of you might be thinking about getting a pet. Consider rescuing an animal by checking out local animal rescue shelters. Be sure you choose a pet that is appropriate for your lifestyle. Don't be surprised if you receive an unexpected invitation to a social event. But make it a point to watch the calories as you are more than likely to indulge in drinks and rich food. If need be, call around early to find a babysitter to ensure your freedom later.

22. SUNDAY. Enterprising. The power and enthusiasm to take the lead in a group venture are yours for the taking. Your adventurous spirit will be ready for any task so long as it relieves the boredom and gives your mind a situation that can excite your imagination. Ideas around making money could be dominant. An interest in restoring furniture, artwork, or plans to run workshops may be your focus. Even distributing pamphlets would get you outside and earn some extra dollars for later enjoyment. If you are involved in group activities, refrain from getting testy with someone who is less adept than yourself. Remain impervious to nasty comments so that you can go home and sleep with an easy mind.

23. MONDAY. Manageable. Focus on your productivity this morning. Pay attention to quality and detail in all your tasks, from the food you serve and eat to the way you file your papers. If you have time, organize your desk for better efficiency. You may find yourself working closely with someone else, a situation you may or may not welcome. Similarly, your point of view may clash with that of your partner. To avoid arguments, it's important to keep everything in perspective. Chances are you will be able to win them over to your side eventually. But this is not the day to attempt this. Wait patiently for the tide to turn. Don't let your boss badger you into working overtime if you have plans tonight. Be true to yourself.

24. TUESDAY. Delightful. With the Moon and Venus together in your house of relationships, you can expect pleasant and loving feelings in all interactions. If you are in the process of negotiating a property settlement with an ex, this is probably the best time to find a satisfactory compromise. Business negotiations should be lucrative. Still, you need to keep your eye on your competition just in case they are not playing fair. There is an indication that you may be caught up in legal matters. It may be to appear as a witness in a case or to serve on a jury. Be sure to dress to make a grand impression this evening. No matter who tries to make eyes at your lover, they won't be able to take their eyes off you.

25. WEDNESDAY. Sensible. Excellent insight and business acumen are your strong points today. A business meeting can give you the chance to air some of your ideas and have them accepted. Beware of being too independent though, as this could be perceived as a threat by your employer. An offer to join up with a colleague in your own business venture would be worth considering. If you decide to say yes, make sure you have a legal agreement to protect your interests. Such a contract will keep you from worrying should your relationship change. Engaged Archers might meet someone very important through a business connection or friend and ask them to be a member of the wedding party in the not too distant future.

26. THURSDAY. Deceptive. It will be all or nothing today since half-measures are very unlikely. Don't be surprised if you have to deal with aggressive customers, clients, or authority figures. Put on your best face and smile because if you react, the result could be far worse. Play it safe with your finances. Don't let any pushy salespeople or so-called financial experts separate you from your cash. Be aware of flashy advertising. Some intriguing products are sure to be fakes. Today's atmosphere is also likely to manifest in the romance department. What seems to be a steamy affair may not last past midnight. Private and secretive liaisons might be favored but proceed with caution. Watch out for compelling strangers who may be dangerous.

27. FRIDAY. Demanding. What starts out as a walk in the park could end up testing your nerves and patience. Do your research before entering into important business negotiations, and you won't get taken for a ride. If possible, get the advice of someone in the know before you get started. An expert can make you aware of what you need to look out for. Check all your insurance policies and be sure you are up-to-date. Some of your information may have changed, and you don't want to give the insurers any reason to reject a claim. A problem on the home front needs to be addressed rather than swept under the rug. If you don't deal with it now, it can become more hidden and grow into an ongoing conflict.

28. SATURDAY. Diverse. Mixed fortunes apply today. Current planetary influences are serving as a reminder for you to slow down and do more thinking and planning before taking action that cannot be reversed later on. An evening event may demand a lot of preparation and running around on your part. Since accidents are a possibility, remember to breathe and relax so that you do not take risks or make mistakes. If you find you are full of tension and anxiety because of nothing to do, go for a jog or a walk. The exercise will release the tension and clear your mind. A potentially exciting date this evening could have you chewing your fingernails, drinking too much coffee, or overeating. Instead have a massage and pamper yourself.

29. SUNDAY. Pleasant. Philosophical or spiritual interests can spur you on to do extra reading and research into fascinating topics. The desire to explore the world from the comfort of your living room is likely to appeal far more than actually flying off to adventure. Hours spent surfing the Internet or watching movies might be the most enjoyable ones you've spent all week. Some of you may be enjoying moments with a new lover, basking in the intimacy of getting to know each other. If you want to get out and about, visit some local markets and enjoy the sights and sounds in the crowd. There is a chance you may run into an old friend and enjoy spending the rest of the day catching up on news and gossip about others from your past.

30. MONDAY. Positive. Expect a slow start to your day. With this in mind you can take extra care to look after yourself, eat a good breakfast, and be ready to face the day with a smile. A significant dream may linger in your heart and mind and would be worth writing it down. You might also jot down any thoughts that come to mind surrounding it. These thoughts can be very useful to you later in the day when you might question something you have taken for granted. By the afternoon your professional life will be back on the agenda. It seems that work is beginning to pile up and will need your attention. Don't get caught on the phone or the Internet by the boss. They may have had a hard night and are looking for someone like you to pick on.

MAY

1. TUESDAY. Difficult. An impulsive career decision may put you at odds with your family. Before you make your decision final, why not talk to an older and wiser colleague and get informed about what lies ahead. With the Moon and Mars affecting each other, you are quite likely getting a little hotheaded about everything anyway. Partnered Sagittarius may have to accompany your partner to a business lunch and can meet up with someone you can do business with yourself. Be cautious about what you tell other people today. You could find yourself the subject of whispers and rumors. Don't be afraid to put forward any creative ideas you have regarding work. Superiors and colleagues alike will appreciate them.

2. WEDNESDAY. Variable. Look after your commitments and let others look after the rest. There will be a lot of talk and bluster on the job. Many of your colleagues may only be interested in feathering their own nests and should be ignored as best you can. Stay close to the ones you trust and do the right thing. No matter how fantastic some offers may sound, you will be proud of yourself at the end of the day. Your loved one could want you to give up some of your independence in your own work to support them in their job. That may be alright on paper, but you do need to look seriously at what it is that you want. Security is a slippery idea and sometimes simply means dependence.

3. THURSDAY. Diverse. Be aware of your expectations before engaging in any negotiations, whether business or social. If you take a deeper look inside yourself, you may find desires that you probably are not even aware of. Don't gauge your progress on how you are feeling because emotions go up and down all the time. For a far more accurate picture, be practical and assess where you are and what you are doing. Ask a favorite colleague to lunch with you and enjoy a break away from tensions of the workplace. It is strange how some romances start. You might find that you have more in common with each other than you thought. Relax at home with friends and enjoy intimate conversations this evening.

4. FRIDAY. Indecisive. You may struggle to make a decision as your head and your heart are telling you two different things. Stop trying to sort it out this way and think laterally. Instead of looking at points for and against, try art therapy and begin drawing. A course like this might give you a different take on the situation. Or you can simply wait until tomorrow when the choice will be obvious. A new romance may not fit in with your lifestyle. You and your lover may work opposite hours or might come from a different culture or religion with opposing values. Don't just quit. Take it slowly when you can, and you might find change happens while you are not looking. Taking on extra responsibility on the job might work in your favor.

5. SATURDAY. Guarded. Maintain strong boundaries today. There is much activity in the cosmos, suggesting innuendo and intrigue edging in on your consciousness. Although you may have a lot of social engagements, you would be far better off spending some time alone. Hidden matters can come to light through meditation. Such a silent observation can help you more than ever now. With the waxing Full Moon in Scorpio in your twelfth house, it is a time to review the past two weeks and assess whether you have been true to your own goals. Some of you may need to look after an ailing elder. You might enjoy talking to them about the past and their life's experience as you help them.

6. SUNDAY. Subdued. As this day dawns, many of you may be wrapped in the arms of a lover and want nothing more than to hide from the world and whisper sweet nothings all day long. If you are on your own, you could prefer to get out of the house and explore the countryside. You might decide to visit a distant relative and take a tour off the beaten track. Pretend you're on a holiday and enjoy tourist sites along the way. Some Archers may be on vacation in a country very different from your own. Take this opportunity to enjoy the sights and sounds of a market that is stocked with all sorts of exotic foods and wares. If you are lonely at home, you might volunteer at a local charity.

7. MONDAY. Favorable. A boost of confidence is likely as the emotive Moon now lights up your own sign of Sagittarius. Expect to make a stellar impression, as you are gifted with even more charm and magnetism than usual. You may find that increasing pressure in your career and in your closest relationships will keep you on your toes for the next two days or so. Don't be swayed by the emotions of others. Just look after yourself and let other people worry about themselves. That doesn't mean you have to be coldhearted. At the same time, don't put your needs on the back burner since this is the best time to get a personal project off the ground. Pamper yourself with a massage or a lovely hot tub scented with sweet-smelling oils.

8. TUESDAY. Restless. As the Sun closes in on Jupiter, your ruling planet, over the next couple of days you could suffer from a severe case of itchy feet. Whether you want to change jobs, move away, leave your partner, or take off overseas, give yourself a few days to think about it first. If you still feel the same this time next week, then you probably should go ahead. Try to keep your head should a disagreement with a loved one incite you to do something impulsive that makes matters worse. Instead, find a mutual friend who can be a mediator for the two of you and help you to find the middle ground again. Volunteer work can be very satisfying for you now, and you may learn a valuable skill as well.

9. WEDNESDAY. Trying. The Moon collides with lusty Pluto in your sector of finances, which should be taken as a warning to watch your cash. Be wary of theft and fast-talking salespeople first and foremost. You might want to review your budget as well and ensure you are getting the most from your investments. Messenger Mercury moves into Taurus and brings an enquiring attitude into your house of work and health. You are more inclined to make to-do lists, pay bills, and sort out clutter now. Health concerns can be on your mind also. Consider scheduling a checkup or begin researching ways to improve your health. You are inclined to want to learn new job skills or improve your output in terms of work.

10. THURSDAY. Tricky. Loving discussions can turn sour without any warning. You will be better prepared for situations if you don't assume that your partner holds the same values and priorities as you do. Whatever upsets occur, they will only be minor, so don't have a major blowup over it. Business Archers should double-check contracts and agreements before signing on the dotted line. It would be wise to ask a lawyer to go over the details first. Home buyers should also arrange a building inspection before buying. There could be hidden structural damage you are not aware of. Be moderate when purchasing a gift for a loved one. If your partner is worried about your finances, an expensive gift won't be appreciated.

11. FRIDAY. Expressive. Think first before speaking, and you can avoid unnecessary problems. Archers do suffer from the proverbial foot in mouth disease, so use tact and diplomacy when saying anything to another. Be receptive to your partner who may be having a few problems that you are not aware of. Any support from you will be gold to them. This is a good time to get involved in your local community. You could make new friends and also add valuable contacts to your business network. Volunteering your skills to the local rescue squad, fire brigade, or a charitable organization will be rewarding. Your help will also enhance your reputation and sense of self-worth. Practice kindness in all your affairs.

12. SATURDAY. Starred. There are very good aspects tied in with a few tense ones, so don't expect something for nothing. Remember that no matter how hard a situation may seem, it will work out in your favor. If you have ever fancied yourself as a writer or journalist, now is the time to have a go. For those of you setting off on a long trip around the country or overseas, travel journalism might be worth considering. There are strong Sagittarius vibes with the Sun and Jupiter side by side. With this aspect, you can expect whatever you are doing to be done in grandiose style with opportunities for plenty of overindulgence. In fact, dieters do need to be especially diligent. You may gain weight just looking at a chocolate.

13. SUNDAY. Accomplished. Yesterday's party could continue on today if you are not careful. As those around you can get testy, more chances are there for arguments and frayed tempers. Know when to call it quits and settle into your domestic routine again. With the Moon in Pisces shining its loving light into your home and family sector, the home front is where your heart is. If you have a backlog of work to catch up on, get into it early in the day so that you can have the afternoon free for sports and games. Many of you will be in the process of beautifying or refurbishing your home. You are likely to enjoy wandering through department store showrooms gathering ideas on how to improve your home to fit your budget.

14. MONDAY. Challenging. Archers might consider working from home at this time. Keep in mind, however, that work is work no matter where you do it. If you have children who demand a lot of your time, you may find that both your family and your work suffer unless you can properly organize your space. You can be particularly resourceful now in finding efficient uses for the materials you have at hand. Rules and regulations could be your bugbear now, especially if you have friends or colleagues around you pointing out your deficiencies. Practice patience and bite your tongue. What they don't know won't hurt them. Tonight is perfect for enjoying your home, your belongings, and the fruits of your labor.

15. TUESDAY. Steady. Take it easy this morning as there are likely to be delays in your schedule anyway. Enjoy a leisurely breakfast before the daily grind begins. Take the time to be personal with your loved ones and leave home with a smile on your face. Archers might see an opportunity to expand your income and need to call in a few favors from old friends. Let them know as much as they need to, but keep the main game plan to yourself until you get it off the ground. Venus, the goddess of love, starts its retrograde motion in Gemini and your house of partnerships. This passage can cause some disappointment in your current relationships. Counseling might be the best way to renew the shine.

16. WEDNESDAY. Bumpy. A sleepless night may put you on the wrong foot from the word go this morning. Rather than let more irritation take hold, stay away from others until you have regained your equilibrium and enthusiasm for life. This is one of those days when you might want to chuck in your job and move away from it all. You also may be thinking of a vacation overseas. If so, you should seriously think about making arrangements in the destination of your choice right away. A lover's quarrel can be healed if you are willing to say you're sorry. But if you find that too hard, consider whether you want to get tangled up with this person for any length of time. It might be better to call it quits now before you become too committed.

17. THURSDAY. Tiring. A long-time family problem could start to drag you down. You may have a loved one who is unwell. Your worry and concern for their well-being is overriding anything beneficial that may happen around you. At some point you need to look after yourself, so why not plan some time out for something you really enjoy doing. Consider an art, music, or drama class. Or it could be uplifting to read to your children or just socialize with a few friends. With the Moon in your house of fun, lovers, and children, avoid getting bogged down with work and worries. Lighten up and have a good time. At the end of the day if you don't feel happy, then your skies are always going to look gray.

18. FRIDAY. Practical. The Moon joins savvy Mercury, expansive Jupiter, and the shining Sun in Taurus and your sector of work, service, and health, putting the focus on the routine details. The more tidy and efficient you are today, the more successful you will be. Organize important papers so that you are not trying to find them at the last minute. You'll be embarrassed if you are caught unprepared. Eating right, getting moderate exercise, and sticking to a sensible sleep schedule will go far in helping you to get ahead in life. This is an excellent time to start training in an area of work that will boost your income and job satisfaction. Look at working in fields involving travel, advertising, or hospitality.

19. SATURDAY. Creative. Enjoy the simple things in life today. It is an excellent time to make repairs and start renovations or restoration work to beautify your environment. Shopping at your local markets or mall and dining at a pleasant café can put you in touch with friends and connections that will give you ideas for fun and relaxation. You will enjoy tending to the things you love and adding an artistic touch where possible. As the day progresses it is likely to get quite hectic. It's likely you could be out on the road quite a bit. Pack some relaxing music to keep you calm in traffic and help you order your thoughts. If you have worries, meditation might be your best treatment.

20. SUNDAY. Vibrant. The Sun has now slipped into your opposite sign of Gemini. Your focus will turn to relationships both personal and professional. Consider that those close to you provide a mirror through which you can see yourself. When you do, you will notice that over the next month, you will have experiences that make you aware of aspects of yourself that are not being fulfilled except in relationships. On the other hand, you may find that your relationships are encouraging you to display qualities that you may feel are negative. If in doubt, visit a counselor to help you make adjustments and redefine the boundaries in your relationships. Social engagements will offer a chance to meet and mix with fascinating people.

21. MONDAY. Lively. Beware of impatience and irritability in you and in others. With so many things going on, you and those around you are bound to get flustered from time to time. The vibes are perfect for sharing with your spouse or lover. Talk over your long-term goals so that you understand your differences as well as your similarities. If you can accept each other the way you are, compromise and cooperation will be far easier in the future. A social obligation might not be an enjoyable duty. But if you put a smile on your face and accept responsibility for your role, you might end up enjoying yourself far more than you ever expected. Steer clear of shady business deals and you won't get burned.

22. TUESDAY. Important. As the Moon dances with Venus in your sector of partnerships, many of you may be given to thoughts of a past love or dreams of what could be. A loved one may need your support and a few hours of tea and sympathy. It would be wise to organize your schedule to get the important things done beforehand. Legal matters could be postponed and give you extra time to get your case together. All manner of situations can occur that will cause you to breathe a sigh of relief. Young lovers may be talking about moving in together. Now is a good time to start the ball rolling. Don't rush into joint responsibilities too quickly though. Try to maintain control over your own finances for the time being.

23. WEDNESDAY. Tense. Don't let your mind get too caught up in details this morning. Sagittarius is far better at looking at the big picture. Sort through your facts but don't get hung up on them. If you use meditation to step back from your mind and move into your heart space, you will find life far more peaceful. An important business meeting could test your mettle and question your belief that you know what you are doing. Don't be concerned. The situation is likely more a test of who you know than what you know. If you are concerned about your bills and credit card repayments, do something to give yourself a break. Arrange to pay your bills off or call the bank or card company and ask for a payment package to give you time to recoup.

24. THURSDAY. Spontaneous. Quick-witted Mercury joins the Sun and Venus in Gemini and your sector of partnership, putting the focus on your communication skills. Over the next three weeks you will seek intellectual stimulation and conversation in all your encounters, ranging from cheerful banter to spirited debate. Even arguments and controversy can be interesting. They certainly will be preferable to no stimulation at all. Archers need to be conscious of what you are saying and to whom. You are advised to use tact and diplomacy, something you are known to have trouble with. This is a good time to enter into contracts or negotiations. If you are struggling with a property settlement, get professional mediation.

25. FRIDAY. Revealing. Keep your desk in order, as superiors may be watching you closely. It's nothing personal, just part of the normal review process. Keep the personal phone calls to a minimum. Also keep your ears open for important information you can use to your benefit. It's definitely an all-business day. Try to listen more than you talk too. Someone close to you may try to tell you how they feel. If you don't keep your ears open you won't hear it. Interesting gossip around the watercooler could give you food for thought as well as spark a few ideas for your own business deals. The mystery of a first date can excite all sorts of fantasies and romantic notions. Make sure you look your best, and you will sparkle.

26. SATURDAY. Spirited. A strong desire to get away from it all could be a signal to do just that. Why not schedule a weekend away with your lover and enjoy a romantic interlude at an exotic retreat. Or you may go to a weekend workshop and learn about something that fascinates you. Spiritual and philosophical subjects will be exceptionally enjoyable. Check out the local papers for any talks or seminars given by visiting intellectuals or spiritual masters. Some of you may be planning to marry a person from another culture. You can find yourself engrossed in trying to sort out a wedding ceremony that accommodates both families and friends. Take in the theater or a concert this evening for extra inspiration.

27. SUNDAY. Enriching. Life is likely to be picking up lately. Archers could feel as if you have made some progress toward your long-term goals. You may want to take some time this morning to think about the direction in which you are heading. Domestic responsibilities can dictate your activities for most of today, so enjoy what time you get to yourself. News from a partner or loved one can arrive from overseas, or you may spend some time on the computer chatting face-to-face with a foreign Internet date. A new business venture could be in the air, requiring a social gathering with your associates. Ironing out any potential difficulties should be lots of fun. Overindulgence in food and drink might be your one vice.

28. MONDAY. Disruptive. Cosmic forces are not very helpful today as a restless energy pervades the air. Insecurities on the home front might put you in an irritable frame of mind at work. If you have a child who is sick, put the young one first and don't worry about what the boss says. But, make a serious effort to explain the problem and be calm and rational. In all disputes err on the side of caution, and you should end the day on a positive note. Your partner might not be happy with the way your relationship is going, causing you to rethink your own happiness. A superior might pick you for a promotion, which could cause some envy among your colleagues. This is par for the course and most of them will get over it.

29. TUESDAY. Opportune. The going gets a little better, although the cosmos continues to send Archers testing conditions. Step up to the plate in all matters. By doing so, you will build confidence and self-worth simply by tackling each task as it is put in front of you. If you seek out support from your elders or people in the know, you will be well prepared for what is ahead. Be honest with your loved ones, and you can work through any problems between you now. Honesty is the key to success in many areas. Remember that if you tell the truth, you can't forget what you are meant to say next. A change of residence may be in order, but don't try to do it all yourself. Check around for a reliable, professional mover.

30. WEDNESDAY. Uneasy. Business propositions could be tricky and contracts can fall through today. Stay in the moment, and you will deal with whatever upset comes your way with diplomacy and professionalism. The moment you let your mind torture you with negative projections, situations will get a lot harder. As the Moon moves through Libra and your sector of hopes and wishes, you should take the time to write out a list of your hopes and dreams and ask your angels for help. You are generous and kind, compelling you to try and help those close to you. You may even offer help to a person much less fortunate than you. Join up with a local charity and volunteer some of your time to make a difference in an area that matters.

31. THURSDAY. Varied. Group activities can give valuable experience as well as take your mind off your own problems. If you are asked to join a group with a friend, go ahead and don't worry about the expense. The enjoyment and skills that come your way will be well worth it. Trust your instincts now, especially if you are discussing a new business enterprise. If you feel uneasy and apprehensive each time you have to deal with a particular character, then don't trust them. A lunchtime meeting can be lots of fun, but you could be inclined to drink too much. Be careful and don't give away the game. Socializing is sure to bring romance into your life. If you are partnered, take your loved one out on a date.

JUNE

1. FRIDAY. Dreamy. Go ahead and let your imagination run wild. But be aware of letting unreasonable fears paralyze you. Today is perfect for dreaming about the future and visualizing where you want to be in the coming days. Your home situation may be really comfortable at the moment, but there could be an unconscious rumbling regarding your self-expression. Don't push dissatisfactions under the rug. Instead find some quiet time to spend alone. Consider a leisurely stroll enjoying nature or sit in your garden and meditate on your inner space. What is your heart telling you? Listen to your own inner voice on all matters for the best advice. Don't beat yourself up about sitting around and being quiet and reflective.

2. SATURDAY. Indecisive. Yesterday's introspection continues today. If you keep letting other people make the decisions for you, you can't complain about your circumstances, can you? You don't have to rock the boat, but you do need to get in touch with your own needs and self-expression. A large social engagement could be the talk of the town. Left to your own devices, however, you probably would rather stay at home. If you maintain a low profile, you may end up talking to someone who inadvertently gives you their pearls of wisdom. The universe speaks in all things, so all you have to do is be willing to listen. Do not make any commitments in love at this time. Let events unfold for a couple of weeks before deciding.

3. SUNDAY. Emotional. More and more the celestial influences are pushing you to rethink who you are, what you want, and where you are headed. Don't let your moods get you down. If you explore where your emotions are leading you, it is likely that you will discover the root cause. Unconscious issues are like monsters in the dark; once you turn on the light they disappear. So don't be afraid to go after your own inner demons in this way. A business partnership could be stifling your creative self-expression. You may feel the need to make a change, or your partner may be having trouble with their work and wants to leave. Don't let finances stand in the way of making the right decision for your well-being. You will see that the situation will improve.

4. MONDAY. Motivating. Try to avoid infantile outbursts today. It seems that you want to scream and yell to be heard. With this morning's Full Moon lighting up Sagittarius, you are probably looking for a bit of attention. Work on self-assertiveness without standing on other people's toes. Finding a balance between autonomy and dependence is what this Full Moon is about for Archers. Whether you can succeed as a leader could be tested now. This is happening because you are bound to be more popular than usual, and others are looking up to you for direction. Pressures in business dealings can build up to a crescendo. If your partner is in disagreement with the way you want to handle the matter, you will have to sit down and thrash it out.

5. TUESDAY. Challenging. Your earning capacity may come under the microscope as you consider how achievable your long-term goals are. Take all areas into consideration. Include such factors as your family and relationship commitments, your health and physical fitness, and your talents before you start fantasizing about what you are going to do. Personal debts could be another issue on the agenda today. If you are having trouble keeping up with your payments, then it is essential that you work on a budget plan. Adjusting your lifestyle to match your income is not simple. You will be required to be serious about changing your habits and behavior. Remember that creating new habits can't be done overnight. Waiting too long will only make your situation more difficult.

6. WEDNESDAY. Reassuring. Your social life could be fairly hectic and can work at cross-purposes with the need to attend to your daily work and routine. Be selective about whom you say yes to. Being cautious in this regard will make your life a lot less complicated. A social event can become fairly costly if you have to shop for a costume. Don't hesitate to ask around among your friends and see what they have in their wardrobes that you can borrow. What turns up might be absolutely fabulous. Make the most of who you know in all aspects of your life and enjoy the benefits of your network of friends and associates. Undoubtedly they will be happy to oblige you since they can then call on you for a favor when they need it. It's a case of you scratch my back and I'll scratch yours.

7. THURSDAY. Sensitive. Expect an emotional day ahead. Tact and diplomacy are not usually your strong suits, especially if the people close to you keep pushing your buttons. The time for talking is when other people are listening. If you notice that they are talking over your head, you are missing the point. Avoid the whole situation until everything cools down. Delays and heavy traffic on the roads are a reason to leave early if you have an important appointment or meeting. Mercury, the planet of communication, moves into Cancer and your sector of joint finances and other people's money. This phase signals the right time for discussions or negotiations concerning finances or property, particularly those held jointly.

8. FRIDAY. Cooperative. Stay focused on what is important because today should progress smoothly. It is a good time to work with other people for a shared outcome, as you can achieve far more than going it alone. In business this is a good time to consult experts in whatever field you have become involved. The same applies to your personal life, in which you may benefit from counseling. Advice from professionals can give you an independent perspective against which to measure your own views of the situation. A female relative could play an important role in your life now. If you need someone to mediate among other family members, she could be particularly helpful. Watch your pennies at the stores and remember your budget.

9. SATURDAY. Cautious. Self-discipline may not be your strong point today. Reflect on major decisions before you overcommit yourself in any area of life. A trip to stores or speciality markets could be lots of fun. But it seems you might be more attracted than usual to expensive art pieces or antiques. Consider your budget and restrain yourself. Social activities may take up most of the day. Single Archers be aware that you could have fun flirting with other singles. But avoid going too far with anyone you don't know well, and you won't regret any indiscretions. House hunters can enjoy property auctions now. But be careful you don't get caught up with the excitement and hustle. Make sure you really want the place before you go overboard in the bidding.

10. SUNDAY. Disquieting. The focus could be on finding a balance between your personal security and your personal relationships. You may have been involved in a myriad of outside activities and commitments or have been working late most nights. If so, you certainly should expect and understand that your partner may not be happy. It could be that a compromise is not possible unless you both can agree to seek out a mediator or counselor. Possibly you are both trying to live beyond your means. Consider that you may have to start tightening your belts to ensure a happy home life and a loving relationship. A possessive or obsessive relative might make a family get-together difficult. Be assertive but tactful if you want a positive outcome.

11. MONDAY. Powerful. Dynamic celestial influences can bring change into your life through others today. Try not to be rigid in your thinking, as this attitude will only make matters worse. Many of you may feel like breaking out of your routine and perhaps much of your life. But the restrictions you are feeling could come from within rather than without. It is important that you be especially careful when deciding what to get rid of. You don't want to throw the proverbial baby out with the bathwater. A business colleague could try to use coercion to force you to bend to their will. Whatever you do, don't engage in a battle over the situation. You should know whether or not this person has any scruples. To protect your reputation, walk away and don't look back.

12. TUESDAY. Important. Shades of yesterday can leave anxiety and a touch of fear in your heart. Impulsive actions may be an unconscious reaction to your nervousness. You need to reassess your decisionmaking process and try to bring sanity into the mix. Infatuation with a new love can have single Archers in another world of fantasy and excitement. In fact, socializing is likely to bring all sorts of weird and zany people into your orb. No matter how interesting and refreshing this may be, don't commit yourself to any wild ideas that you might live to regret. Wait until another day and see if you still feel the same before deciding. Self-expression can be powerful. Express it through creative outlets.

13. WEDNESDAY. Complicated. There are many conflicting influences swirling through the heavens. Trying to please other people could be your biggest mistake, so make sure you factor your own needs into all decisions. Be creative and don't worry about what others think. Avoid being irresponsible, however, because that will cause you more problems that you don't need. An irritating boss or boring vocation might give you reasons for wanting to quit. Before making any decision, you need to keep your priorities in order. Expansive Jupiter, your ruling planet, is now in Gemini and your sector of partnership. This phase makes a fortunate and happy time for business and love, as you will meet positive and influential people.

14. THURSDAY. Stable. Watch overindulgence early in the day. You could be inclined to drink far too many coffees to remain calm for what's ahead. Partnered Sagittarius should take extra time with your partner to show your love and care. Soft, loving, and intimate words spoken now can stay with you all day, clearing the way for kindness and compassion for all. Pack your own lunch for work with a salad and fruit. You will give your body a boost of fresh nutrients to keep your clarity of mind and quick reflexes on the job. One of your co-workers may have problems at home. If you can lend them your ear over lunch, you'll have a friend for life. Don't hesitate to show a new colleague the ropes either.

15. FRIDAY. Accomplished. Your charm and quick wit will help to inspire and motivate your colleagues on the job today. This might be a good time to use your charm and flattery on someone higher-up for positive results. There could be a pay raise in the pipeline for you. It may come sooner if you are seen to be doing excellent work. Be careful of any jealous or possessive tendencies toward your lover, or you might end up in an argument. Be sensitive to their feelings and enjoy the love you have together without unnecessary problems. One of your parents may not be feeling well and needs your help around the house. If you are thinking about moving them in with you, double-check with the family.

16. SATURDAY. Productive. This is a good day to put your house in order. Prioritize what's important and organize your life to follow suit. Go through your closets and clear out all your unwanted junk. You might consider a garage sale and let someone pay you to take items away. Whatever you are doing now, you will want to do it properly and allow plenty of time for what is important. Pets come into the spotlight also, reminding you that it is probably time to pay attention to their health and grooming. Do some research on their dietary requirements and other special needs. You can eliminate a lot of expensive visits to the vet by being knowledgeable. If you are not feeling well, pay attention to your digestive system first and foremost.

17. SUNDAY. Bright. A confident, positive outlook prevails. The moody Moon joins expansive Jupiter, romantic Venus, and the shining Sun in Gemini and your house of partnerships. This passage can turn up the volume on communication between you and your loved one. Any problems that have been bubbling away beneath the surface will come to light and give you and your partner the opportunity to practice compromise and loving understanding. Deep and meaningful conversations are the norm on a day such as this, so don't try to avoid the inevitable. Competitive sports might grab your fancy and give you an outlet for frustration. If something more romantic is on order, consider the ballet or theater.

18. MONDAY. Busy. You won't want to be home alone on a day like this. Interaction and communication will be the name of the game. Business negotiations can be revealing. It is important that in meetings, you make sure information is based on facts and evidence. If necessary, ask for as much time as you need to consider any propositions. Reflection on many areas can give you valuable insights. A legal situation may be better dealt with through the courts if the other party involved wants to employ bullying tactics. This type of behavior loses its edge in front of a judge. A new relationship could be experiencing a rocky time simply because another has been making eyes at your sweetheart. Consider that the biggest problem may be your jealousy.

19. TUESDAY. Harmonious. The New Moon in Gemini brings to the fore issues around sharing and partnership. An increased awareness of the need for someone significant to consult and rely on can surface. This is a good time to make contacts with others or to make something public, such as announcing your engagement. Be diligent at work and avoid stepping on the toes of those above you. It is one thing to try to do a good job, but you need to make sure you do it the way your boss wants it done. Your intuition can give you a hint about how people are feeling. Act accordingly for smooth sailing. Business discussions will be successful when you ensure that everyone gets to have a say.

20. WEDNESDAY. Constructive. Do not waste time and energy on unproductive matters. If you and your partner have an issue over money, talk about it right away. It won't get resolved if you keep skirting around it. The situation can be exacerbated if you enjoy shopping with the joint funds. Don't make excuses, just be honest. Keep in mind how you can tend to lose patience quickly when your loved one tries to cover up some of their faults. Remember that they can feel the same way about you when you aren't forthcoming. An opening to work in the accounting or banking sector might be a great way to climb up the corporate ladder. For your own sake, ensure full transparency if you are dealing with other people's resources today.

21. THURSDAY. Meaningful. You are likely to find meaning in everything as the Moon colors your rational thoughts with emotion. This is a good time to talk about your feelings, especially since communications with women should be very beneficial now. Small issues can overwhelm you because you may have a tendency to think small and find yourself caught up in all the fine details. Use your Sagittarius understanding of a situation and look at the big picture to ease the burden of details. The Sun moves into Cancer and may bring worries over joint finances or borrowed funds from a financial institution. This is not a good time for you to lend any significant amounts of money. You may not be paid back any time in the near future.

22. FRIDAY. Expansive. Stay objective with any business negotiations you get caught up in. When something affects your pocket, it is easy to get upset. A state of panic won't help matters today. Broaden your horizons and look further afield for answers to your problems. If you are not happy with your income or present employment, consider returning to some studies in your field. You can give yourself the skills to demand a better income and job satisfaction. If it is a faster rise you seek, you are better off finding a mentor who can show you how to manipulate the system and pull strings in your favor. An interest in philosophy or religion might encourage you to pack your bags and head off overseas to explore different aspects of life.

23. SATURDAY. Happy. Since Archers are well respected for your easy demeanor and love of freedom, your friends are likely to give you all the support you need. A duty to friends, a club, or a fellowship could take up some of your time. Even so, you should have a lot of fun taking part. A connection with an older person may put you in touch with a community action group that inspires your allegiance. Many of you might want to help out the needy by working with a volunteer organization to make a difference in the lives of some. The desire to travel could combine with your urge to do good and send you off to volunteer abroad. A job teaching a language overseas might give you the opportunity you are looking for.

24. SUNDAY. Pleasurable. Sagittarius desiring a sea change could find some interesting listings in the Sunday papers. The more distant and exotic a property sounds, the more you are likely to want to have a look. Perhaps you can mix business with pleasure and plan a weekend away with your lover while you inspect possible purchases. The desire for a beautiful, more glamorous home might make you dissatisfied with your present surroundings. With a little imagination and a splash of paint you could make your home much more desirable. Shop around for some flowering houseplants and watch how the beautiful colors and scent put a smile on the faces of your loved ones. You might plant a vegetable garden while you're at it.

25. MONDAY. Efficient. Today's peaceful vibes can get you off to a good start. Focus on your domestic chores before you go anywhere. Be assured that you will feel contented and happy with a clean house and car. Use your eye for detail to purchase the appropriate attire for an interview or meeting. Your reputation will get a boost if your presentation is just right. Business negotiations can go much smoother if you use your connections. It is not always what you know but who you know. Plans to start your own business may include your partner. If so, you need to get a legal contract drawn up to protect both of your interests. Don't fall into the trap of thinking nothing is going to change. Change is the one thing you can always count on.

26. TUESDAY. Lucky. Whatever situation you may face today, you are sure to land on your feet. Have faith in the universe and follow your heart. Last night's dreams can follow you in the daylight hours and take your mind miles away from the job. To ensure your safety, don't do anything you are not sure you can handle. Savvy Mercury glides into Leo and your ninth house of travel and higher learning. This phase may spur you on to return to a course of study or take off overseas. A hoped-for windfall could come from an unlikely source. Sagittarius writers should concentrate on finishing your manuscript over the next couple of weeks because the current aspect is favorable for a lucrative publishing contract.

27. WEDNESDAY. Harmonious. Maintain a balance of relaxation and activity in your life today. Include in your schedule stimulating activities that provide exercise and social enjoyment. Just be careful that your social activities don't infringe too much on your home life and incur your partner's wrath. Venus, the love goddess, moves forward again in your house of partnerships, suggesting your need to focus on your real desires rather than imagined or illusory expectations. Now the small irritations between you and your partner will fade into the background, allowing real dialogue between you to begin. When you know what to ask for, others become the resources that you would like them to be.

28. THURSDAY. Exacting. Feelings of loneliness or depression can result simply because you are tired or hungry. Ensure that you get plenty of rest and eat good wholesome protein food such as beans, eggs, and dairy combined with salads. Carry nuts such as natural almonds in your pocket and eat a handful when you notice your energy levels starting to wane. Start replacing coffee and tea with water and juice, and you will notice a change after about a week. Take a look at your commitments. You need to decide if you can let go of some to give you more time to smell the roses and kick back with family and friends. Spending time with a friend in need will take your mind off your own problems and also bring some peace.

29. FRIDAY. Helpful. Save money and stay close to home today. Time spent with loved ones will be worth every second for your peace of mind and a chance to talk from the heart. Airing your problems and listening to those of others will help to heal hurts and resentments. Some of you may be caring for an elderly parent or a disabled child or relative. If would be wise to make some changes around the house to ensure a safer and easier access to household facilities. This would certainly take some of the pressure off of you. Check in your local directory for charitable services for respite or simply to have someone come round for company and a talk. Sharing the load is sometimes hard, but it is often simply a matter of asking.

30. SATURDAY. Solid. Practice moderation in all your affairs for the best outcome today. Spiritual practices such as yoga and meditation would be the best way to start your day. Focus on what you hope to achieve and then let the universe worry about the rest. Enjoy being in the moment as much as you can. Any chance you get to enjoy the outdoors or take part in a favorite sport will be welcome. The effects of fresh air and nature are beneficial now. Exercise will energize your body and mind and allow you to gain clarity on a confusing issue. A restless mood may cause you to become dissatisfied with your home or lover. Rather than act on an impulse, go for a long walk and see how you feel when you get back.

JULY

1. SUNDAY. Opportune. A quick wit and sense of humor can win friends and influence people. But you do need to remind yourself to be sensitive to the moods of others. Otherwise you may inadvertently hurt someone you love. With the Moon now in your own sign of Sagittarius and making contact with the Sun, Mercury, Venus, Mars, and Jupiter, you are likely to be the veritable center of attention for everyone. With this popularity comes a certain amount of responsibility, so try to be especially aware of what you are doing. This is a great period to get a personal project off the ground. If you are trying to get a new business started, this is the perfect time to advertise and get your message out to the public.

2. MONDAY. Adventurous. Listening to the stories of other people's exploits might be all you need to catch the travel bug and start organizing your own trip abroad. You may be politically minded at the moment and attracted to overseas destinations for further education or social action. A fascination with other people's dramas can take you out of yourself for a short time. Be aware, however, that you could become embroiled in others' problems and become the scapegoat of another. Focus on your own life, and you can renew the romance. Love in is the air for single Archers. Don't be surprised to find that you experience the excitement of distant lands in the arms of an exotic and fascinating foreigner.

3. TUESDAY. Intense. It may be impossible to have a light conversation this morning. No matter with whom you talk, you may find yourself burdened with their troubles. Still, this can have the effect of brightening your mood by the simple fact of knowing that your life is not so bad after all. Lend a hand to friends in need and watch the positive results. The Full Moon in Capricorn shines its light on your house of money and values, highlighting the differences between your values and those of others. You may experience a financial setback, possibly because of fluctuations in stocks or bonds. Apparently this is not a good time to risk your cash. Love and desire are strong motivating factors tonight.

4. WEDNESDAY. Promising. There are many conflicting celestial influences suggesting that for best results you should focus on what is in front of you and avoid getting sidetracked. Mars, the planet of action and energy, is now in Libra, highlighting your house of associations, hopes, and wishes. This is the time to formulate your goals and start to actively pursue them. You are more aligned to the future now and will want to work today for the sake of what you can bring about tomorrow. This is also not a good time to be a loner. You will achieve your goals much quicker if you work cooperatively with others. Use your connections and work on building a network of associates on whom you can call.

5. THURSDAY. Influential. The thoughts and opinions of others will have a stronger effect than usual on your decisions today. Try to stand apart from others when making any important decisions so that you can be clear on your own needs and desires. Your power to move people when you speak will be an asset in business. Don't let your shyness or self-doubt stop you from having your say in the proceedings. You might end up getting the credit for a great idea or for using successful tactics. The communication channels between you and your partner are especially good this morning. Be sure to discuss important plans and goals while you are assured of being able to come to a happy compromise.

6. FRIDAY. Positive. An overactive mind could be the root of all your problems. Try not to think too much, and the day will become much more pleasant. Look around for a group in your neighborhood that practices meditation and yoga. You will enjoy making new friends while ensuring health and well-being for the rest of your life. As a Sagittarian you will always be searching for the truth, and spiritual practices are the best way to satisfy this desire. Your friends, neighbors, and relatives should be a great support to you now. Don't hesitate to ask for help with any problem around the home. If needed, repairs can be easily attended to by asking a friend who is a plumber or builder by trade and has the know-how and the tools.

7. SATURDAY. Renewing. Memories from the past can invade your thoughts and put a sentimental outlook on your day. If you are feeling grief or loss, don't hesitate to call a sympathetic friend and let your tears flow. You may have a neighbor also call on you for an understanding chat. Together you will find that through talking, you both often share the same ideas and outlook on life. An attraction to antiques or mementos from the past might take you to a flea market where you can pick up all sorts of bargains worth restoring. You may even bag a bargain that brings extra cash if you check out websites that buy and sell items. A lucrative sideline might be the result. Parents might begin a family tree for the benefit of future generations.

8. SUNDAY. Comfortable. A conspicuous lack of aspects makes for a relaxing and stress- free day. As the Moon settles into Pisces and your sector of home and family, this is where you will want to be. Get the whole family involved in tidying up the house and yard. You might plant a garden together, giving the children their own special plants to tend and enjoy. Some of you may be away for a romantic weekend, spending all your time holed up in a cozy cabin in the mountains or by the sea. It might be the perfect setting for a proposal. Others of you could be organizing a large celebration. If so, you will be busy connecting with friends and relatives to ensure the smooth running of this important function.

9. MONDAY. Stimulating. A love affair can toss you into the deep end, especially if you both have children from another relationship.

There is a lot of literature on the subject of blended families, which might be worth consulting if you want to make this relationship work. You may be trying to find a happy balance between independence and your new-found love. Be aware that you might have to settle for some gentle ups and downs as you and your partner proceed to work out your affair. Be creative with your self-expression and watch your sense of self grow. The impulse to speculate with your hard-earned cash should be avoided. After a few small wins, you might lose the lot.

10. TUESDAY. Manageable. Juggling family, work, and a busy social life can take edge off the sparkle. Avoid pushing yourself too hard. Resolve to make one day a week a day of rest and enjoy doing nothing or at least not very much. An imminent vacation can consume your thoughts as you start planning what you can do on a limited budget. You probably don't have enough money to fly away to an exotic destination. If so, consider a less expensive road trip to places you have never been. Contact friends or relatives who may live along the way and enjoy some free accommodations. Assure them that you will be happy to return the favor when they travel. This is a good time to start a family, especially if you are in a romantic mood this evening.

11. WEDNESDAY. Varied. Practice caution in any decisions to do with a relationship battle. Until you can both find the middle of the road, you need to be very careful not to overreact and make matters worse. It might be better to involve a professional mediator and save yourself a costly court battle. Some of you may be caught up with plans for your child's future. If you are not sure which college would best suit their needs, consider visiting each in person. Getting a firsthand view of how they are operated will put your mind at ease. Finances can start to look up. You might decide to use some extra funds to get involved in a team sport to keep your fitness at an optimum level and also make new friends.

12. THURSDAY. Opportune. Job seekers may get the opportunity to start some new work. Don't worry about whether you will like it or not at first. Start the job, and this alone will add to your chances of being chosen for a job you will like. Good relations with coworkers can make this a fun day for most Archers. If you are invited to lunch by a gorgeous associate, don't hesitate. In fact, with the Moon harmonizing with Pluto in your money house, it might be a great time to speak to your boss about a raise. With your practical approach at this time, you can budget very successfully. An exciting social event might take up a lot of your thoughts during the day, so remember to stay focused when working with machinery.

13. FRIDAY. Pleasant. You can show your love today through service, even if it just means cleaning out closets and doing laundry. Small things can mean a lot. Shopping in out-of-the-way places can reveal a few unique shops that carry the sort of interesting items that catch your attention. Don't go overboard with your purchases. Arrange to lay away one item at a time and enjoy being on top of your budget. New business attire and new ideas can bring success as you become far more valuable to your superiors. Networking with someone in authority can be promising, especially if you are looking for a change in employment. Take the dog for a long walk when you get home and enjoy the time to digest the day's happenings.

14. SATURDAY. Auspicious. There is a plethora of celestial blessings for Archers this weekend. The mood for travel might overcome all your other plans, and suddenly you are off on an adventure. Couples should speak to your loved one about escaping for a romantic interlude. Suggest a spot where you can explore different customs and landscapes and bring inspiration into your lovemaking. If you are struggling with a business partner who won't listen to your ideas, perhaps it is time to branch out on your own. Before you approach your partner, get an idea of what may be involved. Speak to a relative or friend who may have legal knowledge about extricating yourself from the partnership.

15. SUNDAY. Stimulating. Romance and good vibes are definitely the order of the day as the Moon dances with loving Venus in your house of partnership. Sporting or other social activities can keep you busy for most of the day. To avoid any chance of injury, however, ensure that you don't take on any physical activities for which you are not ready. Single Archers can receive a surprise invitation from a gorgeous friend, possibly someone you have been secretly admiring lately. Don't be shy about letting friends and family know. Take the opportunity as it comes and enjoy the moment. A visit to your grandparents might be a pleasant break from your routine and give them a wonderful surprise. Don't be surprised yourself if they have an heirloom to give you.

16. MONDAY. Constructive. Give your routine a shake-up and put some sparkle back into your daily life. Smokers might want to seek help if you are trying to give up the habit and nothing seems to work. Try a self-help group and get support from people going through the same process. You will be amazed at the difference it makes. The same applies to any of you who may be going through a marital breakup. You are probably finding it difficult to dispel the depression and grief that are part and parcel of this experience. Joint funds can come under scrutiny today. You might be surprised to discover that there is more in the bank than you realized. Take this opportunity to discuss your joint budget plans for the future.

17. TUESDAY. Intuitive. The dreams of last night may leave strange thoughts in your mind. You are wondering if they could be psychic in nature. Dreams tell us a lot about what our subconscious wants to make conscious. Pay attention to the clues your sleeping mind has given you. You may be especially sensitive to the moods and emotions of others, especially if you have an inkling about who is calling every time your phone rings. Being enthusiastic about your ideals doesn't mean that others will agree with you. Don't be disheartened about this. Surf the Internet and find like-minded souls with whom you can converse. Singles may enjoy socializing this evening and meeting a very attractive stranger.

18. WEDNESDAY. Rejuvenating. There is a feeling of mystery as the New Moon activates your house of transformation, bringing the greater cycles of life and death to center stage. This is a time for new beginnings and a time to close the door on the past without regret. Clear away your skeletons and be ready to be born anew. This is an excellent period to enter psychotherapy and explore the depths of your soul with an experienced guide. Investments can accrue over the next month. But you need to be wise about finances. Keep your finger on the pulse and don't become complacent about any shares you may have on the stock market. Couples can move into the next level of love and commitment and may decide to renew your vows.

19. THURSDAY. Stressful. A restless mood can make it hard to concentrate on what you need to accomplish. Dissatisfaction with your lot in life can be used as a motivator to find a direction that does give you satisfaction. Don't use restlessness as a reason to whine and buck the system. As Mercury travels retrograde in your solar house of Leo, it is time to give the details their due so that they can serve your larger purpose. By doing so, you may discover a better version of your own vision as well. Don't hurry because you do have time. Rushing along can bring awkward situations with some very irritating people with whom you could clash. Tap into resources you've ignored, and you can reach your objectives.

20. FRIDAY. Inspiring. A new friendship or love affair can change your way of thinking and open up so many more possibilities for your future. Higher education would be a very wise move if you can swing it. You should research institutions that offer the sort of courses most suited to helping you reach your goals. Archers are likely to be mixing with people from many cultures. You will be delighted and enlightened by the different world views that you can explore through contacts with these people and their families. Many of you may start a serious relationship with someone from an entirely different culture. A possible plan to visit their home country to meet their family is an opportunity to view their way of life through your lover's eyes.

21. SATURDAY. Easygoing. Take it easy when you wake up this morning. Allow yourself the time to relax in the comfort of your bed and reflect on your progress during the past week. A dream may come to mind that you can record in your dream diary and wonder at what your subconscious is telling you now. The day ahead is likely to take you away from home with the promise of achieving one of your goals. It would be pleasant then to spend the morning with loved ones and enjoy the camaraderie of belonging. A large celebration might have you giving a speech. If you are afraid that you might get tongue-tied on the podium, jot down reminders to jolt your memory. Relax, as you're likely to wow the crowd.

22. SUNDAY. Rewarding. Parents or in-laws could be number one on your agenda today. If a family member is feeling down, bring them to your home for the day. They will love to see their grandchildren and no doubt will enjoy watching you in your everyday life. You could be surprised when they offer a helping hand. The Sun moves into Leo and shines its loving light into your sector of travel and education. But be wary of flashy advertising. You don't want to find yourself scheduled for a week at a resort that is inexpensive but shabby. A chance for exciting entertainment could come when you check out local events. A lecturer or performer you've always wanted to see may be nearby. Don't miss an opportunity to attend.

23. MONDAY. Positive. Be early to work this morning, and you will impress the boss. There is the prospect that you may receive a promotion or a raise some time soon. If you are willing to take on a leadership role, you will enjoy the challenge and add to your talents and skills. Some of you may be lucky enough to be offered extra training through your workplace. Get a head start on important appointments or business meetings by allowing plenty of time. Traffic delays and public transportation holdups are likely. In fact, don't expect business deals to come off easily or business negotiations to go as planned. Until savvy Mercury starts moving direct on

August 9, nothing of importance might happen. Take this downtime to research a better deal.

24. TUESDAY. Expansive. Office banter at work can turn into a stimulating debate about philosophical or spiritual issues, inspiring your desire to learn more. An enhanced inclination to gain knowledge can encourage you to join a group or association with special interests. When you do, you are likely to meet like-minded people and bring them into your circle of friends. Single Archers may be surprised to get an interesting invitation from a supervisor. Should it include a social get-together, take them up on it. You will be curious to find out what might develop. Group commitments could take up a lot of time after work, especially if there is a committee meeting. It is permissible for you to let members know that you have a time limit before you get started. Chances are that you will become so involved, you may stay longer.

25. WEDNESDAY. Demanding. There is bound to be numerous items on your urgent list, so get started early. The more you put things off, the worse you will feel. Guilt over postponing tasks can nag at you until you get your tasks done. You may have inadvertently let a friend down and need to give them a call to make your apologies. Simply pretending a misstep didn't happen won't make it go away. It will only fester beneath the surface. Students can get valuable research done now when you determine to find the answers you need. If you are unsure about asking a fellow student or teacher for help, don't be. Once you break the ice, a very rewarding relationship can develop that will benefit both of you. You can be very influential among your friends when you express your ideas.

26. THURSDAY. Indecisive. Personal concerns over your choices in life can drag you down. You may be so concerned with pleasing others, or simply fitting in, that you are not aware of what you want. Get in touch with your gut feelings by spending some time alone and talking to your heart. Sometimes our head is so busy worrying that we forget to tune into this important center of the soul. Even if you have a busy day ahead, try to stay out of the limelight. You could be influenced by the opinions of others. The Moon is now in Scorpio, signaling your lunar low cycle. Over these next two days you need to recharge your batteries and make important decisons. You will want to be ready when the new cycle begins.

27. FRIDAY. Exacting. Fall back on your friends in times of stress. Unexpected problems can cause unnecessary anxiety when all you need to do is confront the problem and do what is necessary to fix it. With the help of your friends you can do this. The upside is that you may learn quite a bit about yourself while you're at it. Buying a gift for a friend or lover could be a chore in itself, especially if you are on a budget. Be realistic. Think of something small that they will use each day to remind them of your love. Parents should keep an eye on your children, as accidents may be more likely than usual. Especially supervise their Internet activity to ensure you have the necessary censures in place.

28. SATURDAY. Positive. Don't be afraid to speak your mind this morning. Little irritations can build into large resentments if you don't address them right away. You will likely be pleased with your partner's reaction. Sagittarius is known for your ability to see the big picture, and you can make far-seeing plans now. Trust that you understand how it is with a situation and act on your instincts. You can't go wrong when you do. A lunch date with a few good friends will be a real treat. The conversation is likely to open your mind to ideas for a new project. Cook a special meal for your loved ones tonight. Why not make it a party to show them how much they mean to you?

29. SUNDAY. Enjoyable. This should be a fun day, no matter what you have on your agenda. Your popularity is on the rise, and you are likely to have a choice of social events to choose from. Single Archers could have second thoughts about a new love. It might be a good idea to take the weekend off to do your own thing. Start off at some shops and look for an exceptional item to take home. You might even find a good bargain. An invitation to go away for the weekend will be right up your alley now. You will welcome the chance to get away by yourself and enjoy entertaining yourself. Don't be surprised if you are inundated with text messages from the love you've left behind. Take them in your stride.

30. MONDAY. Tricky. Dealing with more than one strong personality could make you feel like the filling in a sandwich. You can remain there and try to handle the situation as best you can. Or you can make your apologies and take off. Some of you may be away trying to get a business idea off the ground. To your consternation, you seem to be missing important information or can't get in touch with an important player. Either way you will probably have to call it quits for the day. Don't let frustrations eat away at your insides. Go for a long walk in the fresh air and clear your head. You never know who you might run into while walking in the park or just airing the dog. Anything can happen and probably will.

31. TUESDAY. Delightful. An abundance of celestial activity makes this a very unusual and interesting day, which is just the way most Archers like it. New and interesting people come into your orb who can give you some great new ideas for your future. Vacation plans could get a push when a friend has tickets for a trip that they can't use and wants to sell them cheap. Money matters can be first and foremost on your mind as you grapple with your budget. A business idea might need cash to get started. You will have to investigate what you can borrow and how much you can afford to pay back. Usually your bank can offer financial advice, so check with them before proceeding.

AUGUST

1. WEDNESDAY. Rewarding. Whatever you have planned to do today could be subject to some changes. Not that you'll necessarily mind. It is almost certain that plan B will turn out to be more enjoyable than plan A as long as you are philosophical about any change that unfolds. There is also the possibility of sudden travel, giving you an unexpected weekend away. Writers may get an opportunity to publish some of your work. Don't be shy about digging out some of your other work that may be languishing in your desk drawer. If you are in an ongoing partnership and romance has gotten a little stale, be creative. Put a little devilment into your routine and enjoy the result.

2. THURSDAY. Bright. Friends and neighbors can love being with you because you lighten any situation with your lively mindset. You are now in tune with others' needs. This could put you in the role of a leader, either at work or in a group situation. Don't be surprised if you get nominated to serve on a group's committee. Since you sometimes think you can handle more than you can cope with, be honest about how much time you can devote before you accept. If you have a flair for technology, you can be in your element in online networking or games. Photography is also an area where you could shine now. Try your hand at some family portraiture at your next party.

3. FRIDAY. Encouraging. Philosophizing on the job can be inspiring for Archers this morning. A new workplace health and safety policy could have the whole place buzzing with different views and genuine concerns. There may be a consideration that needs to be taken to your superiors. You could offer to be the front person for your fellow employees. The boss might be pleased with your performance and initiative and offer a promotion and leadership role. Excitement about meeting intriguing people takes over when you receive an invitation to a prestigious gathering this evening. The chance to rub shoulders with attractive people can give you a fresh outlook. An old love can resurface and rekindle the passion of yesteryear.

4. SATURDAY. Frustrating. There is a strong chance that you will find yourself interacting with parents this weekend. Be aware, however, that if you try to get out of a family invitation, you could cause a serious offense. Responsibilities and obligations can please or frustrate you, depending on your current situation or need for space. Some of you may be on vacation away from home and are finding your traveling companion less than cooperative. It may be that your interests are not compatible. Or you could be stuck with handling luggage or organizing the itinerary. It will be up to you to resolve any issues with an honest, forthright talk. Student worries regarding a study program can be solved by talking to those who have prior experience.

5. SUNDAY. Interesting. Those friends who tend to be a little bit zanier and less hidebound than you can be a breath of fresh air. That doesn't mean that you want to drop everything and take off on one of their harebrained adventures, or does it? Whatever you do, you do need to let go and just enjoy what comes your way. In fact, the less control you apply to events, the better. Don't get too dejected if your partner has promised to do something and has forgotten all about it. Consider how busy they are and the amount of responsibility with which they have to cope. Make sure you express your disappointment in a rational way, and give them the chance to respond. Your heart will know if it's the truth or just an excuse.

6. MONDAY. Exhilarating. With the Aries Moon joining quirky Uranus in your house of fun, nothing will be too boring. If it does, you or one of your friends will find a sure way to liven things up again. Your creativity is high today. If you have any great inspirations, write them down quickly. You won't want to forget them. Dreams of going to a university can come true with your acceptance for enrollment. All you have to do is organize the rest of your life to follow suit. If your lover has to move away to study or work, don't try to stop them. Their leaving could be the beginning of journeys for you too. This is an excellent time to follow up on any hobbies and possibly turn one into something lucrative.

7. TUESDAY. Intense. Before you get caught up in an argument, be aware of conflicting desires within you. You are likely to be experiencing a need for independence but at the same time have a possessive attraction to another. With Venus sweeping into Cancer and your house of sex and transformation, sexual relations can go beyond the physical act and become a vehicle for transformation and inward change. How to balance such intense desires with the need to be free is the question. Honest communication is a good place to start. The next four weeks are a good time to seek a loan or other financial support. Recycling and restoring some of your old furniture can also bring in some extra money.

8. WEDNESDAY. Significant. This day may appear mundane from the outside. But inside your head, the landscape is likely to be futuristic and inventive. Don't be afraid to share some of your creations with your coworkers. They may adopt one of them and hail you for being a genius. Work in computer technologies or on the stock market could be right up your alley now. Don't hesitate to take a course to help you get started, as you could be a natural. Setting up a business from home might be harder than you think, especially if you are considering working with a partner. Be patient and work through all the problems and legalities before you sign on the dotted line. It could save your sanity as well as your money.

9. THURSDAY. Productive. This is a perfect day for tidying up around your home and getting your garden under control. If you are out shopping, you are quite likely in the stores looking for items to spruce up your home. Plans that have been coming together over the past few weeks will shortly have a direct effect on what people are saying about your career plans. Don't toss off your ideas lightly. Mercury, the planet of communication, moves direct in the sign of Leo, bringing more activity, discussions, and exciting new plans for travel or study. Delays in legal matters, travel visas, or agreements should disappear, leaving the way clear to follow through with your business plans.

10. FRIDAY. Promising. With the Moon now in your house of health, it is also an auspicious time to start an exercise regimen and implement a healthy diet. Don't go overboard as Sagittarius people are known to do. Be content to work up to your optimum gently but thoroughly. The same goes for diets. Be sure not to get taken in by false advertising and start a fad diet. Instead, eat sensibly. When you indulge in fresh salads and homecooked meals as much as possible, your energy and zest for life will return. Talk to your subordinates and tell them your plans before you do anything today. What you presume they know might be news to them. Reserve your evening for romance and take your lover out for a quiet dinner for two.

11. SATURDAY. Bright. Harmonious vibes among friends, family, and lovers will conspire to make this a special day. Your generosity makes you a soft touch. Use your head, not your heart, before you make promises that you probably can't keep. Take this opportunity for a honest talk with your partner and enjoy the heightened sense of intimacy that is created. If you have social commitments that may call you away, ask your partner to go with you. Once they get to know your friends, you may be able to share more relaxed time together enjoying the same interests. Some of you might be in the public eye at the moment. If you have been doing volunteer work, you may receive some form of acknowledgment.

12. SUNDAY. Smooth. Today promises to be full of fun and social activity. Many hands make light work when getting chores done. You won't have any shortage of people you can call on for help and support. Some of you may be feeling a little jealous of your lover's interests and feel left out. Don't keep these feelings to yourself. If you open up to your partner in a loving and honest way, they won't be able to do anything else but answer in kind. A marriage celebration can bring your whole family together. You are bound to enjoy catching up with some of your relatives whom you haven't seen for a long time. This enjoyable interaction can give you a stronger sense of who you are and warm the cockles of your heart.

13. MONDAY. Stressful. Avoid pushing yourself too hard no matter how enthusiastic you are about your work. Take the approach that it is better to get a few tasks done well than it is to do a lot of things badly. Ensure you have time off during your workday to relax and let off steam. If you don't, you could suffer serious burnout and be unable to do anything. The Moon snuggles up to Venus in your house of partnership, suggesting that art, music, nature, and spiritual pursuits would suit you better on a day like this. Sagittarius artists are likely to have an opportunity to display your work and may be stressing over minor details. Try to relax and have faith that your work is already perfectly yours.

14. TUESDAY. Uncertain. Patience is required in all your affairs, especially with a loved one who is being difficult. Some of you may be going through a sticky divorce settlement and are experiencing a sense of grief and loss over a broken home. Don't try to get through this period on your own. Seek out the support of a good friend or get counseling from a professional who comes with expert qualifications. All business matters should be perused thoroughly. If you find that you can't balance your books, you will have to go back over all your credits and debits to find the leak. You may find yourself in a tough position when you realize that it is you who has been overspending.

15. WEDNESDAY. Eventful. Work on resolving problems before you start anything new today. Discussions relating to shared profits can be productive. Refrain from concentrating on others' weak spots. Rather, stay focused on their strengths, and you will bolster confidence and cooperation among your peers. Curb a compulsion to spend money on frivolous items. Now you can enjoy watching your bank balance grow for a change. The mood will lighten as the day progresses. Philosophizing with those around you about everything from politics to shopping prices will be immensely rewarding. You could find it so enjoyable that you will consider joining a debating team to further advance your skills and sharpen your memory.

16. THURSDAY. Puzzling. Business opportunities might open up spontaneously, so be ready to maximize the benefits. Luck favors the brave, and adventurous Archers will be equal to any task now so long as it is inspiring. Nevertheless, consider those who are not so inclined. Being too critical of others who don't meet your standards can keep you from finding what might be of benefit to you. Some of you could prefer to socialize with your friends and associates rather than roll up your sleeves and apply a bit of elbow grease. Consider your future before you slack off. Your partner may become critical to the point of being obsessive. But that doesn't mean you should be confrontational. Think about a situation before you take the easy way out and miss an opportunity to resolve a problem.

17. FRIDAY. Sparkling. Make an effort to initiate new projects or activities. When you do, you will expand your mind, feed your spirit for adventure, and stretch your imagination. With the New Moon in Leo highlighting your solar sector of travel and education, you will feel renewed by a new perspective on life. This means it is an excellent time to implement changes and start reaching for the stars. Money problems could be your only glitch. Do your research, and you can find a way out of your problems. It all depends on how badly you want something as to how hard you will work at achieving it. Start with small steps, and before you know it you will have traveled miles. Speak to your elders for a dose of wisdom.

18. SATURDAY. Important. Recognition for a job well done can come from your peers. But if you have other issues going on at home, you may not be in the right mood to take the credit you're receiving. Dissension may be rife among family members, catching you up in the moods of others. Assert your own intentions and stand your ground on issues that are important to you. You will be surprised at how much simpler life can get. Peace of mind comes from being honest and developing confidence in your own truth. A business investment can pay dividends and allow you to manifest a dream. Don't argue with your partner over the issue. Just follow through.

19. SUNDAY. Comforting. Good feelings among friends and family combine with creative talents to make this day relaxing and productive. Even if you are just lazing around your home, you might have a conversation with a loved one that clears up many issues. Or you may be able to pass on the benefit of your experience to a child and enjoy watching them make practical use of this knowledge. An elderly parent who may be having trouble living on their own could need your help today. Consider taking them around to local retirement villages to help ease their possible transition into full-time care. Just spending time with a loved one who is ailing will give you more personal satisfaction than an expensive outing.

20. MONDAY. Powerful. Strong aspects between the Moon, impulsive Uranus, and controlling Pluto will ramp up the volume on the freedom or closeness dilemma for Archers today. The trouble will come from trying to control your own spontaneous drive to fit in with others or trying to control others to fit in with you. Either way you likely lose the battle. Power comes from knowing who you are and letting others take care of themselves. If you find those around you are trying to control you, then you might simply let them know your own mind. Arguing will be useless. A strong intuition can bring out some startling creative work on your part. Don't be afraid to shut the door and get into it.

21. TUESDAY. Constructive. It may be time to push the reset button on a close friendship. Rather than cut the tie between you, however, it might be better to honor the bond that makes that person worthy of another go-around. The trouble is can you let bygones be bygones. This might give you some intriguing concepts to reflect on. Look inside yourself rather than blame others. With a change of perception, all can look rosy again. Your ambitions may force you to lie to your parents if you feel they won't support you to reach your goals. This can cause a sense of guilt that you don't need to have. Speak to an older relative who is impartial and receive the benefit of their objectivity on the issue.

22. WEDNESDAY. Challenging. This might be your last chance to get something you are trying to achieve. Let other activities wait while you give it all your concentration and energy, and you will finally win out. You can learn from previous mistakes now and move on to the next level of growth. Legal matters can be finalized satisfactorily. If you receive an offer out of court, this could be your best scenario. Try not to quibble over details. The desire to get away from the daily grind might give you the impetus to plan a solo overseas adventure. Sometimes it is better to follow your heart than wait around for a friend with whom you can share a venture. You are likely to meet some great companions in your travels.

23. THURSDAY. Sensitive. Spend some time alone today. You need to allow the many thoughts and ideas going around in your head to move into a more cohesive pattern. Reflection will give you the chance to meditate on your inner motivations and sensitivities that underlie outer drives. The shining Sun has now moved into Virgo and your solar sector of career and long-term goals. This area of your life will become more important to you over the next month. Focus on your career, your role in the larger society, and your standing and reputation within the community. You may be called upon to take over the direction of a task or project that can give you considerable power. But remember that the responsibility will be great also.

24. FRIDAY. Confusing. With the confident Sun connecting with the undermining energies of Neptune, difficulties around assertiveness could arise for you and everyone else. This effect can give you an uneasy feeling. Your intuition seems to be picking up the feeling that what is being said is not what is meant. Let your intuition guide you. It may show you more about what you truly desire than all your best thinking can. People around you are likely to look up to you for advice. Here you need to practice caution also. Only give advice on matters you know about when it comes to the feelings of others. You are aware that in relationship issues everybody is different. Just give them your ear. Romance can be truly divine this evening if you let it.

25. SATURDAY. Satisfactory. An eventful day lies ahead, with the possibility of an interesting situation arising. Although your popularity is on the rise, don't expect everyone to view you with favor. Your penchant for talking about your thoughts and feelings is usually found to be entertaining, but some may take offense at your open and straightforward manner. You will need to be diplomatic. Mars, the planet of action and energy, slips into Scorpio and your house of solitude. This period suggests that you will be better suited for working in the background or as part of a team over the next couple of months. Working in a social service field in order to help others would be very satisfying right now.

26. SUNDAY. Variable. A strong motivation to improve your social standing and your earning capacity will drive your actions today. You are likely exuding a powerful drive that will make you stand out from the crowd and attract good things. Archers who belong to a social or sports group may find yourselves on a fund-raising mission. If so, you will enjoy working in a team and learning new skills. Be cautious about involvement in any late-night celebrations. It would be wise to restrict your drinking and the time you stay around. With some others the fun could deteriorate into arguments and innuendo at the end of the night. Check out local sales, as you might pick up a bargain on a household appliance that will make life so much easier.

27. MONDAY. Volatile. Your mind is likely to be constantly occupied with new ideas and plans to make money. Be careful that you are not too possessive about your possessions and ideas. Otherwise, you may not be able to see the good in opposite views. This is not a good day to go shopping. Your emotions can rule your logic and put holes in the budget you have worked so hard to control. A disagreement with your partner about your spending habits might present you with a challenge to prove yourself right. At the end of the day, however, they may be right. Let them show you that they have a valuable perception from which you can benefit greatly. For better cooperation and a chance to learn something of value, listen as much as you talk.

28. TUESDAY. Troublesome. A job or deal may not be moving as fast as you would like. Before you start cutting corners, remember that haste makes waste as well as can give you a reputation for sloppy work. Seek your instructions from your superiors. Remember that they are paying you and can make your work life uncomfortable. It will be more advantageous for you to work their way and avoid confrontation. Follow up on all your paperwork and keep copies of all receipts. You may have to justify your actions sometime in the not too distant future. Traffic delays or road rage can make travel across town unpleasant this afternoon. Tune into meditative music to take your mind off the stress and arrive home refreshed. Get an early night for the best rest.

29. WEDNESDAY. Promising. A new job may offer a good salary and prestige. But consider whether it gives you the opportunity to express your creativity and take initiative. Sometimes you have to juggle issues in too many areas. If you are snowed under with bills and financial commitments, then letting the creative ball drop for now might be a means to an end. Once you have gotten yourself sorted out and in a good financial position, you can apply for a promotion. Or you might decide to look for a job that will give you what you want. Everything comes to those who wait. A nosy neighbor could become a boon to you since they keep an eye on anyone who comes and goes while you're away. Take them a gift and get them on your side.

30. THURSDAY. Useful. A sensitive mood prevails. Poetry and art, especially escapist art or literature, will appeal more than ever. A struggle between your head and your heart may be appeased through writing your own poetry. A recent lover's quarrel may be dispelled and smoothed over by sending a love poem to the one you care about. Appreciate the simple pleasures in life, and don't make things too difficult with complex issues. You might find that they sort themselves out while you take a deserved break. Go home early and put your feet up. There may be nothing more soothing than the sounds of your neighborhood. Say hello to your neighbors and fellow commuters and enjoy being just one of the crowd.

31. FRIDAY. Reassuring. Today's Full Moon in Pisces shines its loving light into your sector of home and family, suggesting that this is the place to be. The last two weeks have found you working hard toward your career goals and in other public matters. Now the demands of your personal life are paramount. Striking a balance between energy spent on work and energy spent on domestic matters is essential to your health and well-being. Balanced attention to your public and personal lives is what you need to focus on. It's time to prioritize. Otherwise, you run the risk of overextending yourself. A home, family, or property matter could grab your complete attention at this time.

SEPTEMBER

1. SATURDAY. Advantageous. Joint plans can come together without a hitch, as you and your partner should be able to agree on anything. Home renovations or repairs could be on the agenda. Ask your family members who have talents in this area to help. Later, you will enjoy serving up a hearty meal and celebrating all the good work you've accomplished together. Family gossip is likely to be fairly revealing. Still, it may leave you feeling as though you should be able to do something to assist the people involved. Your interference is not likely to help. The best you can do is to be there when needed. Mercury joins the Sun in Virgo and your house of career, turning your thoughts to improving your opportunities for success.

2. SUNDAY. Helpful. Caution is needed because you are likely to jump into something that you might regret later. Be mindful of the company you keep and what you want to achieve from any given interaction. Archers have a strong creative bent, but you might hold yourself back in a bid to save cash. This is only a form of self-undoing. Be aware that your creativity will give you far more joy than a fat bank balance ever will. Children can be a lot of fun, but their activities could get expensive. See if you can steer them toward playing baseball in the backyard. For the most fun, invite the neighbors over and make a real game out of it. You can make new friends as well. Whatever you do, don't gamble.

3. MONDAY. Sensitive. Your self-esteem and confidence can desert you when you really need them. It will be necessary to persevere with the problem. It is only through facing up to these tests that you will build your self-confidence. It appears that your inner feelings are making you think that others are not being supportive of your goals. Be assured that those around you do want you to succeed. You could be working hard on a personal project and haven't gotten around to seeing your friends lately. Remember to give them a call and find out what is going on in your circle. There may be someone you need to help. Boredom can be alleviated by joining a group or sports club in a creative pursuit. Joining an amateur theater company could be fun.

4. TUESDAY. Fulfilling. The simple comforts of your daily routine could be your best medicine today. Enjoy working with your co-workers as a team and experience the pleasures of being a team player. Sometimes you just don't need to be noticed. This could be one of those days. Start to think about the food that you put on your table. What you eat has a lot to do with your health and your moods. There are classes in all kinds of cooking that might strike your fancy and give your cooking skills a boost. Thai or Indian cuisine could add some spice to your dining The family will enjoy the change from the usual fare, and you may lose a pound or two in the process. Keep reading the jobs section in your local paper. There is the possibility of a more fulfilling job for you.

5. WEDNESDAY. Outstanding. There is a certain amount of intensity in the celestial atmosphere now. If you can turn your thoughts to the things you love, the passion and intensity can only enhance your experience of the day. Personal relationships are sure to be harmonious. A partnership that seems to be less romantic now can be more fulfilling if you decide to be more assertive and talk about it. Young lovers might plan to marry and wonder whether a full-page announcement in the newspaper is too extreme. Nothing is too extreme if it is a true representation of your emotions. Go ahead and express yourself. You may not feel much like work today. But Archer students may need to do some studying so that you don't fall too far behind.

6. THURSDAY. Significant. A practical approach presides today. Go ahead and get your chores done early so that you can plan for more enjoyable pursuits later in the day. Job seekers might turn toward the armed forces, giving you the opportunity to train while you work. And keep in mind the extra perks that can come with the military. Venus, the goddess of love, slips into Leo and puts some romance into your sector of travel and philosophy. This phase suggests that through love, or the experience of beauty in art, you will have a consciousness-expanding experience that will broaden your horizons and bring about personal growth. Find a cultural venue where you can experience something entirely new.

7. FRIDAY. Problematic. Today's celestial vibes are up and down to say the least. Expect change, and you can't go wrong. Many Archers may have the proverbial itchy feet, encouraging you to get out of town or maybe leave your lover. This desire could go even further if you are not getting along with your boss or don't enjoy your daily routine. It may be time for a serious look at number one. It might be wise to visit a counselor to find out why you feel this way and to help you understand this aspect of your personality. An impulse to spend some money may alleviate the restlessness a little. But take care. When you get home, you are likely to look in the mirror and see a poorer you.

8. SATURDAY. Lively. Tension concerning having to appear in public could give you the nervous jitters. Since most Archers would prefer to take a backseat, you might request a less public position. Work in a voluntary capacity could take you all over town, making it likely you will meet some very interesting people along the way. Fortunate opportunities can come your way while in the throes of helping another. You may have some romantic ideas as you watch a gorgeous stranger who has crossed your path. Play your cards right and you might end up with a date. The scenario could even be more exciting than the proverbial ships passing in the night. Partnered Archers don't need to miss out on romance either. It's your call.

9. SUNDAY. Tricky. Sleep in for as long as possible and relax as much as you can. As the day progresses you may have to put your hand in your pocket far more than you would like to. Nevertheless, some things must be done, especially if it is the necessary repair of a home appliance or some faulty plumbing. Chances of running into your ex while out and about with your new love are likely. After your initial shock, communication may be quite amenable. Don't be surprised, however, if your partner looks askance at your friendliness. You may have to spend some time reassuring them that you are only trying to alleviate an awkward situation. You may have to spend the evening giving further reassurnces.

10. MONDAY. Disconcerting. Worries regarding your present budget suggest that you should look at refinancing your loans. You might also think about selling a large item if you can't afford the repayments. Archers can get caught up in a shady business deal trying to make a few easy dollars. But the reality is that this type of money usually brings more problems than it's worth. Something that is broken or not working very well can be mended. But before it can be repaired, the fault has to be identified. This is the type of scenario that you can find yourself in now. It can be a metaphor for something going on in your life. Once you know what is wrong, you can fix it and start over.

11. TUESDAY. Steady. An upcoming opportunity for promotion may have your colleagues all jostling for a place in line. Nevertheless, you might not feel like becoming one of the crowd today. Instead, you might do something to stand out from the crowd. Take some goodies or flowers into work for coworkers. Better yet, finish your work in double-time or simply turn on your brightest smile that really impresses the boss. Luck is on your side in most matters, so you won't have to try too hard. Some of you may have spotted a spiritual workshop that is being run in some distant location. You can be very tempted to take the journey. If you are determined that you want to leave, make sure you involve your partner in your plans. If you explain your needs, they will no doubt support you.

12. WEDNESDAY. Productive. As the Moon collides with loving Venus in your travel sector, you are sure to be dreaming of distant shores. Many of you may be mixing with people from other cultures, and will just enjoy the political and philosophical discussions that ensue. An invitation to a cultural event is not to be missed.

The new ideas and perspectives you can gain will stay with you for a long time. Business plans to expand into the import and export trade should be researched thoroughly. Make sure you check out all the political implications that might be involved with the countries you are looking at. Research as well any local regulations regarding such areas as tariffs and quarantine times.

13. THURSDAY. Harmonious. The desire to stay close to home and enjoy the simple pleasures can make this day very pleasant. Even in the workplace, you may not be so interested in the politics that goes on among your colleagues. You are determined to concentrate on getting your work done. With an organized routine, you can probably get a large backlog of projects out of the way. The boss is sure to be pleased. You might be asked to represent your company at a meeting outside your workplace. This will give you the opportunity to make new and valuable contacts and extend your talents. Singles could impress a few people at the meeting and find you can pick and choose those with whom you want to network later on.

14. FRIDAY. Promising. The ability to be in the right place at the right time is a valuable asset to you today. Whether you planned it or just got lucky, you won't miss out on a thing. A job offer could come from one of your social associates and send you home to discuss the lucrative offer with your loved ones. Even if you have to relocate, the benefits are likely to outweigh the negatives. An artistic talent you didn't really know you had can come to the fore and open doors into an exciting new reality. Don't reject an offer for extra training, even if it does cost a bit. Chances are you will be in a position to earn dollars training others as time goes by, giving you extra income.

15. SATURDAY. Challenging. Experience can teach you to be careful with whom you talk about an experience or situation. Approach acquaintances with caution. You will then be more able to gauge the mood of the exchange before you go too far. Sagittarius is known for your lack of tact and diplomacy because you are determined to tell it how it is. For your own sake, you don't need to put people off. The New Moon is in Virgo today, giving you a heightened sensitivity to your standing in society and your goals for constructive progress. This is a good time to develop a new business plan that can reinvigorate a positive approach to developing your potentials. Public responsibilities give you an opportunity to build a positive reputation.

16. SUNDAY. Helpful. A social event could sound really lively. Unfortunately, it seems to have turned out to be the opposite. Be good to yourself and choose those who you know will be lots of fun in any situation. The stress factor at home might be more serious than usual. Instead of leaving and closing the door on the issue, try approaching the problem from a different angle. Think laterally and be creative, as the underlying cause may simply be a need for attention. Singles may be asked out on a blind date. It could have all the potential of being quite exciting as long as you don't have any expectations. If you feel like staying home, invite people over for an impromptu gathering for some fun. It's possible you will attract a new acquaintance to your circle of good friends.

17. MONDAY. Fortunate. Go with the flow, and your generous nature will attract in kind. You are much more group orientated today and will enjoy other people's company rather than being alone. It seems, however, that you will also be quite picky about with whom you want to share your time. Your partner may have a proposition for you that gives you plenty of food for thought. If it is something to do with travel, you will probably run with it straight away. If, on the other hand, it is a business proposition, don't make a snap judgment. Get some advice from your contacts in the know before making any firm decisions. For those of you wanting to get a business off the ground but who lack funds, now is a great time to look around for a partner who has the money to do just that.

18. TUESDAY. Complicated. Focusing on any one matter or issue could prove challenging this morning. Partnered Archers may find your loved one quite annoying. Either they want you to do more work around the house, or they are complaining about your bad habits. Either way you may feel that you don't really need this right now. Relax in bed a little longer and reflect on last night's dreams for some insight into your psyche. Are you being true to yourself? Or are you just lazy? These might be the sorts of questions you will ask. But if you are honest with yourself, you already know the answers to both these questions. Perhaps it might be better to accept life and yourself along with all the imperfections.

19. WEDNESDAY. Mixed. Neither a leader nor follower be might be an apt description of your mood this morning. A strong desire to do your own thing may cause you to be quieter than usual, prompting questions concerning your health. Be open to others, and your day will be a lot more enjoyable than otherwise. You could have a close friend or relative in the hospital and feel duty bound to visit them. Even if this makes your heart heavy, be cheerful and keep your conversation on an optimistic note. A small gift to show your love would no doubt be welcome. The desire for some flashy entertainment can steer you toward a favorite night spot. But don't be surprised if once you get inside, you start thinking about going home.

20. THURSDAY. Changeable. Take time with your morning routine, as you might find that all early appointments are delayed. Ensure you get your chores and paperwork in order before you leave for work. You will want to be well prepared for a hectic day. Once you get warmed up, a surprising clarity of mind combined with intuition can make you a winner, giving your popularity a real boost. Young female Archers might be asked to join a beauty pageant. If you accept, you are sure to enjoy the compliments and attention that come with this position. All Archers can receive offers that will aid personal growth. As with all good things, however, there is another side that can demand hard work. Consider all aspects before accepting.

21. FRIDAY. Striking. Archers exude a powerful vibe now. It is one that will see you stand out from the crowd and attract many benefits. A strong drive to be free from responsibilities doesn't mean you should exclude your partner from hearing your plans. Otherwise, they are sure to worry, and you will have inadvertently hurt them. Be honest and caring and be ready for a surprisingly positive response. Since there is a danger of overindulgence in anything you do, practice moderation at all times. Careful shopping can turn up some great bargains and find you looking like a million dollars. Your motivation will be to better yourself and improve your earning potential. Work on your own initiative to achieve this.

22. SATURDAY. Shining. The Sun cruises to Libra and turns the focus onto your associations, hopes, and dreams for the next month. You're charmed at this time for making connections. As part of the scene, you are sure to gain the recognition you crave. This is a happy, goal-oriented cycle, so focus on your dreams and watch them come true. Attach notes of what you want onto your fridge to remind you daily of what is coming. Being part of a group is important. But among your friends, strive to establish who you are. Without becoming demanding, you should let others know the kind of person you are. When you do, you can fit into the group dynamic without violating your integrity. Get an early night for your health's sake.

23. SUNDAY. Stimulating. Getting value for your money is important, but not at the expense of the other things you value. You may need to spend a little extra on a big-ticket item so that you have what you want. Setting up a lifestyle that makes you feel good is what counts. If you scrape by on budget clothes and other goods, you are really telling yourself you aren't worth the luxury items. Go ahead and spoil yourself, and you will start to feel like the star that you are. Consider buying a new car that is cost effective to run and kinder to the environment. If wishing to purchase a gift for your loved one, spare no expense. You want to show them that nothing is more important than their love.

24. MONDAY. Bright. Your ability to think outside the box could put you in the good graces of your employer. Many opportunities are opening up to you. Make sure you are clear about what you want so that you can make the most of these opportunities. Idealistic dreams are good but should not be carried too far. A secret yearning to travel overseas should be acted on. See that your passport is in order and then take a short trip first to enhance your confidence. After that, there'll be no holding you back. Some of you may be thinking about further training or studies to help you get the work you prefer. Some sacrifice for a couple of years will be well rewarded when you earn big in the future.

25. TUESDAY. Beneficial. The heavens are working in your favor. There shouldn't be too many distractions or interruptions to upset your concentration. Students may find your present subject quite absorbing. For a change, you don't have to force yourself to hit the books. It can come as a surprise that you are grabbing every spare minute to get into the subject. Be willing to help out a neighbor and find your good deed returned three-fold. Your neighborhood may be having problems with unemployment, especially among young people. Consider joining a community group that works toward organizing job-training workshops. You may discover a talent for teaching and find that you can learn as much from young people as they can from you.

26. WEDNESDAY. Fruitful. Exercise self-control, and you avoid any nasty scenes. Petty irritations are not worth holding onto. Reflect on what it is that is triggering this feeling and learn something about yourself. Archers who have moved to a new neighborhood could find that your new neighbors have trouble speaking your language. Instead of getting frustrated, show an interest in learning their language and make some valuable friends. Car trouble may force you to use public transportation. You will have a look at how many other people travel in comfort without a car. A conversation with a fellow raveler could absorb your interest well past the end of the journey. Leaving the car in the garage might become a regular habit.

27. THURSDAY. Rewarding. A task that you have been dreading might be performed without a hitch. Now you are wondering where the fear came from in the first place. The comfort of your home will be your preferred place to be, encouraging you to rearrange the furniture for more space and comfort. Talented Archers can decide to turn your journal into a biography or transform part of it into a novel. You are bound to have fun playing around with ideas and format. This work has every possibility of being published as well. A shopping trip can do wonders to quiet your mind. The chance of discovering a quaint curiosity shop can delight your love of history.

28. FRIDAY. Unpredictable. All one-on-one encounters and intimate relationships will be occasions for surprising events. Arguments between lovers can upset the status quo. It may be that one of you will do something quite unexpected that disrupts your connection and forces you to face a new aspect of your relationship. In a business or professional partnership, you may have to do some radical rethinking because of an unexpected factor. An inner restlessness can be a sign that there are certain elements in your life that you need to change. Look inside yourself to find what it is you really want. Then you can begin making the necessary adjustments. Take care in any potentially dangerous situations when accidents can occur.

29. SATURDAY. Exciting. A high-energy day is promised. The Full Moon joins electric Uranus in Aries, bringing lots of activity and fun with friends, lovers, and children. Nothing is likely to run smoothly, although the challenge of juggling several different projects at once can be stimulating and exhilarating. This is one of those times when you can fall down laughing and beg everybody to stop all the jokes because you can't laugh any more. Take the kids to a fun park and release the pent-up energy with some wild rides. The young ones will love you for it. And you will be happy to see them so enjoying themselves. Whether single or partnered, romance is definitely highlighted as well.

30. SUNDAY. Spirited. Your creative talents and skills are likely reaching a new level of expertise. Don't hold yourself back because of shyness or an unconscious need to be perfect. Begin doing whatever it is your heart desires. You may be interested in starting a new hobby or playing a team sport. You will be aware that the hardest part will be getting yourself started. An interest in the stock market might inspire a small speculation on some shares. Be happy to start small. You may be able to make a profit from your investmentt once you know what you are doing. An important social function will not only be entertaining but can put you in touch with some valuable new connections. An attractive stranger could be part of the mix.

OCTOBER

1. MONDAY. Serious. A hangover from the night before should prompt you to seriously rethink your current lifestyle. Are you trying to fit in with the in crowd but finding it unrewarding? Or are your worries about your health because of your current diet and lack of exercise? If you answered yes to either of these questions, you need to begin making a few changes. You are concerned about who you really are and how you feel about your life. A competitive colleague at work can keep you on your toes. You may realize that you need to pull your weight and make changes in some areas. Reorganize your paperwork and ensure that you are on top of all your tasks. It's important that you maintain with clarity a practical overview of what is important.

2. TUESDAY. Practical. Job prospects are likely to be on the rise. Apply yourself to improving your talents and skills so that you will be noticed in the workplace. A new employee may need help learning the ropes. If you can give them your time, you will have a friend for life. Although you may need to work hard, be sure to take a decent break during the day for your health's sake. Simply getting out of the office, even if only for a short walk or a few minutes of window shopping, can make an amazing difference. Being refreshed with a break will greatly improve your concentration during the afternoon. It would be wise to avoid too much caffeine as well. You don't need to add to any jitters you may feel now.

3. WEDNESDAY. Significant. Get up early, dress well, and be ready for anything the day brings. When you are well prepared, you won't miss out on any opportunities that come your way. Regardless of what your usual job entails, the chance of becoming involved in artistic matters in the workplace is possible. Design, layout work, or creating special advertisements may be included in your projects. If your work is promising, you may get promoted into another area that interests you more than your usual work. Singles may be attracted to an older person or someone whose social or financial position is higher than your own. They can be someone who can help you learn more about getting ahead in life. But don't let mercenary motives be your incentive.

4. THURSDAY. Demanding. An eye for detail will be an asset today. But it isn't necessary to tell everybody everything you know. Keep your information to yourself and act on it when you realize the time is right. This is an excellent period for work that entails precision of thought and planning. Because you are acutely sensitive to flaws in the arguments of others, you can be inclined to make a huge issue over small details. A friend or colleague whom you have admired for some time may fall off their pedestal today. Try not to let disillusionment worry you too much. In the next couple of days, you will gain more understanding. Buy some of the family's favorite takeout food on the way home, and you will be everyone's darling tonight.

5. FRIDAY. Excellent. The Moon and your ruling planet Jupiter interact in Gemini and your sector of partnerships, adding a gentle touch of kindness and generosity to all your one-on-one relations. This is a great time to expand a business partnership or delve into foreign trading. What you must watch for is an overly strong sense of optimism that can override your usual financial astuteness. As savvy Mercury swims into the deep waters of Scorpio and your sector of the unconscious, your intuitive faculties are strengthend. Listen carefully to your instincts before coming to any important decisions. This is a perfect time for doing research and for quiet reflection. Take a class in meditation and enjoy peace of mind.

6. SATURDAY. Auspicious. Saturn, the planet that is also called the teacher, slips into Scorpio and your twelfth house. It will stay for the next two and a half years, triggering a reappraisal of what you are doing and where you are going. You will deal with endings rather than new beginnings during this transit as you shed outdated attachments. You are likely to be more introspective at this time and isolate yourself from others in some manner, a process that tends to come naturally. Health issues, generally of a psychosomatic nature, may come to the fore. You could be attracted to more idealistic and alternate ways of living. Self-study fields such as psychoanalysis and philosophy will also be appealing.

7. SUNDAY. Enterprising. Mars, the planet of energy and action, moves into your own sign of Sagittarius, where it will stay for the next six weeks. This passage will give you the energy to be more assertive and act on your plans, even moving them forward. During the first half of the day, Mars interacts with nebulous Neptune and may cause doubts about your own potential. But if you use this time to reevaluate your ideas, you are likely to iron out any problems before they arise. Involvement in work with religious or spiritual groups is possible. Or you may decide to engage in charitable or social work helping those less fortunate than you. You might make plans to volunteer abroad and combine your ideals with further learning.

8. MONDAY. Distracting. Social activity can take you away from important work. Regardless of how tired or slightly unwell you may feel, the sooner you get your work done the more your energy will return. Your partner may ask you to accompany them on a business lunch. Business discussions turn into an afternoon party as everyone enjoys philosophizing about the economy, politics, and a thousand other topics. It is flattering when someone you hardly know begins flirting with you. But be aware that your partner is taking notice. A joint business account could be due for an audit. If any discrepancies are found, clear them up right away. A serious discussion between you and your partner is called for.

9. TUESDAY. Expansive. The opportunity to move forward with a personal project can reinvigorate your inspiration. Some Archers could be impulsive today and act on a hunch that turns out to be wishful thinking. Be willing to double-check your ideas before taking any precipitous action. Conversations around the watercooler at work can be especially inspiring. It may be because a new worker is in your midst. If you ask this person to have lunch with you, a lasting and valuable friendship could be formed. A new romance could be gaining momentum as you are invited to meet your lover's parents. Be cautious about talking too much. You would be wise to listen and learn.

10. WEDNESDAY. Productive. A legal matter that has been keeping you awake at night can suddenly look very positive. Don't get carried away just yet though. Be patient. Solving the problem should be a sign of better things to come. An opportunity to form a business partnership with an active and interesting person may become a source of social and intellectual interaction and not just an income. Some of you might decide to go into a business partnership with your lover. Be aware that you will need to define your separate roles clearly. This way you can avoid bringing your marital issues into the business. Single Archers can meet your future spouse through a friend now, so don't reject any invitations to go out this evening.

11. THURSDAY. Complicated. A number of celestial influences are impacting your solar chart. This event suggests that you might need to give yourself more time to develop clarity of purpose before trying to push through your plans. Consider taking on extra training to enhance your knowledge of and expertise in the new technology. Some colleagues may be spreading gossip behind your back. You need to face the situation at once before it gets really serious. It will probably be necessary to confront them no matter how unpleasant it will be. Aggressive salespeople will also rile you today. Your interest in ideas may get you caught up in long conversations that make you terribly late to an important appointment. News from overseas can cheer you up later tonight.

12. FRIDAY. Delightful. The Moon dances in harmony with loving Venus, making this a very loving day for Archers. An easygoing attitude can hold sway. Even your employer might be in a good mood for a change. You can enjoy a tremendous surge of optimism and enthusiasm for what your future holds. If you are currently unsure about your long-term direction, your positive outlook will make any uncertainty much less of a problem. An achievement may bring you unexpected honors and open doors into an area of employment that truly interests you. If you are purchasing a special gift for a loved one, jewelry should be at the top of your list. The simple saying that diamonds are forever is very true, ensuring your gift has long-lasting value.

13. SATURDAY. Useful. Pay attention to the small details and forget about long-term plans for now. You cannot know just what the future will bring. The more you apply yourself to immediate concerns, the calmer you will feel. Your reputation can precede you as you look forward to a social event. Don't be surprised if you find people lining up to meet you. This supportive recognition from others will encourage you to maintain your moral integrity and humble approach. If you are receiving an award for your achievements at a public event, ensure that you are properly attired and well prepared. It will be for your own benefit as well as for those you are representing. A family dinner can get boisterous unless you intervene.

14. SUNDAY. Fair. Expect a routine day. The sociable and solitary sides of your personality need to coexist in balance. Don't be shy about canceling a social engagement that doesn't really appeal to you. A reclusive mood is suggested for Archers, so you are well within your rights to close the door and please yourself. Partnered Sagittarius might want to hide from your partner's nagging. A better outcome will be achieved by being honest and letting them know you're not happy with their behavior. Don't worry about satisfying others' requests because if you can't do it without rancor, it would be better not to do it at all. A new romantic attachment could be a great reason to get away from it all and enjoy your intimacy in loving privacy.

15. MONDAY. Cooperative. Working with groups of people is highlighted. The New Moon in Libra is pointing your focus toward networking and establishing connections through friends or organizations. This is an excellent time to connect with like-minded people in a concerted effort to improve humanitarian or environmental projects locally or across the globe. If you have stepchildren, this is a perfect time to invent some new activities that you can share with them. Sharing will help break down any barriers that may be making your relationship more difficult than it should be. Whatever you do though, don't rush them. Let them come to you in their own time, and you will build a solid friendship. A community event can be a lot of fun now.

16. TUESDAY. Useful. Communication is highlighted today. Some of you may spend the day on the phone discussing some intriguing gossip with friends or neighbors. But avoid spreading malicious rumors no matter how much you might desire to repeat what you have heard. Chances are they are not true, and you would be doing the people involved a disservice to repeat unfounded gossip. Enjoy your simple routines without fuss. The opportunity to have an honest discussion with your lover will allow you to share those thoughts and feelings that may be confusing. Listen carefully to what your loved one says. They will likely want you to clarify some important issues that have risen between you. It is a great day to finish off artistic projects and listen to music.

17. WEDNESDAY. Favorable. Keep your business and personal plans private today. With so many different views and ideas circulating, talking with others might only leave you confused. It would be more beneficial to suit yourself and let others go their own way. Keep your mind on your dreams and your ears open, and you will learn something that will give you an opportunity to reach for the stars. Don't lose your concentration at work. It appears that a particularly ambitious colleague has their eye on your job. Stay under the radar and work in privacy to avoid interruptions. A desire to delve deeper into spiritual philosophies might give you the impetus to begin studying an esoteric subject.

18. THURSDAY. Hectic. It may seem as if everyone is out for a piece of you, making it very difficult to concentrate on any one task. Don't let the pressure upset your equilibrium though. Stay level-headed and eventempered, and you won't put yourself on display losing your cool. All areas of your life may need attention now. Trying to cover your bases in relationships, family, and career simultaneously can test your mettle. Multitasking is a skill that can be learned. If you know someone who is very good at it, have a talk with them. Where there is a will, there is always a way. A satisfactory end to the day will see family Archers at home relaxing, while single Archers are likely to be out on the town.

19. FRIDAY. Good. Working in seclusion could be anathema to you. If, however, you want to get some valuable work done, you might have to do it on your own. Promise yourself that you will get out after you've finished. Plan to do something exciting, and your seclusion won't seem so onerous. In fact, Sagittarius needs to do something special for yourself today. Even if it is just enjoying a massage, it will improve your sense of well-being. Go shopping for new clothes that are made from materials that feel great against your skin. You can delight in the pleasure of being so well dressed. Clean up around your home too and reorganize the furnishings to afford more comfort as well as space. You will be glad you did when friends drops over for drinks.

20. SATURDAY. Intense. Today's energies would make for a very fruitful session with your therapist. Deep feelings and resentments can bubble up to the surface and turn a quite normal exchange into something far more unpleasant within your own mind. Determine to focus your thoughts on what is real and practical. Money worries or other causes of personal insecurity could be the root cause of unrest. Address these problems because trying to push them beneath the surface will only make matters worse. Avoid gambling or any other speculation at the moment. The stock market is always a risk and can let you down right now. Possessiveness and jealousy can surface in a love relationship, sparking a battle if you are not careful.

21. SUNDAY. Eventful. Harmonious vibes infuse the atmosphere and will be a valuable asset for Archers wanting to make a good impression. Sagittarius needs beautiful surroundings. A strong desire to refurbish or otherwise improve your home will encourage you to find just the right objects to enhance your comfort. A steady flow of emotions makes it an excellent time to announce your feelings to another. Be adventurous in choosing some different and possibly exotic attire, and you are bound to attract their attention. It is a perfect time for lovers to get away together and enjoy a picnic surrounded by nature. Sagittarius salespeople may clinch the deal of the century and go home with a fat commission. Celebrate with a bit of indulgence for a lovely finish to the day.

22. MONDAY. Important. Don't miss the chance to make somebody's day special. A small thoughtful gesture, a kindly act, or a charitable venture can put you in touch with the side of you that is generous and caring. You can also look for a good turn that may be heading in your direction. Ironically, your emotions can feel more raw now than they have for a long time. Some kind of deeper meaning is stirring within you, and you need to listen to what it is saying. This might be a time when you have to stand up for yourself and stick to your guns regardless of criticism from loved ones and others. Personal values are not worth giving up for anyone. In the long run, your ethics will gain you the respect you deserve.

23. TUESDAY. Troublesome. Receptivity to the ideas of others could be a stumbling block when it comes to implementing your own plans. Try to get away from crowds so that you can do your own thing in peace. The Sun moves into Scorpio and your twelfth house of the unconscious today. This four-week period is an excellent time to look back over the past year to see how well you have managed the art of living. But you do need to watch any inclination to fall into self-pity or resentment. Be honest with yourself and own up to your part in how situations and events have played out for you. An important meeting may be deferred, giving you time to forward your case and prioritize the issues for the best results.

24. WEDNESDAY. Creative. Last night's dreams are likely to be a strong portent of what is brewing in your life at the moment. Take the time to mull over your thoughts and impressions. Perhaps you will even write them down so that you can refer back to them at a later date. Listen to your ideas because you could be ahead of your time with some of your creative thoughts. Be cautious if you are involved in a property deal. There may be something important that has been overlooked. It is also possible that you may need to go over the small print and be sure that everything is in order. It is a wonderful time to beautify your home, as your artistic side is bound to achieve stunning results.

25. THURSDAY. Happy. Sagittarius is renowned for your adventurous spirit. Today you are likely to be dreaming about traveling to far-flung corners of the earth. These dreams can interfere with your sense of responsibility or make your routine that much harder to endure. You might consider organizing the weekend to be away with your lover. Setting off to a entirely different landscape can bring delight in a change of scenery and a chance to renew your spirit. Doing whatever you please will make all the difference to your enjoyment of daily life. Some of you might decide to save up for a recreational vehicle and take your home and family with you in your travels. Try your hand at travel journalism and perhaps earn some extra money.

26. FRIDAY. Rewarding. Keep on your toes today. If you find that you are tired or under the weather, take short breaks to exercise. It would be wise to also refrain from overeating. Several small meals rather than two or more large servings will help keep your energy levels on an even keel. An ailing elderly relative may have to go into a nursing home, and you will want to ensure that she has the best accommodations. Try to share this responsibility with all your family members. It would not be fair if others did too little while you take on most of the burden. If you notice that you always want to do tasks yourself, consider whether you may have issues centering around control. This attribute usually stems from being a perfectionist. Remember that life and people are not perfect.

27. SATURDAY. Enjoyable. Take the day off for fun. Archer parents should try to get out of having to escort your children all over town to their parties and sports. You do need time for yourself now. Getting together a car pool of parents could be the perfect answer to the problem. Competitive sports could be a lot of fun, with some of you reaching your personal best. Think of it as a reward for all the conscientious training you have been doing. If your home is large enough, you might decide to rent out a room and earn some extra money. Put plenty of thought into it first. You want to ensure that sharing a space doesn't impose on your own lifestyle. Enjoying the dance circuit tonight can introduce you to some new and fun friends.

28. SUNDAY. Challenging. This is a time for new beginnings in love, so be open to a romantic renaissance. A picnic by the shore or in the park will start matters on the right path. Be willing to make the effort and it will pay off. Your artistic urges are powerful, and if you aren't dabbling in painting or music, you might be considering a career in writing. Your skills for organizing and expressing your ideas and feelings can stand you in good stead at this time. It might be a good idea to talk with someone you may know in the publishing business. Venus slips into its own sign of Libra and highlights your solar house of wishes, giving you a nudge to start promoting your own talents. Or you might consider working in a more creative and exciting field than your current work.

29. MONDAY. Disconcerting. Your bad habits are likely to come to your attention and upset your equilibrium. Your health and your lifestyle could be adversely affected unless you make some changes. Smokers should consider throwing out your cigarette and declare that it is your last pack. Dieters also could think about swearing off junk food for good. With the Full Moon in Taurus shining the spotlight in your sector of health and work, you are bound to notice even the little flaws. Use this surge of emotional energy to make positive changes in your life. Avoid blaming others for your own state of discontent if that is how you are feeling. Make an attempt to improve your work conditions if they are annoying you. A talk with the boss may be in order.

30. TUESDAY. Fair. Whether you commute to an office or telecommute from home, it's important to start the day off right. Try taking a brisk walk or even a run before breakfast. If you have been eating too much junk food, this is the day to detoxify your body. Eat only fresh, healthy foods and drink plenty of water. You might even consider a day of fasting if your health will allow it. You may appreciate any opportunity to simply serve and work where you are needed. Many of you have had too much time on your hands to think lately. Chores that involve very little skill will be therapeutic. You might even have a chat with yourself about your problems while doing household chores.

31. WEDNESDAY. Demanding. What appears to be true may not be so. Be diligent and thorough in all you do, and you won't be fooled by anyone. You may be looking for a change of jobs. If so, you shouldn't ignore opportunities around your current workplace. Your willingness to take on extra tasks is sure to impress your boss. There might even be a promotion down the road. You might ask for some overtime. Any boost in your pay will make a difference in what you can do with your free time. This in turn can lessen your general dissatisfaction with your routine life. A higher-up might make advances toward you at work. Although this may be very flattering, accepting such behavior is certainly not in your best interests.

NOVEMBER

1. THURSDAY. Surprising. The next two days are fine for dealing with important issues, even if you don't have the time or the inclination to proceed. But thanks to lordly Jupiter and delightful Venus, today has a fortunate undertone. Your partner can shock you with news of a career change. Whether you agree or disagree with their decision, it is best that you concentrate on giving them support rather than thinking about what you want. You may receive an unexpected gift from an admirer. Although you could be thrown off guard, it is quite acceptable to allow your pleasure to show. It is important for you to express who you are and not try to be what you perceive another wants. You don't want to let resentment rule you.

2. FRIDAY. Revealing. You are primed for action, but moderation is the key. Take extra care to avoid impulsive behavior, as it can lead to disaster. A professional partner or an employer may have difficulty curbing their behavior, becoming manipulative and unpleasant. As much as it would be understandable for you to react angrily, you are much better off removing yourself from the situation. It might be wise to report their actions to a colleague or a higher authority. Do not let loyalty get in the way of your own well-being and doing what is morally right. An artistic project could receive public recognition. Even if it is only displayed in your employee or student magazine, it is most probably a sign of things to come.

3. SATURDAY. Challenging. Nervous energy reigns as the Moon and Pluto clash. Make every effort to stay on an even keel. If possible, take yourself away from any situations that seem problematic. Those Archers who work independently may still find plenty of stress to deal with in your environment. Certain events can bring relationship matters to critical mass. Unless you have Scorpio Rising, most Archers will find today's events strenuous and somewhat distasteful. Intensity is not your favorite characteristic, especially when it is exhibited by an emotional partner. Could it be that your actions, or perhaps lack thereof, have brought on this firestorm? A desire for a new adventure may see some Archers out on the town tonight. Just be sensible and you won't have any trouble.

4. SUNDAY. Sensitive. A very late night or overindulgence could keep you in bed for the morning. Once you realize you have commitments, you are likely to snap out of your lethargic state. Some of you may still want to indulge in sweet intimacy with your lover and will be reluctant to end your shared communion. Nevertheless, family matters are calling. And you may feel torn and frustrated at having to be satisfied with dealing with issues that could dull the enjoyment of your day. Inner irritability toward others can make major decisions difficult to resolve. Don't jump headlong into decisions just to get an unpleasantness over with. Take time to sort out your inner desires and needs as opposed to your wants. It might be difficult to talk honestly with some of the main players in your life. Write down your thoughts for later reflection, adjustment, and expression.

5. MONDAY. Helpful. A strong urge to get out and travel could inspire you to embark on a trip away from your usual stamping grounds. Be open to new opportunities in your travels because you are likely to encounter a profitable and interesting experience along the way. House or property hunters can find a property with potential and begin negotiations for the right price. Since it is a good time to enter into agreements or negotiations, you will be happy with the outcome. Your mind is quite clear now. But you need to take care that it doesn't run away with an idea before you have thought through all the angles and really know what you want. Otherwise, look forward to a pleasant and profitable day.

6. TUESDAY. Pleasing. Most Archers will feel upbeat as you meet the challenges of the day. You prefer to look on the bright side of life now. An inner restlessness suggests that it is a good time to change your routine. Introducing some new activities can go a long way toward raising your level of excitement. Take a look at some of the social groups or clubs that you can join. Not only will you meet new people and perhaps even a new love, but you can learn new skills and have fun while you're at it. Those of you living far from your place of birth may find you are being profoundly changed by your new surroundings. This is a propitious time to start studying. You might even be contemplating learning a new language to expand your horizons.

7. WEDNESDAY. Varied. This may very well be one of those days when nothing you do seems to go right. Don't let unconscious resentments trip you up while the Moon battles Pluto and Neptune. You may find yourself saying things you really mean but didn't want to express. Biting your tongue will be necessary to avoid trouble. The Moon is in your ninth house, which rules writing and publishing. Have you ever considered writing your memoirs? You don't have to be famous to write and publish the highlights, and low lights, of your life. Consider taking up your pen for those who come after you.. Diaries and journals are often the most treasured possessions of children and grandchildren. You will enjoy leaving a legacy for them.

8. THURSDAY. Intriguing. A fascination with unusual people can be positive or negative, depending on the people. Be aware of your attraction to others, but don't be foolish with your trust. Your lesson may be to recognize that you find these people alluring because you are projecting your own artistic and spiritual potential onto them. Be wary of being manipulated. A business venture that could be in the pipeline means it's up to you now to take control. Allow yourself enough time to do the job properly. You don't want to find yourself rushing around looking for any missing facts. You are likely to be in the limelight today. Even if you aren't that aware of your popularity, others know your talents and are watching you. An old friend may resurface just at the right time for you to gain the benefit of their advice.

9. FRIDAY. Pressured. Practicing self-control might be very hard, as those around you keep pushing your buttons. Think about what those buttons really are. Apparently there are vulnerable spots in your character you aren't aware of. Instead of blaming others, use this experience to learn more about yourself. Superiors could be watching your moves, which will put you under pressure. Keep in mind that the less others can ruffle your feathers, the better you will be able to concentrate and stay cool. Be aware of any tendency to slough off suggestions from others or let important matters slide. An attitude like this will only work for a short time. It is imperative that you focus your thoughts and finish your work. A major business deal is likely to fall through, so ensure that you have a backup plan.

10. SATURDAY. Disquieting. Trying to balance your emotions with your intellect might not be easy. This is especially true if circumstances and people keep changing the game plan on you. If you count on the unexpected upsetting your plans, you will be well prepared for the day. Surround yourself with those who share ideals so that you can avoid unnecessary squabbles. It is not your place to change another's perception, nor is it theirs to change yours. If you make that your primary philosophy, you will be on the right path. Dedication to a worthy cause can keep you busy all day. You have good reason to be skeptical of demands for loans. Money matters are not likely to go smoothly now. If you are in a financial bind, look after yourself first.

11. SUNDAY. Amicable. Distant relatives can arrive in town and need a place to stay. Even if you feel that your space will be a little cramped, you are sure to enjoy their company a lot more than you expected. Social functions and group fund-raisers are all likely events on today's calendar. Mixing and mingling with many different people is one of your stronger points. But a quiet mood might be a good reason to make your apologies and go home early. A new romance can keep you out longer than you expected. It seems you won't mind at all since you're enjoying a lively conversation. If you haven't been home since yesterday, you should let others know where you are. They could be worried about your well-being and need to know that you're safe and sound.

12. MONDAY. Sensitive. You could feel rather haunted today, literally or figuratively. Dreams and visions may be disturbing you. Take the time to analyze them. You will find they are a great tool for personal and spiritual growth. Avoid negative places. Rather, surround yourself with objects and people that comfort you. You need a time to hide once in a while and be in your own safe, private place. The practice of meditation will give you peace of mind, aid relaxation, and provide an escape from your fears. A spiritual workshop might take your fancy, allowing you to heighten your awareness. You can enjoy rest and relaxation while following a healthy regimen.

13. TUESDAY. Renewing. The New Moon in Scorpio and solar twelfth house of solitude and secrets signals a period of review, letting go, and recharging your spiritual and physical batteries. The focus now is on fulfillment through service, empathy, and awareness of others' needs. But, in a social sense, it can also be a time of withdrawal and some sort of retreat. Soul-searching can bring up some issues you haven't been conscious of and can now do something about. In a manifest sense, it is a good time for renewing your environment. Throw out those things that are no longer of any use or that hold unpleasant memories of the past. You need to let go of these and prepare now for your future.

14. WEDNESDAY. Spontaneous. It is a good day for showcasing your leadership skills. Don't be afraid to take over the reins when needed. After the last couple of days, you may feel like a butterfly emerging from its cocoon as the Moon enters Sagittarius and your first house of personality. Since tonight can be an interesting time to share with friends, consider going out to dinner and enjoying lively conversations and plenty of laughs. Your relationships can be benefited by this transit, especially if you are willing to talk about your vulnerabilities. The next two days are high energy ones for you. Determine to make the most of this upbeat time period. Those of you who feel more moody should spend time helping others. Sharing joys and sorrows can be the best cure for the blues.

15. THURSDAY. Confusing. Trickster Mercury, the planet that rules your mind, is moving retrograde in Scorpio and your house of the unconscious, bringing a hard aspect to dreamy Neptune. Right now it would not be wise to trust your thinking. A tendency to don your rose-colored glasses might give you the wrong messages in any situation. If you are trying to sort out an important matter, you would be wise to avoid haste. You should wait to research and revise the situation until you are sure about the facts. On another note, you are likely to be charming and empathic, allowing you to enjoy increased popularity among your peers. Take care with your appearance and you will outshine everyone.

16. FRIDAY. Successful. Business matters progress as you pursue excellence today. Keep your cards close to your chest, and don't discuss details with people who don't count. Trust your abilities. You have been putting in the hours these last couple of days, and now it can pay off. Break away for lunch with someone special. You will appreciate the benefits of taking your mind off work by delighting your senses with good food and lively company. Archer parents might have to leave work early to attend to a child. If you worry too much about their care while you are absent, it might be worth considering changing the work environment. Starting your own business or possibly working from home may be the answer.

17. SATURDAY. Pleasant. Getting to know people and mixing with crowds from all walks of life will suit you well today. Check your local newspaper to investigate some activities that are offered. You don't want to miss anything interesting. A love of luxury and pampering yourself could lighten your purse. It might be wise to leave your credit cards behind if you are shopping and want to keep your costs down. Indulgence in food and drink might be something else to avoid if you are dieting or need to watch your health. Try not to cave in to old habits. The ability to change your behavior is not an impossibiity. You have the capacity to develop a latent talent of your own.

18. SUNDAY. Difficult. Mars, the planet of action and energy, moves in Capricorn and your sector of money and values until December 27. This transit often indicates wasteful spending. And you are likely to turn your actions toward holding onto possessions that you view as a projection of your self-worth. You must be careful not to make unwise and impulsive purchases. You appear to feel that you must have material goods to gratify your ego and not because you actually need them. Disputes over the ownership or use of property leading to estrangement from others is another possibility. On a positive level, you are willing to work to establish and defend your values regardless of the opinions of others.

19. MONDAY. Cautious. This is a day for communication. You can be on the phone calling others, or the phone never stops ringing. It seems that you can't stop talking with your friends. A major purchase might be worth looking for on Internet auctions. If you find just what you are looking for, carefully check out the payment method. It is wise to be cautious about making payments online. An overseas purchase might have added costs and be more expensive than you expected. Choose your confidantes carefully today. What you say could be used against you. Make sure only your tried and true friends are privy to your secrets. If you are shopping for a secondhand car, be skeptical about the salesperson. Get your own mechanic to check out the vehicle check before purchasing it.

20. TUESDAY. Taxng. A strong urge to stay under the radar should be heeded. No matter how busy you are, pace yourself to stay on top of your tasks. If you race ahead, you will make mistakes that you would rather you hadn't. Ensure you have several snacks of protein-rich foods throughout the day to maintain your energy levels. Otherwise, you could feel groggy and listless. Leave work early if you can so that you can rest. Expect mix-ups and misunderstandings in communication. It is important to avoid making silly mistakes. Possibly you are having problems with a roommate and don't feel like going to your home. Think about staying over at a friend's place and enjoy the break with someone with whom you can talk.

21. WEDNESDAY. Satisfactory. Take a few deep breaths and count to ten as many times as you need to today. Yesterday's problems may be improving, but you probably feel a bit frazzled from all the stress. One of your parents may be unwell or in the hospital. Try not to let your concerns interfere with finishing your work. Your first priority is to make sure they are comfortable and have everything they need. You might find that once you see them, you will be able to relax again. At the same time, don't let a parent press you into doing more than you need to and can humanly do. Your home is your haven while the Moon is in Pisces. Skip the nightly news or dull television programs. Curl up on the couch and keep the world at bay with a good book instead.

22. THURSDAY. Auspicious. Late yesterday afternoon the Sun entered your sign of Sagittarius. Happy birthday to all of you Archers! Now the celebration of your personal year can start. Under the Sun's transit, you are able to recharge yourself for the remainder of the year. Personal matters, rather than the world at large, will be your focus now. Venus, the goddess of love, joins reflective Mercury and serious Saturn in Scorpio and your sector of solitude.

This phase suggests that this is a period for quiet introspection balanced with your gregarious lifestyle. An attraction to secrets and gossip could be something to watch out for and avoid. At the very least you will enjoy intimate social gatherings and long for romance behind closed doors.

23. FRIDAY. Fair. Stressful activities that you have been dreading could be called off or, conversely, could go easily and smoothly. Either way, you will be able to breathe a sigh of relief later in the day. Stay under the radar as much as possible. A group of planets in your sector of solitude might be too much to face and could test your nerves. A new romance could be proceeding smoothly, but that doesn't mean you can't suffer from lovesickness. With thoughts of love and desire overriding all other practical matters, you might not be able to accomplish anything. Boredom can be your worst enemy as well. Try to complete tasks before you start something new, and you will gain an inspiring sense of achievement.

24. SATURDAY. Constructive. Focus on personal issues rather than spread yourself too thinly. Friends are valuable but will understand if you decline to join them. Let them know something that is important to you has surfaced to interfere with your plans. This doesn't mean you have to become depressed and avoid all social contact. One-on-one contact will be the most beneficial. If you are going out with a lover or spouse, be honest with them. It is important that blocked emotions don't manipulate your behavior. If you are picking up mixed messages from your partner, chances are they need to get something off their chest also. Let your compassionate side take over and enjoy being able to help.

25. SUNDAY. Gratifying. Enjoy a slow start to your day. Sleep in, if that turns you on, or simply pamper yourself by doing exactly what pleases you. There may be some conflict between your wanting to please the important people in your life and pleasing yourself. Take a deep breath and please yourself. If others care for you and understand your needs, they will still love you. Be determined. A close friend can give you some good advice about how to resolve any conflict. Once you decide to venture out into the community, your kind nature can lead you to give help and support where it is needed in a way that pleases you too. If you prefer to stay at home and get your chores or repairs done, you may discover a lost item.

26. MONDAY. Assertive. This is a good time to work as a leader with groups of people. While you have a consciousness of aims and objectives, you are also sensitive to the needs and feelings of others.

A strong desire to improve your income might spur you on to work harder now. But you must watch your own physical well-being. Don't push your body to a point where it will start complaining by giving you aches and pains. Get your affairs in order. You need to get a clearer picture of your financial situation and an idea of where you are heading. Keeping a journal would be helpful to you. Just the action of sitting down and organizing documents and accounts can bring the clarity of mind you are seeking.

27. TUESDAY. Intense. With energetic Mars joining hands with powerful Pluto in the heavens today, most people will be a lot more pushy and ambitious than usual, including you. Use this energy to make progress toward your goals. But in your desire to succeed, be wary of standing on the toes of others. The best course of action would be to have a plan that takes all situations into account before you start. A coworker might become abusive, and you will need to protect yourself. But don't let their anger ignite yours. Step back and instead seek a way to avoid confrontations. A powerful sexual attraction to a colleague is also possible. If you wish it, an encounter with them might lead to a romantic evening.

28. WEDNESDAY. Disruptive. Strong ego energies can upset well-laid plans and won't be conducive to cooperation or compromise. With the Full Moon in your opposite sign of Gemini, your need for independence could be at crosspurposes with your need for love and closeness. Emotional energy is high, and attempts to discuss thoughts and feelings may simply stir up more emotions. Unless you feel clear enough to listen to another without reverting back to your own wants and desires, leave the scene. You need time off until later in the day when everyone has had time to calm down and think. With passion running hot, however, be careful that you don't become involved with an acquaintance on a whim and live to regret it.

29. THURSDAY. Positive. Archers are likely to be center stage today. An opportunity to take a public position might boost your earnings and give you job satisfaction. A legal matter can be resolved successfully and give you cause to celebrate. When it comes to spending, strong vibes indicate indulgence and overspending on unnecessary items that will upset your bank balance. The best way to avoid such spending would be to leave the plastic at home. Be wise, and only take with you what you are willing to spend. A row with your partner can be smoothed over now. To celebrate, enjoy an evening at your favorite restaurant to renew those loving feelings. Don't hold back on the apologies if you owe one.

30. FRIDAY. Dramatic. Complicated influences prevail. Hidden agendas are likely to cause unexpected problems and upsets to your plans. The more people with whom you are involved, the worse the situation can get. Keep things as simple as possible for the best results. A secret business merger could be be flawed or even illegal. Check all the fine print before you get involved. An unexpected bill can blow your budget, putting your future plans up in the air. Arguing with your partner over excess spending will also be fruitless. Accept that the disagreement has happened and move on. Now, decide that you both need to have a firm agreement in place regarding your spending. Plan a goal as an incentive to make saving easier.

DECEMBER

1. SATURDAY. Energetic. The celestial influences suggest an interesting day, offering you a challenge to accomplish all the activities on your agenda. Don't assume your spouse or partner understands how you feel. There may be issues that you are sidestepping in a push to get what you want done. Be fair and take the time to be honest and open about your desires. Be assured that you will be happy with the results, and so will your loved one. Renovating or beautifying your home could become a nightmare if you and your partner both have different ideas. Talk it over calmly and rationally. There is bound to be a compromise to which you both can agree. At the end of the day, whatever you are trying to do, compromise will get it done faster.

2. SUNDAY. Fortunate. A sense that there is more to life than the material world might give you a push to seek a psychic counselor or begin studying one of the esoteric arts. Trust your instincts because your sensitivity in this realm is high at the moment. Being well prepared for a large family gathering will assure a pleasurable time for everyone. The saying that you can choose your friends but not your relatives may well apply to relationships among your family members. Since you can't exclude some and invite others, it will be up to you to ensure that key players are comfortable with one another. Some of you may be preparing for surgery or a series of tests. The time is auspicious now for a positive outcome.

3. MONDAY. Rewarding. After the last few days, today will be a breeze. Fun and excitement can follow you into the most mundane places. You are likely to find that your attitude toward many of your usual activities and associations will begin changing. Perusal of your accounts or an unexpected tax refund might surprise you. It will be a relief to know that you now have the funds to realize one of your dreams. Restless Archers may want to start checking out fares and accommodations involving distant destinations. More stay-at-home Archers might sign up for a study program. Love is also part of the day's plans. A recent lover's quarrel might now be the prelude to a more exciting and deeper form of intimacy. Your horizons are expanding, so let go and enjoy.

4. TUESDAY. Encouraging. Be careful if you are planning a child's education. You could be inclined to project your unfulfilled dreams onto a young one. It is in the best interests of both of you that you allow them to follow theirs. Concentrate on your own goals and don't let peer pressure keep you from realizing your ambitions. You don't need others to tell you how to enjoy your life. You're quite capable of doing that on your own. If you find that your ideals clash with those of your in-laws, you may have to have an honest discussion with them so that you aren't sending mixed messages. This applies to couples as well. Don't agree with your partner for the sake of peace when secretly you are disheartened with their choices. To be free, you must be willing to say no occasionally.

5. WEDNESDAY. Beneficial. Your mind could be a thousand miles away today, making it very hard to stay focused on your job. If you find that you are not feeling well, take the day off regardless of how this might interfere with your finances. In the long run, looking after your well-being is more important than money and possibly creating a problem on the job. Since your sensitive feelings are heightened now, use these emotions to listen to others. You have a compassionate side to your approach and are able to help those around you feel better about themselves. A job offer to work in a human relations department might not be what you had planned. It could prove to be a stimulating change.

6. THURSDAY. Lucky. The nurturing Moon makes many favorable aspects in the heavens, ensuring cooperation and good vibes with others. Some Archers might decide to cut back on one of your hobbies or interests in order to save money for this year's festive season. A desire to buy expensive or many gifts to please your loved ones seems to be more important than your own pleasure right now. Luck and good fortune are also looking your way. A lottery ticket might be a worthwhile investment. Don't be surprised if your boss singles you out for a pay raise or decides to select you to travel to another venue for a conference. Job seekers could find the right job and suddenly feel flush for the holidays.

7. FRIDAY. Bumpy. Make a slow start and ensure you have everything you need to do a proper job. Just looking after the kids could take up much of your time, as they all need different things for their day's activities. If you have to take the day off to care for a child who is unwell, don't let an insensitive boss persuade you differently. Your spouse or lover may have to go off on a business trip and leave you feeling saddled with all the responsibilities. Take it in your stride. You know they would do the same for you. If you are experiencing domestic problems and your partner is threatening to leave, then perhaps you should call their bluff. If they storm off, don't panic. They probably just need to blow off steam.

8. SATURDAY. Favorable. Dissatisfaction can be caused by expectations that are too high. You may be pushing yourself too hard, which in turn is sapping your enjoyment in life. Be happy that you have the time to socialize with your friends and family for a change. Your partner may have an invitation to a large social affair and you could be invited too. The event will give you a chance to show yourself at your best and meet some valuable new contacts. It will be enjoyable for you both to share the fun and laughter and go home with something to talk about. A new business may start to make a profit and give you a boost of confidence. Don't let this give you a false sense of plenty though. You could be tempted to celebrate in such style that the profit doesn't last long.

9. SUNDAY. Varied. A generous overtone to this day suggests that if you are not doing the giving, then you are doing the receiving. Try to return any good deeds you receive, if you are helping a friend; be assured that your good deed will be returned to you in kind when you need it. Pleasing your partner may seem harder than usual. You really need to speak up if they are pestering you to go out and you don't feel up to it. Let them know that you love them and will be with them in spirit. But make it clear that you need some space alone. Try to make yourself comfortable at home. This is a perfect day for lying on the couch and watching movies or reading a good book.

10. MONDAY. Introspective. In some ways, life is easier, more fun, and more exciting than it has been recently. But paradoxically, you may also be feeling an inner angst. There are influences around you that are encouraging you to learn from the difficulties you have faced in the past. Don't see these as failures, but rather value the battle scars that prove you can triumph over adversity. Unconscious patterns of behavior can surface. If you enjoy lavish entertaining, planning a grand dinner for friends could take your mind off yourself. But be aware that it could add to any financial woes. A new love affair may cause difficulties because you are trying to impress your lover. This can only produce a relationship that could be too unrewarding. Think carefully before you carry on.

11. TUESDAY. Frustrating. Your thinking is likely to speed up and keep you on the ball as you jump from one thing to another. This can create a certain amount of restlessness. And you could find it hard to focus on one thing at a time to get your work done. Try to factor in breaks so that your mind can have a rest and will continue to feel refreshed. Mercury, the messenger god, moves into Sagittarius today, bringing an ability to multitask and accomplish more than usual. At the same time, your mind can get stuck on one problem. Instead of assessing the problem and settling on a resolution, you are likely to be obsessing over it. Going over the same old details from all different angles will stress you out. Get away for a long break.

12. WEDNESDAY. Active. A challenging day ahead could be inspiring. Lots of new opportunities seem to be coming the Archer's way. Stay on your toes, as there may be some strife among those surrounding you. Mixed messages can put you on the wrong path if you don't pay attention to what is going on around you. Be prepared to finish off loose ends as part of the process of initiating new things. An unexpected happening early in the day could throw your plans out the window and dictate a new approach to whatever you have in front of you. Do what you love and love what you do for the best success. If you are finding it hard to get enjoyment from your present employment, then it is time to look elsewhere.

13. THURSDAY. Rejuvenating. This morning's New Moon signals the start of a new lunar year for Sagittarius. It's time to reinvent yourself to keep pace with your dreams and goals. Find the time to reassess your present situation in light of personal satisfaction and whether it will take you to your goals. If you don't find any discrepancies, you will be in great shape. But if you should find some stumbling blocks, now is the time to begin new plans and change your method of attack. The urge to travel may be foremost in your mind. It may be hard for you to concentrate on issues and tasks close to home. Perhaps taking a short trip will satisfy your itchy feet. If you are unsure about where you want to go, talk it over with some friends. You might even invite someone to go with you.

14. FRIDAY. Cautious. A positive approach to your daily grind will put you in front of others. Don't cut corners on any job, whether it is cleaning out files or supervising many people. The care you take will have a positive effect on your self-esteem and boost your image in your own eyes. Taking risks doesn't mean a negative outcome. You can win the game as long as you know the odds. Be wary, however, of believing everything you hear. If finances are involved, remember that fraudulent offers abound, and someone could be trying to pull the wool over your eyes. You often have a trusting nature that could lead you astray until it is to late. To defend yourself, listen to your razor-sharp intuition. It will tell you whether to carry on or go forward.

15. SATURDAY. Successful. A plethora of planets in your sectors of solitude, self, and values suggests this is a prime time for soul-searching. Begin from a positive stance. You will be content to enjoy life by treating yourself as well as you treat others. Indications are that you may need to focus on your budget to get your social and professional life back on track. Don't worry about long-term plans. Determine to get your daily financial affairs in order. You can then watch the rest grow from there. Be prepared to take baby steps in any endeavor, and you will succeed. There may be those around you who are trying to push you into decisions or actions that you don't feel comfortable with. You would be wise to say no.

16. SUNDAY. Starred. Venus, the planet of love, is now in your sign of Sagittarius, adding beauty and charisma to Archers everywhere. Your attractiveness to others can add to your friendships and give you the edge over your competition. Your ability to compromise is strong now. You will easily make peace with those whom you may have been out of sorts with. Smoothing over problems and making life so much more pleasant for everybody will be the result. A love of the high life can kick off the festive season on a joyful note. Don't be surprised when you become a popular and sought-after partner on the dance circuit. Communication is also highlighted. The time is ripe to get on top of your paperwork and send out your holiday greetings.

17. MONDAY. Difficult. Be careful that while chatting with friends or colleagues not to let an important secret slip out. Someone close to you might be counting on you to keep their confidence. Betraying their trust will cause them to lose faith in your integrity. E-mails and phone calls can keep you busy all day. Expect interruptions, and you will be able to stay on top of your workload. Important arrangements for the holidays might involve going behind someone's back so that plans work out best for everyone. The happy result will overcome any sense of guilt you may, and will bring joy to the other person involved. Remember to send a card or visit a close friend or relative who may be in the hospital. It will make their day.

18. TUESDAY. Challenging. Be ready for a very interesting day as informative Mercury, loving Venus, expansive Jupiter, and the emotional Moon all connect. Discussions are likely to become intense, and emotions are bound to be triggered as each person argues for their own views. If you are capable of taking control, compromises can be worked out to please everybody. Otherwise, there may be a few hurt feelings that you will need to placate. Family members or those who share the same roof can need some extra consideration. If you are planning a gathering, ensure that you give everyone plenty of warning and allay any fears. Spending can go over the top, so try to practice moderation.

19. WEDNESDAY. Pleasurable. A desire to socialize and be the life of the party can be stronger than usual. Burning the candle at both ends may be fun for a short time but has a nasty habit of catching up with us. So focus on your domestic scene today and enjoy the comfort of home and family. Spend extra time on the housework and cook a scrumptious dinner. You will all enjoy dining together as everyone gets a chance to talk about their day. Loving is about giving, not just taking. The more you do for others today, the better you will feel tomorrow. Phone calls from close by or distant places might come in as plans for a large gathering start to take shape. Make sure you don't forget anybody.

20. THURSDAY. Delightful. Expect all sorts of pleasant surprises as the celestial sphere smiles down on Archers. Romance is a serious possibility if you can get your mind off yourself for a time. An attractive person who has been part of your circle for some time now may suddenly look very appealing and show the same interest in you. You may have to factor in your child's hectic schedule when another parent pulls out of driving. Take your time with everything no matter how pressing your schedule. It is more important to arrive safely a little late than not get there at all. A creative hobby can become an asset. You might decide to design a play set for your children. Or, if you want to save some money, you might find it fun to create your own cards or holiday wrappings.

21. FRIDAY. Lively. Early this morning the shining Sun leaves your sign of Sagittarius and slips into Capricorn, joining forceful Pluto and energetic Mars here in your house of money and values. News from out of town can bring more surprises and perk you up. Whatever you are planning, you are going to have to keep your mind on your work as well. Coworkers might need your support to organize an end-of-year party. You are likely to come up with a quite different entertainment and surprise everyone. Ensure that you get the go-ahead from your boss before you get too carried away. Still, it wouldn't be wise to push too hard for success now. The more you struggle, the more your goal can move away from you. It takes a certain attitude to get to the top. Being desperate isn't it.

22. SATURDAY. Variable. Take the ups with the downs and appreciate what you can manage to achieve. Be careful of what you say in front of others. Your tact and diplomacy aren't abundant right now, and you don't want to cause unnecessary problems. You are going to meet all kinds of people today, some helpful and some not so helpful. But among all the many conversations you have, one is going to be more meaningful than the rest. You can share a vision that excites and interests you. But you need to allow yourself the chance to research your facts before speculating. If you want to lose extra pounds, or reach new levels of well-being, visualize yourself looking fantastic. Every journey starts with a first step.

23. SUNDAY. Steady. Whatever you have planned, you are well organized and ready for it. Put extra hours into your work or project, and you can achieve desired results now. Shopping is starred today. Ensure that you stock up on food and beverages in case of unexpected visitors. You might also have to make a last-minute shopping trip to find a few bargains as the clock winds down to the festivities. Some of you may not feel too well. Be wise and cancel any social outings. You will want to recuperate quickly for the holidays. Research possible treatments on the Internet. If you stick to natural therapies with caution, you may find you will recover with fewer side effects. In case you are thinking of giving a pet as a gift, think twice.

24. MONDAY. Practical. A thorough approach combined with an uncanny eye for detail will help you to get through your workday. Social events throughout the day can interrupt your rhythm but will make work more enjoyable. Expectations of a bonus at the end of this year could be disappointing. It's not a good idea to make a fuss. Joint funds could become a bone of contention between you and your partner at this time of the year. Arguments won't solve the problem. Resolve to discuss the situation rationally, and you can reach a compromise. Focus on what matters most and enjoy your day. If you take part in singing Christmas carols around your neighborhood, you might make some new friends while enjoying yourself.

25. TUESDAY. Merry Christmas! A generous and expansive vibe ensures that this day has a lot to offer everybody. Many of you may be away this year, traveling to a distant destination or getting ready to embark on a trip. For those celebrating at home, you should have a house- full of guests from your circle of friends and acquaintances. Some Archers may also be part of a public function or performance. A great deal of merriment will generate good conversation and even some gossip, creating humorous stores for future enjoyment. Any differences of opinion will be easily smoothed over. However, you are not likely to be tolerant of anyone wanting to change or upset your plans. So bite your tongue and carry on.

26. WEDNESDAY. Social. Archers are likely to be still celebrating today as visitors from near and far keep arriving. You may be visiting others, enjoying meeting some new people or catching up with family members and old friends. Professional as well as personal activities are suggested while you carry on with business as usual. Be aware of your partner's plans so that you can compromise if they clash with yours. Keep up your holiday spirit to avoid any confrontations. Special after-holiday sales are likely to lure you back to the stores to look for bargains or to exchange gifts that don't quite suit you. Ask your partner to go with you. Hopefully the two of you will be a brake on each other's spending.

27. THURSDAY. Positive. The repercussions of the festive season can catch up with you today. If you are lucky enough to be on vacation, lounge in bed for a while and enjoy the extra rest and recuperation. If you have to go to work, keep your head down and avoid whatever dramas are likely to take place. Your grandparents can visit bringing an absolutely fabulous gift for you or the kids. Welcome them warmly. Remember that they are getting a lot more pleasure from giving than you are from receiving. Difficulties with a lover might be based on innuendo and insinuations. Stop the banter and talk about the facts. If you both really love each other, forgiveness and empathy will ensue.

28. FRIDAY. Disquieting. Difficulties between you and your partner can continue and bring up images of divorce courts or separation. It seems that this is only your fears getting the better of you. If you can't find a common ground between you, seek a mediator or counselor for advice and help. Find someone who is objective enough to see both sides without judgment. A desire to hide away from a problematic situation will cause more trouble than it's worth. Face any problems head-on and watch them disappear. The Full Moon highlights your eighth house of joint funds and other people's values. With this phase in mind, make sure you are clear about where you stand in the equation. Whether it's business or pleasure, don't let another force you to compromise your values.

29. SATURDAY. Mystical. Your dreams may reflect your fears about money, power, and sexuality as the Moon stimulates your eighth house. Take this opportunity to analyze the clues your sub-conscious mind is sending you. On the surface, most dreams make precious little sense. Break down the symbols, and you will soon find the answers to many problems in your life. An opportunity to visit a medium or psychic might bring insight and inspiration. Or you might take a class in metaphysics that could develop your own psychic powers. Join a group activity that attracts your interest. It will be enjoyable making friends with like-minded people while you learn something new. A relationship adventure second to none could be yours now.

30. SUNDAY. Stimulating. After a worrisome morning, the Moon blows into Leo, your ninth house of travel and adventure. This stimulates your intellect, urging you to dream about the future. It may be hard to stay on track today. Give yourself frequent breaks in routine and capitalize on your creative energy. Someone new may enter your life, introducing you to different ideas and interests. Some Archers could be packing for an overseas adventure and are hoping to get everything in order before your bon voyage party starts. You would be wise to leave as early as possible. You want to be fresh and alert for what comes next. An evening concert can captivate your imagination and set up a perfect romantic date.

31. MONDAY. Fulfilling. Although there may be unexpected changes to your plans, you won't be disappointed with the outcome. Let go of any need to control your moves and have faith that the universe has grand designs for you. Communicative Mercury joins the shining Sun and forceful Pluto in your sector of money and values. This influence turns your attention to the things you value in life, whether material, intellectual, or spiritual. A situation can occur in which you have to define your sense of values to another person. In doing so, you will discover something new about your-self. You have a canny knack for getting a situation to work out the way you want it to now. New Year's activities should be fabulous as they portend many good things to come.

SAGITTARIUS
NOVEMBER–DECEMBER 2011

November 2011

1. TUESDAY. Deceptive. What you think and what you do can be quite different. Examine what it is that causes this dishonesty in your actions. Often, there is an underlying fear that you won't get what you want if you act true to your thoughts. Stop second-guessing others and find true freedom. You have support from behind the scenes, and may be tempted to manipulate a situation to your advantage. As long as you have the main players on your side, you should be successful. Plans for travel and adventure may be delayed. The current political climate can interfere with where you can go and what you can do there. Be practical, accept that there are powers stronger than you, and let it flow from there.

2. WEDNESDAY. Agreeable. Saucy Venus moves into your own sign of Sagittarius, adding charisma and charm to your attributes. You should make a favorable impression with others. You will be a valuable asset in business meetings and negotiations. You can make peace among others and pay the mediator effectively during this Venus influence. A certain amount of restlessness may interfere with job satisfaction or your daily routine. Try all avenues. Get involved in social pursuits and volunteer work, and you might find what you are looking for. A desire to help others should be strong. Any involvement in humanitarian or environmental issues can revive your inspiration for life, love, and adventure.

3. THURSDAY. Entertaining. Mercury, the planet of communication, joins Venus in your own sign of Sagittarius and stimulates your mind and ideas. Talking and socializing are your forte now. You will gain great enjoyment from mixing with different people. You do have to keep a watch on your focus. Your mind can jump from one thing to another and confuse you as well as others. There is a fortunate aspect for business negotiations and contracts, which adds to your normally adventurous nature. You may find yourself getting around your local area far more than usual. As you travel around, keep your eyes and ears open. You may encounter profitable and interesting experiences along the way.

4. FRIDAY. Distracting. The responsibilities of home and family can seem like lead weight restricting your sense of adventure and inhibiting your dreams. Talk to your loved ones, and you may be able to organize time for personal freedom. Finding the balance between work and play can be achieved with a cooperative approach. You are probably in a chatty mood, and may not get off the phone for most of the day. In fact, you could end up being an impromptu counselor to friends, neighbors, or siblings. Avoid getting involved in other people's drama. Doing that will bring problems you don't need. This is a positive time for a business venture. Collaborate with colleagues over the next move.

5. SATURDAY. Lively. Your creative use of imagination and ingenuity can win you lots of brownie points from those around you. Your mind may tend to be overactive, but you're highly inventive. When anyone has a problem, you are apt to work out ways to fix it. Your artistic urge won't let you down. Get out the tools of your trade and amaze yourself with what you produce. Make your own holiday cards. With your talent, you can make each card a unique message of your love. Social gatherings will be very enjoyable, but watch what you say. In your gregarious mood you could talk to the wrong people about the wrong things and give away important secrets.

6. SUNDAY. Impulsive. Patience is a virtue, but it may be very hard to find in today's celestial climate. Watch your words. Archers can be very tactless at times, and you don't want to hurt someone's feelings inadvertently. If you are not feeling one hundred percent, make an attempt to look after yourself. You are likely to push yourself to the limit and make things worse. Sagittarius parents may have worries about a child. Any attempt at discussing the situation with them now might turn into an argument. Do something exciting together. Break down the barriers through friendship rather than discipline. Shoppers can get a good deal on linens and other fine fabrics.

7. MONDAY. Pleasing. Regular daily happenings can turn out to be full of romance and mystery. A brief encounter with someone who captures your mind and imagination, not to mention setting your heart racing, might dominate the rest of the day. Your thoughts will be focused on engineering another meeting. If you are about to receive an award or honor, don't let the jitters hinder your experience. Chamomile or valerian are calming herbal teas, and a splash of lavender oil will also help. A very helpful colleague may give you a lead on a promising new investment, all the while feathering their own nest. Find out what their expectations are before you get wildly excited.

8. TUESDAY. Disillusioning. All things being equal, your life should be sailing along pleasantly enough. Still, your mood could plummet into a dark and depressed place. This is a good time to sit down with pen and paper and let all your thoughts out so that no one else has to hear. Before you know it, the mood will pass and sunshine will light up your life. Worries over a child could take your thoughts away from your job. Going over and over a problem will not help you solve it. Practice some breathing exercises and relax as much as possible. Concentrate on the work at hand. The future will fall into place. If you try to take control, all you'll do is create more problems.

9. WEDNESDAY. Lucky. Awaited news can bring cause for celebration. Simple plans can lead to important new opportunities. Keep your eyes and ears open. Serendipity treads quietly. Your finances should be in good shape. If they are not, then perhaps you might hope for a lottery win. Luck is yours, so purchase a ticket. Do not procrastinate when it comes to an important meeting, deal, or investment or you might miss out. The mood is such that you may just expect results without putting in the hard effort. This attitude will let you down now. You have to help luck along. Archers looking for work should get an early start and show up first at an audition or interview. It will make a difference.

10. THURSDAY. Irritable. Restlessness on the job may be because you are not being fulfilled and have little job satisfaction. Take a look at your options. Compare them to what your heart desires and what are your long-term goals. If these are not compatible, then it is time to question your values and priorities. Perhaps be prepared to let go and welcome a change. The Full Moon in Taurus shines its light on your sixth house of work and health. If you aren't happy with your daily work, your health is bound to suffer. Consider returning to study. You might be surprised at the options available to you. Sagittarius adventurers might find a course out of the country that fits your budget and fires your mind.

11. FRIDAY. Motivating. Mars, planet of assertiveness, has moved into Virgo and lends energy and action to your house of career. Mars here arouses your ambition to achieve, and you will be willing to work very hard to reach your goals. But you won't tolerate too much authority over your initiative and independence. This is a perfect time to get a business venture off the ground and start working for yourself. Dealings with government officials can be testing. Watch out for competitors in your chosen field. Don't become angry or resentful if anyone achieves more than you do. Any attempt to defeat a challenger could just hold you back from your own objectives in life.

12. SATURDAY. Renewing. Stop thinking about the future and enjoy the present. Cultivate companionship with your significant other. With good insight and fundamental instincts, you can intuit a partner's needs. Renew the deep love that each soul yearns for so much. Cultivate the passion and the supportive commitment that belong to you. Single Archers are sure to be dressing up in your glad rags to meet someone and hoping for subtle cues and magical openings, which are bound to arise. It is all about being in the right place at the right time. If you stay at home, you will miss out. You might be named as a speaker at an important social function this evening, so dress to impress.

13. SUNDAY. Harmonious. The celestial influences favor family get-togethers and reunions. A celebration for a christening, wedding, or anniversary can renew the ties that bind and uncover parts of family history you were hitherto unaware of. Listen to your elders and hear some valuable advice. Charity work will be well rewarded today. Some of you might be caregivers for someone less fortunate, and will discover a friendship and love worth far more than gold. If you have recently experienced a marriage breakdown, make the most of your friends and family ties. Human contact heals pain. It doesn't take long for love to creep back into daily life. Positive thoughts will bring positive outcomes.

14. MONDAY. Helpful. Whatever the cause for concern, don't worry, it will pass. The morning starts off with vibes of competition, financial losses, or a personal setback. But by the evening there should be cause for celebration. A large bill may arrive in the mail and threaten your feelings of personal security. If you call the company and arrange a repayment plan, your fears will drop away. Budgeting will be good for you anyway. After the bill is paid off, you can start saving for something you hold dear. You have good friends and plenty of support around you, so call in a favor if you need some extra help. Don't borrow money to pay back a debt, though, as this is simply moving sideways.

15. TUESDAY. Prosperous. Your career looks to be on the up and up, and you may celebrate with the purchase of a big-ticket item.

Do be sure that you have insurance for all your property and you can live worry free. You may be surprised at what you will end up doing. Inventive Archers might start an Internet business and enjoy the freedom. If you are a fund-raiser for a local charity, put forward your ideas and you may come up with a real winner. So good, in fact, that you might end up with an opportunity to start your own business and build up valuable equity. You may have to take time off work to care for an ill child or a parent. See your employer and ask if you can work from home.

16. WEDNESDAY. Complex. There may be so many things to attend to that you don't know where to start. Begin by changing your attitude from worrying about your abilities to being thrilled by the chase. You will do what you can do. But how you think and feel about it is the difference between enjoying life or not. You may be suspicious if your partner seems to be preoccupied with people and activities outside your home and family. Rather than jump to conclusions, try explaining your feelings and asking your partner. There is likely to be a much simpler explanation than what you are imagining. Many of your problems could be of your own making. Relax and stop fretting.

17. THURSDAY. Upbeat. Good fortune presides over this day. If you are not happy with the usual run-of-the-mill routine, you may initiate change at every opportunity. Playing the prankster should keep people laughing, but might get you in trouble with your supervisors, teachers, or employers. A sudden interest in New Age subjects can introduce you to another perspective on the meaning of life, the universe, and everything. But over time, this might open doors into areas of employment not known right now. Anything that expands your understanding of the world and all its peoples will be of major interest. A course in martial arts might get you fit and give you a spiritual understanding.

18. FRIDAY. Disquieting. A lack of exercise or an excess of rich and fatty foods can cause irritability and discontent. Start drinking plenty of water and taking a walk each day, then watch the improvement. Those near and dear will be the first to notice and cheer. You have many possibilities open to you. Whether it is job advancement, travel, or love, it is up to you. Don't be your own worst enemy and look for all the negatives. With that sort of attitude, you will lose before you even start. Think positive and the world is your oyster. An offer of a leadership role will be beneficial. Feeling shy is normal. Accept the offer and take it as it comes. Your confidence will grow day by day.

19. SATURDAY. Good. A social role or activity might put you in the public eye. You may have the gift of oratory. Your empathy and ability to read the moods of others will endear you to them. Your busy schedule and willingness to take on even more may be the cause of physical lethargy. But while your mind races, you may not want to get off the couch. Delegate others to take care of your most pressing engagements, then relax for a change. Go for a swim or play in the garden. Anything that grounds you and that lets the soothing vibes of nature slow your brain and bring a little bit of peace will be the order of the day. Make sweet love to your lover and sleep well.

20. SUNDAY. Fair. Take a backseat and get as much rest and relaxation as possible. You may want to do a bit of work on your health. Throw out all the instant snacks that are really junk food. Shop at a farmer's market for local fruit, vegetables, and nuts. The nutrition in fresh food will boost your energy and your immune system, and you'll be more alert in no time. A secret attraction to a friend or neighbor could make you feel awkward around them. Come clean and tell them of your feelings. Ask them out on a date and you may not be disappointed. Those of you already in a relationship would benefit by focusing on your lover and letting go of all your other cares and woes.

21. MONDAY. Inspiring. Plans for a new project need your wholehearted attention if you are going to get it off the ground. Shut yourself away from interruptions and finalize your ideas. The peace and quiet will do you good at the same time. This is one of those days when contemplation will allow your intuition to speak to your heart. Start a journal if you don't already have one, and let the pen have a life of its own. You'll be amazed at what comes to light without censoring or editing. One of your friends might ask you for a sizable loan and put you on the spot. You may want to help, but are unsure whether you can trust them to pay you back. Find out if you can get a guarantee.

22. TUESDAY. Energetic. Happy birthday, Sagittarius! Today marks the beginning of your annual celebration. The life-giving Sun rolls into your sign and adds its warmth and creativity to everything you do over the next month. This is a great time to do a personal inventory, assess how far you have come toward your goals, and be grateful for all the good things in your life. This could be a busy day, so make sure you eat a good breakfast. Treat yourself with love, and you will always have a smile on your face. Your ability to make friends and influence people is on the rise. A cherished goal might start to look achievable. Romance will also be a highlight this month.

23. WEDNESDAY. Restless. A chronic case of itchy feet might drive you out of the house in search of adventure. If you have a sick day to use, now is the time to take advantage and hit the road for a change of scenery and a spontaneous adventure. Visit a museum or an exhibition heretofore unseen. Take a drive to a town or cultural spot that you haven't visited before and give your mind something new to think about. If you don't get out, you are likely to stay at home alone and surf the Net or watch television all day long. Beware of retail therapy. Instead, examine your thoughts in order to understand what is creating this inner need for self-gratification.

24. THURSDAY. Unsettling. Beware of the temptation to gloss over bad behavior. Even white lies can have powerful repercussions. You may want to make a situation look better than it is. Or you may fool yourself into believing what you want to believe. But at the end of the day the truth remains the same. Your denial simple enables what is not kosher to keep on keeping on. The Scorpio Moon signals that you are at a low point in your lunar cycle. Look after yourself now more than ever. Finish those odd jobs and personal projects that are holding you back from going forward. Clear out what is not needed. Then make room for something new and refreshing to come in and take its place. Practice love, and that is what you will get.

25. FRIDAY. Refreshing. The New Moon in Sagittarius today heralds the start of a new lunar cycle, promising happy and creative vibes. Single Archers might have a new romance on the boil, and start to feel that something more will follow. Your love of life gives off a charisma that attracts all sorts of good things into your life. Mercury, the planet of communication, has just moved retrograde in your sign and will stay retrograde until December 14. This will cause misunderstandings and delays to all forms of communication. Contracts and agreements can fall through or get held up during this time. Travel plans are best left until after Mercury moves forward again. Use this time for reflection.

26. SATURDAY. Favorable. Attractive Venus cruises into Capricorn, your second house of values and money, adding love and generosity to your daily life. Loving relationships are apt to intensify and bring you closer to your significant other. Singles looking for love might get more than you bargain for, so watch out for possessiveness and dominating types. You should find plenty of bargains to make your shopping trip worthwhile. An incredible deal on finance can allow you to refurnish your home, with no interest or repayments for years. But don't let this justify the purchase of something way beyond your means. You will eventually have to pay for it.

27. SUNDAY. Dramatic. Watch out for childish acts that say you are not getting enough of what you want, or that reveal your need to please because you don't feel good enough. Resentments are the first sign that something is not right inside. So rather than look at others, take a hard look at yourself first. Your partner might be flirtatious and belittle you in front of others. Do not make a scene about your partner's behavior. This will only put you in the same boat. Instead, you might be better off to state your feelings and simply leave. This will put the ball firmly back in their court. You might be undecided about a work-related decision. Stop thinking about it. When you least expect it, the answer will come.

28. MONDAY. Variable. Work prospects look excellent, as does your earning capacity. Be willing to make changes if you are not satisfied with your current employment. Go back to school, or sign up to volunteer abroad. Even volunteering in local institutions will give you work experience as long as it is compatible with your chosen career. This is a great time to apply for a loan for the purchase of property or a business. Gather up all your references. Before you put in your application, research which financial institution gives the best rates and is reliable. Personal concerns may be your main priority. Perhaps you need time off work to deal with things.

29. TUESDAY. Intuitive. This is one of those days when you need to turn off your mind and let yourself act spontaneously. Trust that your inner instincts know what is right for you and go with it. The more you question yourself, the more paralyzed you will become. A secret attraction to a coworker could come out into the open when they ask you for a date. It might surprise you to know that while you have been slyly checking them out, they have been doing the same to you. The universe is on your side if you just relax and let it flow. Tidy up your paperwork. Then you won't overlook a bill or some other correspondence that also needs attending to. Gossip sessions can have negative repercussions.

30. WEDNESDAY. Harmonious. Despite your current busy schedule, you can remain remarkably cool, calm, and collected. Make the most of your charisma to win friends and influence people, and you will be amazed at what you can achieve. A role as a representative for your workplace or for teammates will bring out the best in you. Don't refuse to do your bit for the group. Sagittarius writers can rely on today's intellectual stimulation to finish a manuscript for publishing. Your material should be welcomed warmly. Those of you home from school can put in valuable study time now. Get assignments ready for submission in order to earn high grades. Just be sure to address all questions.

December 2011

1. THURSDAY. Useful. There is an intensity in the air that will set everybody's passion meters on high. Shoppers are bound to find an expensive piece of apparel that you just have to have, although you don't know where you will wear it. In fact, it might just hang in the closet, but you will always love it. Home renovations will come to the fore with renewed inspiration to beautify your home and make your everyday life that much more enjoyable. You will want the very height of fashion now, so shop around for the best prices before you buy. Your energy level could be a bit flat. You might have to bring work home with you so that you can catch up before your deadline is due.

2. FRIDAY. Challenging. The competition is likely to stretch your abilities and bring out the best in you. Delays can be very frustrating. You may be waiting for a check to arrive, a contract to be signed, or word about a job application. Yet nothing is happening. With Mercury, planet of communication, and Jupiter, planet of abundance, both in retrograde motion, these two aspects of life can't move forward. Meanwhile, concentrate on your preparations for the festive season and be prepared ahead of time. It will take all the pressure off in the final week when the whole world seems to operate in a frenzy. Spend time with your loved ones. Perhaps you could take them out to dinner and have a laugh.

3. SATURDAY. Manageable. Today's message says not to take yourself for granted and don't let precious resources sit idly by when you can put them all in play. Think twice before running out to buy something new. You may already have what you want in the cupboard. Don't be a slave to fashion. Use your creative style and flair to create your own world the way you like it. Give yourself a break from your fantasies and be happy being normal. Play in the garden, visit friends, throw an impromptu party, or just laze around your home. You can do as you please. Romance is not far away for

lonely hearts. Put on your Sunday best and visit new locales. You
never know who you will meet.

4. SUNDAY. Stimulating. Prepare for an exciting day. Romance is
high on the agenda for most Archers, whether you are sleeping in
late with your nearest and dearest or out early visiting your favorite
club. Nestling up close and feeling the nurture of love and desire
will be your main aims. Parents should take your kids out for fun at
a theme park, or for an adventure in the countryside. Be reserved
about bringing along friends, as this may make for mischief and
interfere with intimate contact. A burning ambition might override
all other plans. Even while out with your loved ones, you are plot-
ting and planning your rise to power. Keep a notebook with you for
writing down ideas.

5. MONDAY. Enthusiastic. Incorporate fun into your routine day
and put a smile on everyone's face. Don't be afraid to put your
reputation on the line with a new idea. Your creative abilities are
heightened and your career prospects look very positive. You may
even have some excess cash that you would like to invest. A broker
will have some great ideas for you to think about. Don't delay. Call
and become a client while the aspects say go. Business plans could
be held up until after the holidays. So spend this time refining your
ideas and perfecting all the ins and outs. Young and single Archers
may meet a stunning new love who not only looks gorgeous but
also has money in the bank!

6. TUESDAY. Frustrating. Try not to rush. Then you won't have to
redo as many things. The Taurus Moon makes a strong aspect to
Mercury and to Jupiter, which are both in retrograde motion. This
means slow down. Reflect, review, reorganize, reapply, redefine, re-
examine, repair, reassess. If you are trying to do one hundred things
at once, stop, then start with one at a time. Your day will be so much
more enjoyable. The amount of work you manage to plow through
will be impressive. Enjoy the camaraderie of coworkers and a long
lunch. It will eliminate stress and give you a new outlook on many
things.

7. WEDNESDAY. Positive. You can wake up feeling refreshed and
ready for life this morning. Stop thinking about applying for a promotion or pay increase and just do it. The sooner you do, the sooner
it will come through, and you will need some extra cash over the
next few weeks. Get your holiday card list compiled. Organize your
plans for the silly season so that you won't miss out on anything.
Take your car in for service and check any other mechanical or

electronic equipment you rely on. It will be cheaper to service them than have to repair a breakdown. Research and revise a diet that isn't working. You might prefer to simply cut out fats than give up the good life at this time of year.

8. THURSDAY. Confusing. Plans can change on you and leave you wondering how you can juggle your personal and professional spheres. Perhaps it would be easier if you considered what is most important to you personally. Then make sure that this area of your life is satisfied first. You will find that everything else will fall into place after that. Your partner could be sending mixed messages. Instead of trying to guess, just ask straight out what is going on. At least this way you might circumvent the buildup of frustration that is bound to happen if the situation continues. Satisfy the traveler inside you by dining at ethnic restaurants in your community.

9. FRIDAY. Tense. Steer clear of arguments and any conflict with your significant other. There is no use trying to work out resolutions at the moment. You are more likely to create new misunderstandings. It might be better to send messages of love and at least nurture the good part of your relationship. Write your resentments down on a piece of paper and bury them in the backyard. Give them to the universe and start your day afresh. Forgive and forget is your best motto. A legal matter can be held up and demand more paperwork. Be thankful for this chance to make sure you have done everything properly. If this problem hadn't occurred, a successful conclusion might have eluded you.

10. SATURDAY. Distracting. You could spend hours on the phone chatting, catching up with people you haven't seen for ages, while the housework stays undone. Instead of getting your planned activities under way, you may go out for a game of golf, or participate in some other sport or social interest in your life. Regardless of what you end up doing, you may possess a sense of inner restlessness that tells you you should be doing something else. Consider what it is you are avoiding and how long you wish to keep doing so. At least then you will be conscious of what is really going on. You may be afraid to visit a parent because of unfulfilled expectations. Face up to it and clear your conscience.

11. SUNDAY. Fair. Trust your instincts and don't believe all you are told. Be discerning; don't buy something just because you can afford it. Use the installment plan if you can't afford the total cost up front. Shopping for presents can be challenging as you try to find that special something for the main people in your life. A spiritual or philosophical gathering can be very powerful, touching you with a sense of the magical and mystical. A workshop in chanting or another equally wild art will add a new perspective on the ordinary, and allow you to express the artist within. Wondrous coincidences might occur to remind you that the universe works in mysterious ways.

12. MONDAY. Innovative. The changing face of your social group can give you insight into your own personal growth. You might be acting as a mentor for your partner at the moment and find that your abilities surpass your expectations . You both might decide to join your talents and start a business partnership that allows you both more freedom and initiative. Do be careful of extravagance. Your exuberance for the aspects of life that you love is not based on the practicalities of daily life. Business matters look promising. You have new contacts who can help you restructure your approach toward a wider market. If you are planning to employ others, check out the insurance coverage and costs.

13. TUESDAY. Slow. Whichever way you look today, there is likely to be some sort of problem or blockage. Throw out your timetable and accept that you will need to work through each one by one. Your partner or colleagues could question what you are doing now, and bring your attention to something important you have overlooked. So don't jump to conclusions or get annoyed too fast. You may have been avoiding an issue in the workplace, but today you can't do that anymore. Whether you like it or not, you will be held accountable for past mistakes. A property or investment matter could dominate business discussions. Be prepared to let go of the old to make way for the new.

14. WEDNESDAY. Smooth. Colleagues as well as outside vendors should follow your lead now. Your business manner is persuasive. You can achieve the things you set out to achieve and then some. Plan your day well so that you can cover all aspects of your business. Mercury, the planet of communication, has moved direct. Now misunderstandings and delays can be cleared away. Contracts and agreements, as well as business negotiations, are also likely to move toward finalization. Travel plans can be made, and you are likely to stumble upon a great bargain-basement price for the destination of your choice. A nagging suspicion about a deceitful colleague could prove to be right.

15. THURSDAY. Dreamy. Plans for the future can interfere with your work in the here and now. Keep your mind on the job, and you won't have any slipups or accidents. Furthering your career can open up new avenues of learning that will broaden your mind. You may find that you get a taste for new realms of thought and don't want to stop. Philosophical or religious discussions could get out of hand, as the topic strikes a nerve in the participants. You could be very gullible at the moment, so take everything that is said with a grain of salt. Curb a desire to drink if you are going out tonight. Your energy level would benefit much more from good food and an early night.

16. FRIDAY. Bumpy. Be mindful of personality differences, and you can avoid stepping on the toes of others. Problems during your workday may bring up the desire to find a career that gives you independence and initiative. Sagittarius desires freedom and adventure, and you might find this desire somewhat stymied throughout the day. You and everybody else are likely to take more risks than usual. Keep your eyes open when working close to others or traveling in your car. Do not broach subjects with your family or fellows that demand cooperation and compromise. These attributes might be sadly missing in most discussions. If you can, wait another day to achieve a positive and unified outcome.

17. SATURDAY. Fulfilling. Focus on your appearance and your presentation in public, and you will achieve the results you desire. Working with others in a community event will be starred. You are making new contacts and establishing your reputation among your neighbors. The camaraderie and good vibes will make for a fun-filled family day. Social events and commitments might be so thick that you feel like you only go home to sleep. Family Archers should include loved ones in a day activity, or build the evening around them. In the long run, no matter what you do in your life, these are the people with whom you travel the important years.

18. SUNDAY. Spontaneous. Be prepared for the unexpected, and you won't be surprised. You may have planned a day at home to organize the coming week. Instead, you are bombarded with visitors from far and near. Some might descend and expect a bed for the night. Be very straightforward about what you will and won't do. Don't get sucked into lending money, as you might not see it for a long time. A new relationship could be high-maintenance, and you're starting to wonder how you can escape. Be up front, be kind but honest, and you will avoid more painful times. You could be celebrating a birthday and decide to go to a catered venue. There you can relax, and the house will stay tidy.

19. MONDAY. Demanding. Don't soldier on over a problem. Call on your extensive network for the skill and assistance you need. Developing a team effort in the workplace will also bring rewards. Many hands make light work. You could be working on a large-scale project that demands a lot from you by way of responsibility and commitment. Rather than let this weigh heavily on your shoulders, just take one thing at a time. Breaking it down into smaller components will make it easier to focus on. If this is beyond your scope, consider delegating and play the role of overseer while you get more than one thing done at a time. Service in a humanitarian organization may stretch you to the limits.

20. TUESDAY. Low-key. Avoid overloading your workday. This is a hectic time of year, and you might find that there is no need to do as much as it might seem. Take care of the most pressing matters, and find time for yourself as well. Do what you can to recharge your spiritual batteries, whether you attend a worship service, go for a long walk, or spend hours reading a good book. Time for yoga and meditation will also be a treat. As the sensitive Scorpio Moon passes through your twelfth house of secrets and solitudes, any quiet time you can get will be golden. Meet that special someone for lunch and enjoy a romantic moment in between appointments.

21. WEDNESDAY. Favorable. Luscious Venus has moved into Aquarius, your solar sector of communication, and brings affection and good company into your daily life over the next few weeks. Contact with your siblings, neighbors, and friends is likely to pick up. What might start out as a quick call or short lunch can turn into long conversations full of fun and laughter. You might want to bring art or artistic creativity into your daily life now. If you haven't already begun decorating, there is no time like the present. Involve the whole family in making your own decorations. With paint and glue and sparkles, you can have lots of fun together. Your boss might pass out a festive bonus.

22. THURSDAY. Bright. As the loving Sun moves into Capricorn, your second house of money and values, the Moon moves into your sign of Sagittarius and bolsters your popularity. Put yourself first. Make sure you have your plans truly in place before you get sidetracked into helping others. You may have several invitations for the holidays, but you decide you are not going to do the usual thing this year. Some of you might be taking off on a vacation as soon as your work closes down. If you are well organized, you can relax and enjoy early celebrations. Then you won't have to worry about overindulging that would hinder your upcoming plans.

23. FRIDAY. Productive. Pay attention to your finances. You might want to pay your outstanding bills now and not have to worry over the coming week. If you have any gifts left to buy, do it now and don't wait until the crush of tomorrow. You might go to a small shopping center and find something different from the run-of-the-mill fare available at the malls. Objects of art and specialty wares can seem more appropriate to you at the moment. You are in danger of spending big, so leave your credit cards at home to remove that temptation. You might be amazed at the work you get done in between helping others to finalize their projects. Love and laughter are infectious.

24. SATURDAY. Revitalizing. A friendly and relaxed atmosphere may prevail. The company of your family or neighbors can be particularly interesting, just what you need. Today's New Moon in Capricorn lights up your financial sector and brings opportunity to improve this aspect of your life. A business proposal might arise out of a casual conversation with a friend you haven't seen in ages. Unusual and unexpected fortune can sparkle amid your daily routine. An overly optimistic attitude can prompt you to make promises you can't keep, so be mindful of what you are saying in order to avoid future problems. Stay close with loved ones this Christmas Eve. Savor the love and inner peace.

25. SUNDAY. Merry Christmas! There is a strong spiritual flavor today, with the emphasis on helping those less fortunate. Your kind and generous Sagittarius nature is evident. You will be loved by your fellows for your good cheer. Some of you might be far from home. Catch up with family and friends over the Internet while you join in with the different style of celebrations of a foreign land. You may find that your values are changing. You are enjoying pleasures that money can't buy, and are starting to appreciate certain things you normally don't notice. Be cautious traveling on the roads. If you are going a long distance, check the weather forecasts to ensure you are prepared for what is ahead.

26. MONDAY. Successful. Your ruling planet, benevolent Jupiter, has moved direct. All the blockages to expansion or travel will clear away. Work and business opportunities will become clear. You will know when it is the right time to act. Your intuition is strong, your hope for prosperity is justified. Some of you might have a house full of guests from afar. Enjoy the conversation and gossip while everyone shares the tasks of cooking and cleaning. A neighborhood celebration may take you away from your hearth and into the larger family of the community. Dancing and singing are joyful expressions of shared values and commitments.

27. TUESDAY. Opportune. You might get the chance to make some extra money today. You are likely to be mixing with people who have different ideas from yours, and gain a new perspective on your usual life. Sometimes it is helpful to talk to others about problems in a relationship and get the benefit of their objectivity. Just offloading fears and resentments onto an impartial listener helps you to clear out these negative emotions. You might have to cut your holiday short to return to help a family member or because of a business matter. Perhaps, despite all the festive cheer, some people just can't get along. The return to your usual routine and the comfort of home will be reassuring.

28. WEDNESDAY. Disconcerting. Stick to your original plans, no matter how good an idea sounds. Once you start changing one thing, you'll be surprised at the problems that arise later on. Romantic dreams and ideals might distort reality. Today's vibes are much more attuned to creative activities than pragmatic black-and-white issues. If you have an important meeting or appointment, make sure you have a map and clear directions. Mix-ups and delays are a high possibility, as are breakdowns. The feeling of déjà vu can bring back a dream from last night and add a touch of magic to your day. Call that special someone. Make a date to share intimate moments of tenderness and desire.

29. THURSDAY. Satisfying. Your usual daily routine will be rewarding. Chores around the home might bring deep satisfaction as you use your creative skills to improve comfort and pleasure for the loved ones in your life. The chance to take over the training of new employees might inspire you, adding extra enjoyment to the working day. Concentrate on developing your natural talents, and give up trying to be someone you are not. You might be amazed at the opportunities available to you now that you are not imagining the grass is greener elsewhere. A romantic interlude can lead you to a new social group that offers valuable business contacts and friends from unusual backgrounds.

30. FRIDAY. Diverse. There is no reason why you can't mix business with pleasure successfully today. An invitation to a party could introduce you to new business connections or to a chance to advance your career. You may be trying to juggle your professional and home life. Make sure you take your family along so that your partner can get enthusiastic over all the possibilities. A great property investment might come to light and encourage you to think about selling and moving out of state. Family concerns might consume most of your day. Just getting loved ones to sit down together may be a mammoth task. If there is argument over possessions, it might warrant drawing straws.

31. SATURDAY. Eventful. There is sure to be plenty of nervous energy in the buildup to this evening. Most Archers will want to do your own thing now, and a personal project could take precedence over everything else. Children might demand your attention. You might spend most of the day trying to find a babysitter to free you up for the evening. Take some time out to reflect on the year past. Review your achievements and your regrets. Writing a gratitude list will help you to become clear on where to go from here and on your most pressing priorities for the coming year. This will identify what resolutions are necessary to keep you on a steady course next year.

FREE
PARTY LINE

Make new friends, have fun, share idea's never be bored this party never stops! And best of all it's FREE!

Never Any Charges!
Call Now!

712-338-7722

Only Regular Low Long Distance rates apply where applicable